Political Parties after Communism

Political Parties after Communism

Developments in East-Central Europe

TOMÁŠ KOSTELECKÝ

WOODROW WILSON CENTER PRESS
Washington, D.C.

THE JOHNS HOPKINS UNIVERSITY PRESS
Baltimore and London

EDITORIAL OFFICES

Woodrow Wilson Center Press
One Woodrow Wilson Plaza
1300 Pennsylvania Avenue, N.W.
Washington, D.C. 20004-3027
Telephone 202-691-4010
www.wilsoncenter.org

ORDER FROM

The Johns Hopkins University Press
P.O. Box 50370
Baltimore, Maryland 21211
Telephone 1-800-537-5487
www.press.jhu.edu

2 4 6 8 9 7 5 3 1

Library of Congress Cataloging-in-Publication Data

Kostelecký, Tomáš
  Political parties after communism : developments in East-Central
Europe / Tomáš Kostelecký.
      p. cm.
Reviews the post-communist development of political parties in the Czech
Republic, Slovakia, Poland and Hungary.
Includes bibliographical references and index.
  ISBN 0-8018-6851-3 (hard : alk. paper)
1. Political parties—Europe, Eastern. 2. Representative government
and representation—Europe, Eastern. 3. Europe, Eastern—Politics and
government—1989–   4. Post-communism—Europe, Eastern. I. Title.
  JN96.A979 .K+
    324.2'0943'091717—dc21   2001008239

To my wife, Yvona,
whose work deserves as much recognition
as writing books about politics

Contents

Tables and Figure

Tables

Figure

Preface

In the second half of the 1980s, during my study of human geography at Charles University in Prague, I became especially interested in the study of human behavior. That interest raised a problem, however. To study human behavior while Czechoslovakia was still under a powerful Communist regime, I probably would have had to join the Communist Party, or at least negotiate some arrangement with the ruling class, and I, like the vast majority of my generation, considered involvement in politics very dirty business in those days. In the end, then, I decided to concentrate on the study of the most nonpolitical features of human behavior such as commuting, migration, or other aspects of demographics.

After graduation in 1988, I joined the Institute of Geography of the Czechoslovak Academy of Sciences and began to study the development of settlement structures in Czechoslovakia. I must admit now that I did not have enough imagination to envision the vast scope of the changes on the horizon. The sudden and surprising breakdown of the Communist regime not only brought freedom to the country's citizens, but also lifted all ideological constraints for those interested in the social sciences. Fascinated by the occurrence of the first free post-Communist elections in 1990, I changed the topic of my research to political geography—specifically, the analysis of voting patterns. My decision to join the Institute of Sociology had the effect of broadening my interest from electoral geography to the study of the political behavior of voters and party activists. Later, when I recognized the importance of institutions, I also began to study political parties themselves.

The economic, social, and political changes that followed the breakdown of the Communist regimes gave social scientists an extraordinary chance to work in a kind of living laboratory. The dramatic developments in society that ordinarily would take decades were compressed into several years. Thus European social scientists and others have studied the political development of the former Communist regimes intensely. Indeed, social scientists worldwide have published hundreds of articles and chapters in books dealing with features of political development after the regime changes. Some works have been descriptive, some analytical; most have been based on empirical research in one of the countries studied in this volume. Meanwhile, as one bent on undertaking my own research, I felt lost in the flood of empirical findings and began to think about how to make any meaningful generalizations about what had happened. Is the political development of the post-Communist countries in a state of chaos, as it sometimes looks like from the Western point of view? Is there anything common to the development of party structures in different post-Communist countries? What are the general features of political development and what is country-specific? What is the relationship between the political development of the post-Communist countries and the political development in the Western democracies? This book is an attempt to answer these questions.

Acknowledgments

This book would never have come into existence without the support of several people and institutions, and I am grateful to all of them. Václav Gardavský, director of the Institute of Geography of the Czechoslovak Academy of Sciences in 1988, gave me a chance to start my academic career. Petr Dostál, lecturer at the University of Amsterdam in the early 1990s and organizer of study trips for Czech social scientists to the Netherlands, helped me and others to learn what we were unable to learn in Czech schools under the Communists. I also am heavily indebted to Michal Illner, director of the Institute of Sociology of the Czech Academy of Sciences from 1992 to 2000, who kindly supported my work on this book while I worked at the institute. And I would like to thank my former colleagues at the Institute of Sociology, where I spent most of my time working on topics related to the subject of this book. I learned a lot from them.

This book also would not be possible without the financial support of the Woodrow Wilson International Center for Scholars in Washington, D.C., which granted me a nine-month visiting fellowship from September 1996 to May 1997. I also am grateful to the Japan Society for the Promotion of Science, which financed my one-year stay in 1999 at the Slavic Research Center at Hokkaido University in Sapporo, Japan. I would especially like to thank Tadayuki Hayashi of the Slavic Research Center for being such a kind host during my stay at his institution. Finally, I would like to thank two anonymous manuscript readers for their suggestions and criticism.

Abbreviations for Post-Communist Political Parties, by Country

CZECH REPUBLIC

ČSL	Czechoslovak Peoples' Party (*Československá strana lidová*)
ČSS	Czech Socialist Party (*Česká strana socialisticlá*)
ČSSD	Czech Social Democratic Party (*Česká strana sociálně demokratická*)
DEU	Democratic Union (*Demokratická unie*)
HSD-SMS	Movement for Self-Governing Democracy–Society for Moravia and Silesia (*Hnutí za samosprávnou demokracii–sdružení pro Moravu a Slezsko*)
KDU-ČSL	Christian Democratic Union–Czechoslovak Peoples' Party (*Křesťansko demokratická unie–Československá strana lidová*)
KSČ	Communist Party of Czechoslovakia (*Komunistická strana Československa*)
KSČM	Communist Party of Bohemia and Moravia (*Komunistická strana Čech a Moravy*)
LSU	Liberal Social Union (*Liberálně sociálni unie*), a coalition of: the Czechoslovak Socialist Party, Green Party, and Agrarian Party
ODA	Civic Democratic Alliance (*Občanská demokratická aliance*)
ODS	Civic Democratic Party (*Občanská demokratická strana*)
OF	Civic Forum (*Občanské fórum*)
OH	Civic Movement (*Občanské hnuti*)
SPR-RSČ	Association for the Republic–Republican Party of Czechoslovakia (*Sdruženi pro republiku–Republikánská strana Československa*)
US	Union of Freedom (*Unie svobody*)

HUNGARY

FIDESZ	Federation of Young Democrats (*Fiatal Demokraták Szövetsége*)
FIDEZS-MPP	Federation of Young Democrats–Hungarian Civic Party (*Fiatal Demokraták Szövetsége–Magyar Polgari Part*)
FKGP	Independent Smallholders Party (*Független Kisgazda, Földmunkás-és Polgári Párt*)

KDNP   Christian Democratic People's Party (*Kereszténydemokrata Néppárt*)
MDF   Hungarian Democratic Forum (*Magyar Demokrata Fórum*)
MIÉP   Hungarian Justice and Life Party (*Magyar Igazság és Élet Párjta*)
MSZDP   Hungarian Social Democratic Party (*Magyar Szocial Demokrata Párt*)
MSZMP   Hungarian Socialist Workers Party (*Magyar Szocialista Munkáspárt Párt*)
MSZP   Hungarian Socialist Party (*Magyar Szocialista Párt*)
SZDSZ   Alliance of Free Democrats (*Szabad Demokratk Szövetsége*)

POLAND

AWS   Solidarity Electoral Action (*Akcja Wyborcza Solidarnoscz*)
BBWR   Non-Party Bloc for the Support of Reforms (*Bezpartyjny Blok Wspierania Reform*)
KLD   Liberal Democratic Congress (*Kongres Liberalno-Demokratyczny*)
KPN   Confederation for an Independent Poland (*Konfederacja Polski Niepodleglej*)
PC   Center Alliance (*Porozumienie Centrum*)
PSL   Polish Peasants Party (*Polskie Stronnictwo Ludowe*)
ROP   Movement for the Republic (*Ruch dla rzeczypospolitej*), later called Movement for Poland's Reconstruction
SLD   Alliance of the Democratic Left (*Sojusz Lewicy Demokratycznej*)
UD   Democratic Union (*Unia Demokratyczna*)
UP   Union of Labor (*Unia Pracy*)
UW   Union of Freedom (*Unia Wolności*)
ZChN   Christian National Union (*Zjednoczenie Chrzescijansko-Narodowe*)

SLOVAKIA

DS   Democratic Party (*Demokratická strana*)
DÚ   Democratic Union of Slovakia (*Demokratická únia Slovenska*)
HSLS   Hlinka's Slovak People's Party (*Hlinkova slovenská ludová strana*)
HZDS   Movement for a Democratic Slovakia (*Hnutie za demokratické Slovensko*)
KDH   Christian Democratic Movement (*Kresťansko-demokratické hnutie*)
KSC   Communist Party of Czechoslovakia (*Komunistická strana Československa*)
ODÚ   Civic Democratic Union (*Obĕianska demokratická únia*)
SDK   Slovak Democratic Coalition (*Slovenská demokratická koalicia*)
SDKÚ   Slovak Christian and Democratic Union (*Slovenská kresťanská a demokratickcá únia*)
SDL   Party of the Democratic Left (*Strana demokratickej lavice*)
SNS   Slovak National Party (*Slovenská národná strana*)
SOP   Party of Civil Understanding (*Strana občianského porozumenia*)
VPN   Public Against Violence (*Verejnosť proti násiliu*)
ZRS   Association of Workers of Slovakia (*Združenie robotnikov Slovenska*)

Political Parties after Communism

Introduction

Focusing on political parties and party systems must remain a central theme for assessing progress towards the consolidation of liberal democracies following regime change. A strong system of political parties is a guarantee of the responsiveness and adaptability of the democracy and therefore its viability.

—Geoffrey Pridham, *Party Formation in East-Central Europe*

In Europe, political parties are not very old institutions. The parliamentary factions representing different interest groups within privileged classes (such as the Whigs and the Tories in seventeenth-century England) constituted the embryonic phase of party development. But political parties underwent their most intense development during the gradual broadening of the popular franchise in the second half of the nineteenth and the beginning of the twentieth century, which finally resulted in adoption of the notion of universal suffrage. During that period, new parties were founded, and traditional parties underwent substantial changes. Individualist and decentralized *cadre parties* were gradually replaced by disciplined and centralized *mass parties* oriented toward mobilizing the electoral support of entire social groups (Duverger 1964).

Up to this point, the logic of party development was basically the same in both Western and East-Central Europe.[1] But then the rise of fascist movements in the 1930s and particularly the events of World War II, beginning with the German *Drang nach Osten* (pressure toward the east) and ending with the transfer of East-Central Europe to the sphere of Soviet dominance (and the subsequent establishment of totalitarian Communist regimes), excluded the whole region for almost a half-century from the further evolu-

3

tion of the party system underway in Western Europe. Meanwhile, the mass party in Western Europe was, under the influence of the ongoing change in social structures, "transforming itself into a *catch-all 'people's' party* . . . turning more fully to the electoral scene, trying to exchange effectiveness in depth for a wider audience and more immediate electoral success" (Kirchheimer 1966). Later, particularly during the seventies when many nonparty political movements and organizations entered the political arena, Western parties saw their memberships decline. But the arguments put forth that this development meant the decline of the party per se were wrong and generally misconceived (Selle and Svasand 1991). Rather, the party was changing in its organization and structures. As Katz and Mair (1992) argue, parties do not have a single organizational form and any party has three faces—that is, it serves as a membership organization, a governing organization, and a bureaucracy, each of which may function differently. Based on this characterization, it is proposed here that the balance between the three dimensions of party organization was changing in Western Europe in the last decades of the twentieth century and that, as the membership aspect became less significant, the governing and bureaucratic aspects were becoming more prominent (Lewis 1995).

Political parties in East-Central Europe, however, did not participate in the evolution just described. Instead, immediately after the Communists took power in the late forties most of the non-Communist parties were destroyed, and others were involuntarily "transformed" into satellite parties, controlled entirely by the Communist regimes. Even the ruling Communist parties themselves were substantially changed: they fully fused with the bureaucracy of the totalitarian state. Then, in 1989, after the breakdown of Communist rule, the situation changed dramatically. The regime changes gave political parties a chance to play a crucial role in the post-Communist transformation. Although the other states in postwar Europe also underwent democratization (for example, the defeated fascist states after the war and the transitions from authoritarian rule to democracy in Greece, Spain, and Portugal in the seventies), from many points of view the democratization in East-Central Europe is indeed original because of the unique context in which the regime changes occurred. Unlike the situation in southern Europe during seventies, the newly founded or reborn political parties in East-Central Europe are operating in societies with rather different economic and social structures, which were gradually established under the more than forty years of social engineering by the Communist planners. Under communism, massive nationalization led to the total absence of the class structure that is typical of the capitalist economic system, the state remained virtually the only employer, and most of the people of productive age were forced to work. The self-employed were either rather few in numbers (for example, Polish peasants) or almost nonexistent (former Czechoslovakia). Unemployment officially—and in many Communist countries also realistically—did not exist. Forced collectivization changed the countryside, and massive industrialization and centrally planned housing construction changed the face of the cities. Since those days, the reintroduction of political and civic freedoms, together with big economic changes in the form of the "shock therapy" prescribed by the post-Communist economic reformers, have led to changes in the long-term status quo and to steps toward creating a new type of social order.

Although both the traditional and the newly emerging social cleavages have affected the development of the political system, they do not explain all the changes on the political front. Political parties also have been influenced by several other factors—among them, historical, cultural, and juridical. From the historical point of view, a return to liberal democracy gives political activists an opportunity to reestablish the party system in relation to the pre-authoritarian structure (Pridham 1995). Because the pre-Communist histories of Hungary, the Czech Republic, Slovakia, and Poland are not very similar, differences in party formation arising from this fact can be expected, along with various levels of continuity in party formation. For the latter, Linz (1978) differentiates between the "organizational" and "cultural" continuity of political parties. "Organizational continuity" is simply the existence of political parties as organizations during the Communist period. "Cultural continuity" refers to the ideological traditions (leftist as opposed to conservative value systems) that may very well persist even under authoritarian systems, either through remnant networks at the familial level or through what is called "political memory" (Pridham 1995). The political and ideological traditions of each individual country also are part of the general culture, but they are not the only cultural factors influencing the development of individual party systems. For example, traditions such as the practice of conflict resolution, predominantly accepted moral values, the perception of social justice and political fairness, and general attitudes toward authorities, civil rights, individualism, and collectivism are other influential factors. Last but not least, some researchers stress the importance of the "juridical context" or the legal structure and its role in constraining the political behavior of both voters and political parties (Cox 1979), thereby influencing the process of party formation. Clarc (1981) argues that the "law can be seen both as an outcome of political processes and a set of rules and standards with which political actors must comply." However, parties, even though they are the principal transition actors, are not free to change the juridical system too dramatically, because they are "constrained by historical inheritances, and they are also cautioned by the high uncertainties and the heavy tasks of the transition process" (Pridham 1995).

Objective of This Book

This text looks at party development in the post–Communist era in East-Central Europe from a comparative perspective, thereby avoiding the traditional concentration on domestic problems or "mutual isolationism" often observable even within the academic community of the region.[2] In doing so, it examines the relationships between party development in the post–Communist era and the underlying historical, cultural, socioeconomic, and juridical factors, and then assesses the importance of those relationships both in each country and in the region as a whole.

For many distant observers who live in long-term democracies and who are accustomed to understanding what different parties in their home countries represent or stand for, party development in the post–Communist era may appear quite chaotic. This book, however, will prove that a certain logic exists behind all the party successes and failures, merges and splits that have followed the decline of the Communist Party in East-Central Europe. More specifically, this book will describe how immediately after the collapse of Communist rule, party systems were primarily shaped by historical, cultural, and juridical factors, whereas the importance of socioeconomic factors was low. Moreover, parties have been reflecting "cleavages in people's heads," affected more by the perception of the situation than by the real situation itself. In turn, people's perceptions of the situation have been influenced a great deal by historical and cultural factors. Nevertheless, as the effects of the ongoing transformation have become more visible to and recognized by different groups in society, "value-driven" politics has begun to be replaced by "interest-driven" politics, and the influence of the formerly almost negligible socioeconomic factors on the development of the party system has grown remarkably. Thus the party systems in the four countries studied here are increasingly resembling those in Western European countries, whose parties appear to be political institutions reflecting social cleavages (Lipset and Rokkan 1967).

Organization of This Book

The book is divided into six chapters. Chapter 1 describes the basic features of the economic, social, and political development of both the pre-Communist era and the Communist era. This chapter concentrates on those historical events and phenomena that may have influenced the development of the political party structure after the fall of communism. Chapter 2 is fully devoted to describing political parties in the post-Communist period. In this chapter, readers receive the basic context needed to understand the core chapters that present general findings. Chapter 3 elaborates on the question of the extent to which the development of party systems after communism was influenced by historical and cultural factors. Chapter 4 addresses the relations between social cleavages on one side and the development of party structures on the other. It covers not only the classical four societal cleavages that Lipset and Rokkan (1967) identified as the most influential factors shaping party structures in Western Europe (center versus periphery, state versus church, agriculture versus industry, and class cleavage), but also the role of generational and gender-based cleavages in forming political structures. Chapter 5 deals with rules of the political game—electoral laws—and their influence on the development of party systems. Finally, Chapter 6 summarizes the outcome of this search for general patterns in the development of political parties in post-Communist East-Central Europe.

1

An Overview of Party Development
(1850–1989)

Many students of East-Central European politics believe that any study of contemporary political parties in the region requires at least some insight into the histories of the countries there. In view of the region's dramatic, complex history, however, this chapter will concentrate on the history of party systems themselves and refer to the general historical background in which they have developed only when that context would be helpful.[1] Although the historical circumstances in which political parties have come to life and operated have differed from country to country, three periods are common to all of them: the years up to and during World War I (1850–1917), the interwar and the early post–World War II period (1918–1947), and the Communist period (1948–1989).

The Years Up to and During World War I (1850–1917)

As noted in the Introduction, the origins and the basic logic of party system development in Hungary, the Czech Republic, Slovakia, and Poland, the four countries studied, were basically the same as those in Western Europe. Although examples of political institutions resembling modern parliaments are found even in very distant history (for example, the Sejm in sixteenth-century Poland—see Zukowski 1993), the key period in East-Central Europe is the late nineteenth and the early twentieth centuries, when the first modern political parties came to life in the region, accompanied by vast social and economic development. The situation in all four countries was in many respects similar: not a single country was independent—the Czech Lands, Hungary, and Slovakia were part of the Austrian Monarchy, and

8

Poland was divided among Prussia, Russia, and Austria—and domestic politics was inspired by the romantic concept of the state as existing primarily to serve the interests of whole nation. Yet both the political and the economic situations varied remarkably from country to country at that time.

Hungary

Politically, Hungary was in the most favorable position of the four countries. After the unsuccessful Hungarian revolution in 1848, which was followed by a period of (relatively mild) Austrian oppression, the Hungarians finally managed to secure vast political autonomy under the Habsburg monarch in 1867. A constitutional agreement called the Austro-Hungarian Compromise dramatically increased the status of Hungarians within the Austrian Monarchy. Hungarians were no longer one of several nations under the rule of Austrian emperor; rather, they, together with Austrians, were recognized as one of two nations "constituting the state," and the name of the state was changed from the Austrian Monarchy to the Austro-Hungarian Monarchy. Although the Austro-Hungarian Monarchy formally remained one state, the Austrian and Hungarian parts of the monarchy developed rather autonomously after 1867. The old Hungarian Diet was transformed into a bicameral parliament. Only members of the lower chamber, however, were elected by the electorate, which consisted of just 6 percent of potential voters for reasons described shortly (Kann and David 1984).

The new parliament was granted more power than any other representative body in Hungary under the Habsburgs. Politically, it reproduced the prerevolutionary division of the political elite. Thus the main political streams represented were the conservative Independent Party and the Left Center. Typically, the main political issues were those linked with Austro-Hungarian relationships, such as what position Hungary should hold within the monarchy and what strategies and tactics should be used to reach the common goal of all parties—more autonomy for Hungary.

At that time, political parties were far from representing different social groups. Although Hungary was a multiethnic country (with about 50 percent non-Hungarians), no ethnic minority party was represented in the parliament, mainly because of the disenfranchisement of minority voters by property or tax requirements. For the same reason, neither an agrarian nor a workers party existed at that time. The first sign of the change was the establishment in 1890 of the Social Democracy Party (later also called the Social Democratic Party), the first party to work actively among the workers.

The other example of a party linked more explicitly with some social group within the population was the conservative Catholic People's Party, which was founded in 1895 in opposition to the growing secularization of the state. It criticized the "excessive liberalism" that was introduced in the country after 1867 and that led, it believed, to extreme inequality, the breakdown of the traditional social cohesion, and the disproportionate power of Jews in the country's economic and social life (M. Kovács 1994). In 1906, the Independent Socialist Peasants Party was founded in an attempt to preserve the interests of the peasants.

Even though more parties emerged claiming to represent particular social groups, political parties remained nothing more than "parties of notables" functioning more as "political clubs than as modern political parties" (Dessewffy and Hammer 1995). One of the factors likely contributing to this characteristic was the electoral system, which remained very restrictive; the percentage of the population eligible to vote did not increase until after the First World War and was only 6.4 percent in 1910 (Dessewffy and Hammer 1995). Thus, although urbanization and industrialization were proceeding and social structures were changing substantially, the party system remained unchanged.

Czech Lands

The Czech Lands followed a similar path of political development from 1850 to 1918. The revolutionary year 1848 found the Czech political agenda seeking more autonomy within the Habsburg Monarchy. The National Party (the Old Czech Party), which claimed to represent the entire Czech nation, was the main political machine used for pushing "national interests." The Old Czechs united the conservative, liberal, and radical wings. Unlike in Hungary, however, the party had a predominantly middle-class leadership—that is, it was not one of noblemen. For most the leaders of the National Revival, the aristocracy could not be an ally, because almost all Protestant noblemen were forced to leave the country after the Battle of White Mountain in 1620 was lost, and the Catholic nobility and those Protestants who converted to Catholicism were perceived as too closely connected with the monarchy and too heavily Germanized. In fact, the degree of cooperation with the Bohemian aristocracy was one of the basic issues facing the Old Czech Party.

Meanwhile, a division existed between the political representatives of the two dominant historical Czech Lands—Bohemia and Moravia. Those from the more urbanized, more industrialized, and more secular Bohemia were more radical, while representatives of the Moravian Czechs were more conservative, trying to preserve a certain amount of autonomy even within the Czech national movement. (Later, however, Moravian Czechs abandoned separatism and joined Bohemian Czechs as far as the "Czech question" was concerned—Kann and David 1984.)

Following the Hungarian example, Czech representatives, elected in a curie system[2] on the basis of a rather restricted franchise, tried to gain more autonomy for the historical Czech Lands through negotiation with the Austrian leadership. However, their efforts to obtain for the Czech Lands the same kind of status that Hungarians were granted in 1867 failed. Internal conflicts within the Old Czech Party finally led to its split, and the radical wing founded the National Liberal Party (Young Czech Party), which gradually became a leading political force on the Czech political scene.

Although the Czechs were not very successful politically, the second half of the nineteenth century turned out to be a period of tremendous economic success. Industrialization spreading from north of Bohemia to the whole country rapidly changed the economic base of the Czech Lands. In response to the growing agricultural productivity and the need for more labor in the cities, Czech peasants migrated in vast numbers to the multiethnic urban areas. This inflow changed not only the demographic behavior of the population, but also the ethnic composition of the cities, and later led to the growing political influence of Czechs in the cities and industrial regions. Indeed, the Czech Lands became the prime industrial area of the Austro-Hungarian Monarchy, "its only region comparable to the Ruhr, Prussian Upper Silesia or the British Midlands" (Garver 1978). The initial phase of industrial prosperity based on the food processing industry, mainly beet sugar, beer, and dairy products, was followed by the quick development of heavy industry and, finally, by the introduction of the most advanced technological industry, including electric locomotive, trolley car, and automobile production. As Garver (1978) notes, "By 1990, the Czech Lands ranked first among all lands of the Habsburg Empire in railway mileage, and in its production of iron and steel, hard and soft coal, armaments, transportation equipment, machine tools, glass, ceramics, paper, textiles, electrical goods and chemicals." The inhabitants of the Czech Lands, both Czechs and Germans, benefited greatly from that development (see Table 1). In general, personal incomes in the Czech Lands grew during this period, although not all social groups benefited equally from that success.

During the same period, quickly changing social structures (especially

Table 1

*Shares of Personal Income and Population, Selected Parts of
Austria-Hungary, 1900*

Areas Now in	Share of Personal Income	Share of Population	Ratio of Income to Population
Czech Lands	28.9	20.3	1.42
Galicia and Bukovina	10.9	18.1	0.60
Hungary	14.8	15.4	0.96
Slovakia	5.8	7.2	0.80

Source: Bruce M. Garver, *The Young Czech Party* (New Haven: Yale University Press, 1978).

the growing number of industrial workers[3]), tensions among different social groups, and some reforms of the electoral laws lowering the franchise
requirements prepared the way for the establishment of new kinds of political parties based on broader popular support and on orientation for specific
social groups. Thus the Czech faction within the Austrian Social Democratic Party was established in 1896 (but later, in 1911, the Czech Social Democrats became quite independent), and the National Socialist Party, claiming to represent the interests of Czech workers, was founded in 1889. The
several political organizations of Czech peasants that sprang up after 1899
were finally united under the name the Czech Agrarian party in 1905. In
1901, future Czechoslovak president T. G. Masaryk founded the Progressive Party (the Realists[4]). The party did not attract many members or too
many voters, but it was popular among the intelligentsia and was able to secure several seats in parliament for their prominent leaders. Indeed, the
party served as an influential intellectual group in Czech politics.

In mostly Catholic Moravia, the Catholic National Party was established
in 1896 to represent conservative Catholics. The Christian Social Party,
founded in 1894 and reorganized on a popular basis in 1899, concentrated
on solving the problems of Catholic peasants, workers, and tradesmen
(Garver 1978). Thus the last decade of the nineteenth century gave birth to
a whole spectrum of political parties seeking to use existing cleavages to attract support from different social groups. With the introduction of universal suffrage for men in 1907 in the election for the lower house of parliament, the traditional "all-national" parties gave way to the establishment of
mass politics.[5] In the final two prewar parliamentary elections (1907 and
1911) the Czech Agrarian Party and the Czech Social Democrats emerged

as the strongest parties, and they preshaped the political spectrum of post-war Czechoslovakia.

Slovakia

While the basic aim of Hungarian and Czech politics in the nineteenth and early twentieth centuries can best be described as an effort to gain more autonomy and a greater degree of self-government for Hungarians and Czechs, Slovak and Polish politics at that time seemed to be mostly about how to help the nation to survive under hostile foreign rule. Unlike the Poles, the Slovaks had never had their own state. For hundreds of years, the area of contemporary Slovakia was an integral part of Hungary, never a separate administrative unit. The Slovaks were perceived as a part of *natio hungarica*—that is, the political nation created by the Hungarian nobility regardless of the ethnic origin and native language of their subjects. The situation changed substantially, however, after the romantic idea of nation, as defined by ethnicity and language, was adopted by the Hungarian leaders. Somewhat symptomatic of Central Europe, the Hungarian struggle (against the dominant German language) for the right to use the Hungarian language in public administration and higher education was accompanied by the denial of the same right to ethnic minorities living within Hungary (M. Kovács 1992). The logic of that effort was very clear: the more people who became Magyarized through the adoption of the Hungarian language, the more numerous and powerful the Hungarian nation (and the Magyar-speaking population of Hungary) would be. Thus the more successful the Hungarians were in their effort to achieve greater autonomy within the Austrian Monarchy, the more severe the measures they adopted against the non-Magyar population of Hungary.

After the Austro-Hungarian Compromise in 1867, the power of Hungarians within Hungary increased substantially. Although the Nationalities Law of 1868 formally guaranteed minorities the right to use their native language, in practice Magyarization continued. In 1874 the Hungarian government decided to close all three Slovak gymnasiums founded in the 1860s as the only secondary schools with Slovak as a language of instruction. In the meantime, the only political group in Slovakia—the Slovak National Party—was struggling for the use of the Slovak language and for minority rights, but it was not very successful, mostly because of unfavorable electoral laws that prevented Slovak candidates from gaining more than a few seats in the Hungarian parliament.

For Slovakia and the Slovak economy, the second half of the nineteenth century was not a very prosperous period. Although Slovakia was a relatively industrialized part of Hungary, mainly because of the development of the iron production and the food processing industry, and was far from being the poorest part of the Austrian Monarchy (see Table 1), economically its progress was relatively slow. As a result, Slovakia's share in the Hungarian economy declined, and the old social structures based on the predominance of the agricultural population were preserved (Kann and David 1984). Nevertheless, the wave of political activity, as manifested in new political movements and parties, reached Slovakia at the turn of the century. When the Catholic People's Party was founded in 1895 in Hungary, it attracted support from the ranks of Slovak Catholic priests, stressing as part of its party platform the need to respect the Nationalities Law. In 1897, an agrarian movement formed within the Slovak National Party, and a year later a group of pro-Czech intellectuals educated in Prague and concentrated around the journal *Hlas* propagated Czecho-Slovak cooperation and Slavic unity.[6] In 1905, Slovak socialists created a separate branch of the Hungarian Social Democratic Party. Meanwhile, Catholic conservatives under the leadership of the priest Andrej Hlinka continued to be politically active under the auspices of the Slovak National Party, and later under an independent Slovak People's Party (as of 1913). Because of the continuing pressure for Magyarization, the cooperation of different political groups under the all-national, umbrella-type organization of the Slovak National Party remained a typical feature of Slovak politics. The differences among various social groups in political ideologies and interests had to be overcome in the face of the common task of saving the nation from Magyarization.

Poland

The situation in Poland was even more complicated than that in Hungary, the Czech Lands, and Slovakia. Poland, unlike Slovakia, had a long history of being an independent state, but it lost its independence in the eighteenth century and in 1795 was finally divided up into three parts, which fell under Prussian, Russian, and Austrian rule. Although the periodic upheavals and rebellions in the various parts of Poland eventually restored the independence of the Polish state (which made the goals of Polish "politics" basically the same), the political and economic situations faced by different foreign rulers were so varied that the developments in the individual territories must be described separately.

Galicia, in the southern part of the country and held by Austria-Hungary, was in many respects in the most favorable position. After the political turmoil of 1848, the government abolished serfdom and granted land to some of the peasantry (Tworzecki 1996). In 1861, Galicia became the first province of the empire to have its own constitution and its own parliament, and in 1867 it received rather broad autonomy, including the right to use the Polish language in schools and the freedom to form different political and cultural organizations. Thus various organizations representing the grass roots emerged, including the People's Party—a party established in 1895 to represent the peasants' interests. The Galician economy did not fare so well; it suffered heavily from competition with the more advanced regions of Austria-Hungary. As a result, Galicia (together with Bukovina) was the poorest part of the Habsburg Monarchy (see Table 1) and was less developed than the other two parts of Poland. Indeed, typical of its economic structure, Galicia had a great many peasants and a very low level of industrialization.

The Polish territories under Prussia were the most economically advanced, with a higher degree of industrialization, the most developed infrastructure, and the best-educated population. The problem, however, was the relationship between the Prussian government and the Poles, whom it regarded as a distinct ethnic group. The situation grew even worse when Prussian chancellor Otto von Bismarck instituted his *Kulturkampf,* a policy intended to Germanize Polish inhabitants and to attain cultural homogeneity within the German territories. Education in the Polish language was fully subjected to the state's discretion, and it took extraordinary measures such as a ban on teaching Polish, even as a second language (Tworzecki 1996). In spite of persecution, the political and cultural life of Poland was developing quickly.

The third part of Poland, which was under Russian rule, probably occupied the least-favorable situation. Although a certain level of economic development was evident, especially in the textile industry in the Lodz region (an advantage of the huge Russian market), the czarist government ruled the country in a way that was incomparably worse than that found in the Prussian portion. In 1864, even the name *Poland* was abolished, and the country became an integral part of Russia. A process of forcible Russification was then enforced, political activity was forbidden, and most Polish organizations operated only clandestinely. Even under severe foreign oppression, however, some kind of political activity could be found. The Polish Socialist Party was founded in 1892 in a congress held in Paris. This party, as well as the Social Democracy of the Kingdom of Poland (established among party dissenters a year later), tried to defend workers' interests and operate more (Prussian part) or less (Russian part) openly. Some peasant organizations even secured several seats in the German parliament. The National Democracy Party, which had ideological and organizational roots in the activities of the conspiratorial National League (Blackwood 1990), tried to promote Polish national interest and attracted solid popular support in both the Prussian and the Russian parts of Poland.

The Interwar and the Early Post–World War II Period (1918–1947)

World War I dramatically changed the situation of all the nations of East-Central Europe. The fall of the czarist regime, the Bolshevik revolution and the subsequent civil war in Russia, the military defeat of Germany, and the collapse of the Austro-Hungarian Empire on the eve of the war gave nations in the region an unexpected chance to fulfill their longtime national aspirations. Based on the principle of national self-determination, some states were restored, and some quite new states were created with support from the Western powers.

Hungary

Hungary found itself in the least-favorable position in this respect. After the military setback of the Austro-Hungarian Empire, Hungary declared independence and proclaimed itself a republic in October 1918. But the new regime collapsed quickly under pressure from both internal and external enemies. It was unable to secure either the ethnically mixed territories (Transylvania, Croatia, Vojvodina, Slovakia, and Ruthenia) containing a majority of the non-Magyar population or democratic rule itself. The postwar revolutionary chaos helped the Hungarian Communists, led by Béla Kun, to establish a ruthless Communist dictatorship in 1919, which launched all types of revolutionary terror against the "internal enemy," established a socialized economy, but also attracted some popular support by attempting to regain lost territories. The Communist regime lasted only several months, however. It was overthrown by the Hungarian army, aided by military pressure from two neighboring countries, Romania and Czechoslovakia.

The new provisional government, under the leadership of the former

Austro-Hungarian naval chief Admiral Miklós Horthy, established a conservative "Christian-national" regime aimed primarily at regaining the territories lost by the Treaty of Trianon in 1920 (Dessewffy and Hammer 1995).[7] As for internal politics, the new regime was semidictatorial, rejecting liberalism and introducing some anti-Semitic measures. It limited the authority of the parliament and banned the Communist Party, yet some kinds of parliamentarism and party politics persisted. The ruling bloc consisted of several parties, among them the United Party, the Party of Hungarian Life, and the Party of National Unity, which represented in parliament the conservative and corporatist viewpoints. The opposition consisted of the left-wing Social Democrats, who were allowed to participate in politics after 1922, the National Liberals, and the Smallholders Party.

The most important obstacle to the development of democratic politics was the electoral law, which called for public voting (as opposed to secret ballots) in the countryside. This law helped the ruling bloc to gain the firm support of the rural population and thereby maintain power and regime stability. The importance of public voting for preserving regime stability became more obvious after the 1939 election when the universal secret ballot was introduced. The fascist, openly pro-Nazi and anti-Semitic Arrow Cross Party entered the parliament mainly at the expense of the ruling conservatives and rearranged the power structure there. Although Hungary joined Germany as an ally in World War II, hoping to regain lost territories, the regime did not become openly fascist until 1944, when the Arrow Cross Party was placed in the government by Adolf Hitler's Germany. The alliance with Germany had an extraordinarily important impact on postwar Hungarian politics.

After the military defeat of Hungary by the Red Army in 1945, a provisional government was established under Soviet guidance. It included Communists, Social Democrats, the National Peasant Party, and National Liberals (Grzybowski 1991a), and only "antifascist" parties were allowed to participate in the upcoming elections. Nevertheless, the 1945 election turned out to be the most democratic in Hungarian history. Although war criminals, ethnic Germans, and leaders of fascist parties were expelled from the electorate, an overwhelming majority of the population took part in the election. The Independent Smallholders Party, the only right-leaning party allowed to participate in the contest, received a solid majority of votes and subsequently gained 60 percent of the seats in parliament. The Communists and the Social Democrats both received about 17 percent of the votes, and the rest of the votes went to the National Peasant Party (about 7 percent) and to two other small parties.

Even though the Smallholders' victory would have allowed them to create their own majority government, they (inspired by Soviet advice) agreed
to form a grand coalition government under the umbrella of the formally
nonpartisan Independent Popular Front.[8] Between 1945 and 1947, the
power of the Communists, who held the crucial Ministry of the Interior in
the coalition government and were backed by the Soviet army and the secret police, rose remarkably. By the next election, scheduled for 1947, the
proportion of the disenfranchised, who were mainly from different rightist
groups, had increased to about 10 percent of the population. In the months
leading up the election, the Communists campaigned strongly against the
reactionaries within the Independent Smallholders Party, while encouraging the establishment of other right-wing parties outside the Independent
Popular Front (Christian Democratic People's Party, Party of Hungarian Independence, Independent Hungarian Democrats, and Christian Women's
League), hoping that those parties would gain voters from among the
Smallholders' supporters. Meanwhile, the Soviets interfered directly in
Hungarian politics by harassing the leaders of the opposition parties and
then arresting them on espionage and conspiracy charges. The outcome of
the last relatively free and fair parliamentary election before the Communists seized power completely is shown in Table 2.

The Communists gained more popular support in the election than they
had gathered over the previous two years, but the shift in the political ori-

Table 2

The 1947 Parliamentary Election Results, Hungary

Party	Votes		Seats	
	Number	Percent	Number	Percent
Hungarian Communist Party	1,113,050	22.3	100	24.3
Christian Democratic People's Party	820,453	16.4	60	14.6
Independent Smallholders Party	769,763	15.4	68	16.5
Social Democratic Party	744,641	14.9	67	16.3
Hungarian Independence Party	670,547	13.4	49	11.9
National Peasants Party	415,465	8.3	36	8.8
Independent Hungarian Democratic Party	260,420	5.2	18	4.4
Hungarian Radical Party	84,169	1.7	6	1.5
Christian Women's League	69,536	1.4	4	1.0
Civic Democratic Party	50,294	1.0	3	0.7
Total	4,998,338	100.0	411	100.0

Source: Gábor Tóka, "Seats and Votes: Consequences of the Hungarian Election Law," in *1990 Election to the Hungarian National Assembly,* ed. Gábor Tóka (Berlin: Ed. Sigma, 1995).

entation of the electorate was rather moderate. The ratio between the electoral strength of the left, as represented by the Communists, the Social Democrats, and the National Peasant Party, and of the right, as represented by the Christian Democrats, the Smallholders, and other small, right-oriented parties, basically did not change. An important difference, however, was the decline in the Smallholders' fortunes and the increased support for the right-oriented parties outside the Independent Popular Front. Because the government was again formed by the Front parties, the relative strength of the Smallholders within the government was reduced dramatically. After the Communists joined with the Social Democrats in the Communist-dominated Hungarian Socialist Workers Party in 1948, created an armed workers militia under Communist command and adopted a new electoral law (using the old trick of public voting which offered voters the choice of either approving or disapproving the single list of candidates prescreened by the Front), democracy was definitely over and the period of Communist dictatorship had begun.

Czechoslovakia

Czechoslovakia, produced by the fusion of the Czech Lands and Slovakia, was another new state that emerged after World War I from the ruins of the Austro-Hungarian Empire. Although the idea of creating an independent state was not accepted by either Czech or Slovak representatives before the war, the events of the war changed the situation very quickly. The decisive role, however, was played by various prominent émigrés. T. G. Masaryk founded the Czechoslovak Foreign Committee in Paris in 1915 with the aim of establishing an independent Czecho-Slovak Republic after the war. The organization of Czech and Slovak emigrants finally met in Pittsburgh in May 1918 to sign an agreement on the common effort to establish an independent republic that would include Slovakia as an autonomous territorial unit with its own diet (Felak 1994). At the end of the war, this effort intensified, gaining more support from both parties involved. Thus in May 1918 both the Slovak Socialists and the representatives of the Slovak National Party proclaimed their willingness to join the Czech effort in creating an independent state. On May 30, 1918, another meeting of foreign representatives in Pittsburgh produced an agreement that stated, among other things, that "Slovakia should have her own administration, her own diet and her own courts. The Slovak language would be the official language in the schools, in the public offices and in public life generally" (Felak 1994). The existence of the new state was proclaimed on October 28, 1918, in Prague. Two days later, the Slovak representatives assembled together as the Slovak National Council in the North Slovakian town of Martin declared Slovakia's willingness to join the republic.[9]

At the time, the creation of a common state was perceived by political representatives of both nations as the best solution to their immediate situation. For Slovaks, a common state with the linguistically similar Czechs seemed to be the best way to escape from unwanted Hungarian rule. For Czech leaders, the Slovak population represented a welcome reinforcement of the Slavic element in view of the large German-speaking population living in both the Bohemian and the Moravian borderlands. After all, without the Slovaks the Czechs would not constitute even a simple majority of the population in the republic and would not be able to proclaim Czechoslovakia a nation-state of the "Czechoslovak nation."[10]

By proclaiming itself a nation-state of the "Czechoslovak nation," Czechoslovakia could defend its existence on the principle of national self-determination. In such a state, the German population was considered an ethnic minority. Although Germans outnumbered the Slovaks, Slovaks, as a part of the "Czechoslovak nation," benefited from certain privileges that were not given to minorities—for example, they could use the Slovak language in courts and in dealing with the local authorities regardless of their number in any community. To have the same rights as the Slovaks, Germans would have to constitute at least 20 percent of the local population (Bugajski 1994).

The Czechoslovak constitution adopted by the Czech-dominated National Assembly in 1920 defined the state as uninational with a centralized administration. Although the constitution was basically liberal, stressing civil rights regardless of ethnicity, religion, and language, the centralized solution did not satisfy minorities, not even the Slovaks. Thus the questions of minority rights and territorial administration remained crucial for domestic politics throughout the entire interwar period.

Economically, Czechoslovakia continued to follow the Czech success of the nineteenth century. Although some adaptation problems related to the disintegration of Austria-Hungary definitely existed, the problems were mainly in Slovakia where industry lost the traditional ties with the Hungarian market and suffered from the free competition of the more developed Czech economy. Yet interwar development did not bear out the skeptical prognoses. On the contrary, the postwar chaos was quickly overcome, and the tough deflationary policy of the Prague government prevented the hyperinflation seen in Germany (Průcha 1995). And yet this measure did not stop solid economic growth, which was among the highest in Europe and definitely the highest in the region (Mitchell 1992). Despite the good economic record, however, the republics' economic differences (between the industrialized Czech Lands and agricultural Slovakia) remained unchanged during the entire interwar period.

The party structure of Czechoslovakia reflected two basic cleavages—social and ethnic. The social cleavage reproduced to some extent the prewar situation. The ethnic cleavage was even more important—it divided party system into three completely separate subsystems: the full range of Czechoslovak parties (parties established by Czech and Slovak politicians and supported by Czech and Slovak voters), a German party system, and a Hungarian party system. Because in a system based on proportional representation the electoral strength of the parties reflects more or less precisely the ethnic composition of the electorate and because the majority of population was considered Czechoslovak, Czechoslovak parties dominated politics throughout the entire interwar period. Among them, the most powerful were the five parties (*Pětka,* The Five) that together were repeatedly able to gain a majority of seats in the parliament. Thus they made up almost all the interwar coalition governments.

For most of the period, the strongest party within the Pětka was the Agrarian, a moderate right-wing group claiming to represent the agricultural interests. It was backed by influential grassroots peasant organizations (agrarian cooperatives and credit unions, among others). The most important rival on the left was the Social Democratic Party, which represented the interests of the large working class. The Social Democrats, stressing the need for vast social reforms and the protection of the workers, secured over one-quarter of all votes in the first postwar elections of 1920. Internal conflicts between moderate reformers and radical revolutionaries over the scope of necessary social changes and the manner in which to introduce them finally led the party to split. One faction continued to be one of the governing parties respecting the democratic rules of the game; the other faction founded the strong antiregime Communist Party,[11] which was closely linked to the Soviet Bolsheviks and operated legally until the Nazi occupation of the country. The third party belonging to the Pětka was the centrist Czechoslovak National Socialist Party, which was supported mainly by middle-class urban professionals and small entrepreneurs. The fourth party, the Czechoslovak National Democracy, had tried to establish itself as an all-national party (in accordance with the traditions of the prewar Young Czech

Party from which it sprang). But as the class division of society slowly led the idea of all-national politics into the realm of illusions, the party began to seek its support from the "commercial classes" and the intelligentsia by pushing an agenda of social reforms within the limits of economic reality (Blackwood 1990) and by fighting against both the Agrarians and the Social Democrats by rejecting the right of any particular class to enjoy any privileges within society. The fifth of the co-ruling parties was the Czechoslovak People's Party, the classical sectional party that effectively unified several prewar Catholic parties and gained the stable support of the Catholic population living mainly in the Moravian countryside. It thus also served as a representative of the specific regional interests of Moravia.

During the interwar period, all the governments were based on a grand coalition of ideologically different parties united by their common interest in preserving the territorial unity of the country and the democratic regime. The opposition, by contrast, was a conglomeration of parties, some of whom were not very loyal to the state. Besides the Communists, who openly used the democratic institutions only as an arena in which to prepare the ground for their revolutionary solution to all social problems, the opposition consisted of Andrej Hlinka's Slovak People's Party and a whole spectrum of German and Hungarian parties, including the Social Democrats, Christian Socialists, and Agrarians. The Germans, who abruptly found themselves in the position of an ethnic minority in an unwanted state dominated by the Slavic population, had trouble accepting the existence of Czechoslovakia in the country's earliest years. Similarly, the Hungarians were thinking more about possible revisions of the Trianon Treaty than of their future within Czechoslovakia. As the situation stabilized, however, both German and Hungarian politicians became more loyal to Czechoslovakia, which allowed some interethnic cooperation between ideologically similar parties and some limited participation of Germans in the government in the late 1920s.

The Slovak People's Party, under the leadership of the charismatic Catholic priest Hlinka, also represented another type of opposition. All big Czechoslovak parties had their own local branches in Slovakia. Even Hlinka's party closely cooperated with the Czechoslovak People's Party in the parliament at the beginning, but the distrust of many Slovaks toward the central administration of the country, the unfulfilled promises of Slovak autonomy within Czechoslovakia, and the rising suspicion of Czech liberalism and secularism pushed the party into opposition. The result was an image of the party as a defender of Slovak national interests. Thus the political party spectrum in Slovakia consisted basically of an all-national Slovak People's Party and the whole spectrum of Slovak branches of Czechoslovak parties.

The Great Depression, which hit the country hard in 1929 and lasted until 1933, changed the economic and political situation. In the Czech Lands, the crisis was particularly severe in the German-populated regions with predominantly export-oriented light industry. This hardship, along with the rise of the Nazi movement in Germany, spurred nationalism among the Germans. In the 1935 elections, the new all-national Sudeten German Party, which stressed the right to self-determination, managed to secure an overwhelming majority of German votes and become the biggest party in the parliament. At the end of the 1930s, the Sudeten German Party, supported by Nazi Germany, became one of Hitler's most valuable tools in destroying Czechoslovakia.

The hardship of the economic crisis also increased the activity of both Hlinka's party and the Hungarian parties, but it did not lead to the rise of any significant fascist parties[12] or to a departure from the democratic rules of the politics. Under pressure from both foreign and domestic sources, however, Czechoslovakia first gave up to Germany its borderland containing the majority of the German population after the 1938 Munich Agreement[13] and then in 1939 fell apart when the Czech Lands were seized by Germany and forced to join the Third Reich as the "Protektorat Böhmen und Mähren" (Protectorate of Bohemia and Moravia). The Slovaks established a quasi-independent fascist state under the custody of Germany. The one-party system in Slovakia lasted until August 1944 when the regime was overthrown by a Slovak national uprising, and the country was consequently invaded by the German army.

Despite the military defeat of the uprising, an important message was sent to the Czechs: the Slovaks would like to reestablish Czechoslovakia after the war. And, indeed, Czechoslovakia was immediately reestablished after the end of the war in 1945. The way had already been prepared by the diplomatic efforts of Czech and Slovak political representatives in exile who persuaded the United States, Great Britain, and France to recognize the legal continuity of prewar Czechoslovakia. Although the borders of the reestablished Czechoslovakia differed slightly from those of the prewar country (its former most eastern part, Subcarpathian Ruthenia, was surrendered to Soviet Ukraine), the loss appeared to be only a minor one for the future of the state.

The postwar political situation was largely preshaped by two factors: the liberation of the country from the Nazis by the Red Army and Czechoslovakia's bad memories of the Munich Agreement. These factors led to a reorientation of foreign policy toward the east and an improved image of the Communists. The nearly complete expulsion of the German population from Czechoslovakia to Germany, along with the loss of Subcarpathian Ruthenia, drastically changed the ethnic composition of the country: it became more ethnically homogeneous than ever. The postwar provisional government, composed of only "antifascist" parties[14] under the umbrella of the National Front and strongly influenced by the Soviets, ruled the country until the parliamentary election scheduled for 1946. The election, however, was only semifree. The electoral rules not only disenfranchised all (remaining) "Germans, Hungarians and other traitors," but also did not allow the biggest prewar party—the Agrarians—to participate. Although all the Front parties hoped they would gain the votes of the peasants, none did so, except the Communists who promised vast agricultural reforms in favor of smallholders. The Communists also benefited from the support of most of those people who moved from the city to the borderlands to settle. As a result, the Communist Party secured a clear victory in the 1946 parliamentary election (see Table 3 for a summary of the electoral results in the Czech Lands).

The Czech Lands may have been the promised land for the Communist Party, but the situation was rather different in Slovakia in 1946. Even if the Communists tried to split the opposition by encouraging the birth of new parties (Labor Party, Freedom Party), the overwhelming majority of the non-Communist political elite, which was unified under the name of the Democratic Party, was strong enough to obtain almost two-thirds of the 1946 election vote, which left the Communist Party lagging behind (see Table 4).

The Slovaks' overwhelmingly non-Communist vote could not change the future of the country, however; it was increasingly driven toward dictator-

Table 3

The 1946 Parliamentary Election Results, Czech Lands

Party	Percent of Votes	Seats	
		Number	Percent
Communist Party of Czechoslovakia	40.2	93	40.3
Czechoslovak National Socialist Party	23.7	55	23.8
Czechoslovak People's Party	20.2	46	19.9
Social Democratic Party	15.6	37	16.0
Blank votes	0.4	—	—
Total	100.0	231	100.0

Source: Czechoslovak Statistical Office.

Table 4
The 1946 Parliamentary Election Results, Slovakia

		Seats	
Party	Percent of Votes	Number	Percent
Democratic Party	62.0	43	62.3
Communist Party of Czechoslovakia	30.4	21	30.4
Freedom Party	3.7	3	4.3
Labor Party	3.1	2	2.9
Blank votes	0.8	—	—
Total	100.0	69	100.0

Source: Czechoslovak Statistical Office.

ship. After the elections, another grand coalition government was formed under the Communist leadership. And once again, the scenario was familiar—the Communists abused the police, harassed the leaders of non-Communist parties, and created the People's (meaning Communist) militia. It all ended with a coup. In the subsequent "elections," voters had nothing to choose from except the "unified list of National Front candidates." With that, democracy died in Czechoslovakia.

Poland

The interwar political and economic development in Poland more resembled that of Hungary than that of Czechoslovakia. Early post–World War II Poland was anything but a stable country. The consolidation of the state itself was the main problem of the new republic. Poland was divided into three parts in the eighteenth century, and that division lasted until the end of World War I. Postwar Poland inherited "six currencies . . . ; five regions [with] . . . separate administrations; . . . four languages of command in the army; three legal codes; and two railway gauges" (Davies 1981). Moreover, Poland became a multinational state, with Poles making up only about two-thirds of the total. The remaining one-third consisted of Ukrainians, Jews, Belorussians, and Germans. Even the answer to the question "What is Poland?" was far from simple. This was reflected not only in the different ideas of the two Polish political leaders at the time, the conservative Roman Dmowski and the socialist Józef Piłsudski (Wandycz 1990), but also in Poland's diplomatic controversies and the military conflicts with its neighbors which lasted for several years after the war.

The Polish postwar situation was not very favorable for the development of a political spectrum of the Western European type. The strongest political faction in the parliament after the 1919 elections was the catch-all National Populist Union, a political group dominated by the Polish National Democratic Party which openly rejected Western liberalism as unsuitable for Polish conditions. Instead, it proclaimed a policy stating that the subordination of individual rights and freedoms to the needs of the national state was an unavoidable condition for the survival of the nation (Blackwood 1990). The government, however, was dominated by the Polish Socialist Party, which was supported by several political parties representing minorities. The resulting political instability—in the form of extraordinarily frequent changes of governments,[15] numerous splits of the parliamentary clubs, and economic catastrophe leading to hyperinflation—prepared the ground for the successful military coup led by Piłsudski in May 1926.

The political program supported by the new leadership called for fighting against "the overflow of party politics," introducing moral cleansing in public life, and implementing a package of economic measures that sought to improve the economic condition by balancing the budget, stabilizing the local currency, and reducing unemployment (Dziewanowski 1976). Like Horthy in Hungary, Piłsudski created a political bloc intended to stand above the parties while allowing some party competition. Thus in an effort to legitimate Piłsudski's seizure of power, his Nonparty Bloc to Cooperate with the Government participated in the parliamentary election of 1928, competing with other parties. Although the Bloc was the clear winner of the election, it was not able to achieve a majority of the votes. Therefore, Piłsudski applied more authoritarian measures, including police intimidation of the opposition in the 1930 election, which the Bloc won by obtaining an absolute majority of the votes. This win later led to the adoption of a new constitution that was designed to strengthen the role of the president and thus to stabilize the power of the powerful (Vinton 1993). The late 1930s, however, did not bring any stability. Instead, increasing tensions with neighboring Nazi Germany finally ended with the German military invasion that started World War II. Fifteen days after the German attack, the Red Army also attacked from the east, and Poland was quickly divided between two (momentary) allies.

The Polish political representation at the time of the war was basically divided into two groups: the Communists, who changed their name to the Polish Workers Party and were based in Moscow, and the representatives of the non-Communist parties who created the government in exile in London.

When Germany and the Soviet Union began to fight one another, the Communists and the London groups became, at least theoretically, allies in the fight against the common enemy—Nazi Germany. The resistance movement within occupied Poland was represented by the Home Army (*Armija Krajova*).

During the war, Czechoslovakia was liberated by the Soviet Union, and the Red Army was welcomed by a majority of the population, but the relationship between the Soviets and the Poles at the end of the war was far from easy. For one thing, the Soviets annexed the eastern parts of prewar Poland. Moreover, the Red Army, though often assisted by the Polish Home Army, usually considered its soldiers as enemies, harassed its officers, and tried to reduce its influence as much as possible. Strategically, the Soviets were seeking to increase the realm of communism by creating a belt of satellite states dominated by local Communists loyal to Moscow. Soviet leader Joseph Stalin's tactic seemed obvious: to weaken any imaginable core of possible future resistance regardless of the number of possible victims. The prime example of this tactic was the 1944 Warsaw Uprising, inspired and encouraged by the Soviets, but the insurgents were then left without any military help and eventually were totally defeated by the Germans.[16]

Because the Polish Communists were weak, the Soviets had to seize power a little differerently in Poland than in the other countries studied. In 1944, on the Polish territory already under Soviet control, the Soviets created the Polish Committee of National Liberation, a kind of provisional pro-Soviet government. At the 1945 Yalta conference, the Allies decided, under pressure from the Soviet Union, to recognize the Polish Committee, not the exile government in London, as the Polish government, but they expressed the opinion that the Polish Committee should include some representatives of the London government in exile in order to prepare for the free postwar election. The coalition Government of National Unity established in Moscow in the summer of 1945 included the Polish Workers Party (Communists), Polish Socialist Party, Polish Peasant Party (of Stanislaw Miko-łajczyk), Democratic Party, and Labor Party. At the July 1945 Potsdam Conference, the Allies provisionally recognized the new Polish-German boundary and mandated the expulsion of the German population from the new Polish territories. The new eastern boundary of the country was codified by the Polish-Soviet agreement.

The Polish Communists, who had a strong position within the provisional coalition government, were not very eager to organize a free election, because they were not sure how much support they would draw from the population. Instead, they worked hard to implement their political and economic program, which included a resettling of the "Recovered Territories," land reform, and nationalization. When pressed by the other parties and the West to take part in the elections, the Communists adopted a tactic similar to that used elsewhere in the region: they suggested the creation of a unified list of all parties. But when the other parties rejected the idea of the unified list, the Communists fully concentrated on the electoral contest. They created the so-called Democratic Bloc, consisting of the Polish Workers Party, Polish Socialist Party, Democratic Party, and another Peasant Party (that is, not the Polish Peasant Party of Stanislaw Mikolajczyk). Moreover, they sent two satellite parties to the election—the Labor Party and the Peasant Party "New Liberation." The new electoral law disenfranchised over one million voters by not accepting those who "extracted benefits from economic collaboration with occupation authorities" or "collaborated with underground fascist organization bands" (Dziewanowski 1976). A week before the elections, some opposition candidates' names were stricken from the list, and another 135 opposition candidates found themselves in jail. The circulation of opposition newspapers also was reduced drastically. The results of the 1947 elections, which were probably even "helped" by some instances of electoral fraud, are shown in Table 5.

After the victory of the Democratic Bloc, nothing could stop the Communists. In the summer of 1947, the Communists and the Social Democrats agreed to establish the United Polish Workers Party, which was followed by a new wave of imprisonment for opposition leaders. When Stanislaw Mikołajczyk, the leader of the opposition Polish Peasant Party, fled the country in November 1947 because he feared arrest, the defeat of democratic rule was complete.

Table 5

The 1947 Parliamentary Election Results, Poland

Party	Number of Votes	Percent of Votes
Democratic Bloc	9,003,682	80.1
Polish Peasants Party (of Mikołajczyk)	1,154,847	10.3
Labor Party	530,979	4.1
Peasant Party "New Liberation"	397,754	3.5
Others	157,611	1.4
Total valid votes	11,244,873	100.0

Source: Marian K. Dziewanowski, *The Communist Party of Poland: An Outline of History* (Cambridge: Harvard University Press, 1976).

The Communist Period (1948–1989)

1948–1969

The Communist takeovers drastically changed the political and economic situation throughout the entire region. One-party dictatorships were installed in all countries within the Soviet bloc, the foreign and domestic politics of the satellite countries were directly subjected to the "interests of the socialist camp," and the practical policies of the individual Communist governments were carefully supervised by Moscow. The process of consolidation of the new regime's power followed the same scenario. The first step was liquidation of any type of political opposition. Non-Communist parties were either banned or subjected to a front type of umbrella organization directly under the Communist leadership. Leaders of the non-Communist parties found themselves either in jail as "enemies of the people and socialism" or forced to emigrate. The second step entailed taking on enemies inside the parties themselves. In a series of spectacular Soviet-style show trials, yesterday's comrades were presented to the public as the treacherous saboteurs of the party—all in the name of creating a better future for everyone. Fear and distrust would then spread among the public (How can anybody be safe if even the top officials of the Communist Party are not?). This political terror was accompanied by violent campaigning against whole social groups as the Communist economic plans of massive socialization and ideological unification were pushed forward. Enemies were numerous: the entrepreneurs who were "exploiting workers," the businessmen who were "parasiting on the labor of the working class," the farmers who were opposing the collectivization of agriculture, the priests who were "spreading Middle Age darkness among the ordinary people," the professionals "who do not work manually, hence do not work at all." Although the Communists did permit some features of the democratic system to exist (for example, parliament and local councils), the elections to these representative bodies were anything but normal or fair. On the contrary, the elections became the crucial test of citizens' loyalty to the new regime. Public "approval" of the single candidate list preprepared by the Communists "'legitimized" the regime while giving authorities another chance to identify the opponents. And apparently this tactic was successful, because the official figures show "electoral support" for the regime to have been almost unanimous.[17]

The Communists not only abandoned the rules of democratic government, but also introduced a command economy in which all economic units were nationalized and subjected to a central planning committee. The main task of each unit was to fulfill the demands of the state economic plan put in place by the party. Thus the whole economy in the early fifties was geared toward the development of heavy industry, which was designed to serve the military plans of the Communist bloc. The development of services, infrastructure, housing, light industry, or other "nonproductive" branches of industry was not encouraged.[18]

This kind of uniform political and economic development remained in place in the countries under Soviet dominance until Stalin's death in 1953, which weakened the position of hard-line Stalinists in leadership positions in most of the satellite countries. Then from 1953 onward, the individual countries took more divergent paths. In Czechoslovakia, the system of oppression continued unabated, and the forced collectivization of agriculture as well as the political trials continued until the late 1950s. The Hungarian Communists, however, pledged themselves to a program of political and economic reforms. One of the most remarkable results of the reforms was the termination of the collectivization program in the agricultural sector. As a result, "some 130,000 out of 380,000 collectivized farmers . . . dropped out of the agricultural cooperatives" (Grzybowski 1991a). Meanwhile, the internal struggle between the Stalinists and the reformers inside the Communist Party became more obvious. The events of the Twentieth Congress of the Soviet Communists in February 1956 where Stalin's crimes were denunciated by his follower Nikita Khruschev gave new impulse to the internal struggles between the hard-line Communists and the reformers within the Communist Parties. It also gave hope to the people in the satellite countries that something might change.

The Communists, however, were far from giving up their power at that time. When workers in the Polish city of Poznan protested in June 1956 against the government's unwillingness to de-Stalinize, they were crushed by the armed forces and several hundred of them were killed. An even more dramatic situation evolved in Hungary, where public discontent with the regime finally led to a national upheaval in October 1956 that had to be defeated by the tanks of the Red Army. Although extraordinary measures were taken to suppress the popular unrest, including the execution of Prime Minister Imre Nagy in Hungary, the outcome of the disturbances was more or less positive when compared with the situation at the time of Stalin's rule. The new Communist leaders approved by the Soviets changed party policy substantially. Even the Soviets themselves seemed to recognize that there could be more than one path to communism, and they gave more autonomy to the satellite party leaders. Thus in Poland the "collectivization of agriculture was abandoned, censorship was made less restrictive, and the privileges of party and security apparatus members were reduced" (Tworzecki 1996). Similarly, in Hungary the compulsory work competition movement was abandoned, campaigns against enemies disappeared from the media, and people were not forced to publicly agree with the regime. For both the Polish and Hungarian Communists, the main task was to concentrate on fulfilling the material demands of the population and increasing the standard of living.

In Czechoslovakia, the hard-line Stalinists continued to govern until the late sixties. Beginning in the mid-sixties, however, the society appeared to move toward more freedom and openness. The shift began among writers, filmmakers, and journalists and continued after the Slovak reformist Alexander Dubček replaced the hard-liner Antonín Novotný as general secretary of the Communist Party in January 1968. The result was a halt to censorship of the media, and, indeed, a "new wind" abruptly spread throughout the entire society. Although reformers among the Communists basically wanted to improve socialism (that is, to create "socialism with a human face"), the events of the "Prague Spring" occurred more quickly than they expected. Within several months, independent organizations mushroomed, some of them with clear-cut political agendas. The Social Democrats prepared for a rebirth, and the Club of Involved Non-Partisans represented a sort of proto-party organization with a clearly pro-democracy program. The more open atmosphere also encouraged Slovak Communists to raise the old question of mutual relationships between Czechs and Slovaks in the common state by suggesting the federalization of the state and demanding more responsibilities for the authorities of the individual republics.

Czech and Slovak Communists were not the only ones astonished by these events. The Soviet Communists, even more surprised, decided to put an end to this dangerous departure from the general rules. Several rounds of negotiations between Czechoslovak Communists and their counterparts from the "socialist camp" countries about what constituted socialism, ended in a military attack on Czechoslovakia by the Warsaw Pact armies on August 20, 1968. After the invasion, General Secretary Gustáv Husák, who was perceived as a good compromise between the reformers and the hard-liners, was installed as the country's new leader. It soon became clear, however, that Husák's reformist image was only an illusion. He and other hard-liners, backed by the still-present Red Army, began a process of "normalization," which included the massive expulsion of reformers from the party and the mass layoffs of those who were considered by the special screening commissions not loyal enough to the new pro-Soviet government.

When the dust settled, the only visible outcome of the Prague Spring was the new constitutional law establishing the federal structure of the country. Under the new constitutional arrangements, both republics of the Czechoslovak federation (the Czech Republic and Slovakia) had been granted rather broad autonomy. An important byproduct of the wider autonomy for the individual republics was its effect on the process of normalization. In the end, however, the process had an easier path in Slovakia, because more Czechs than Slovaks participated in the 1968 reform attempts and thus were more susceptible to the severe revenge of hard-liners in the Czech Republic after 1969.

1970–1989

In the seventies, the situation in East-Central Europe was already remarkably different. Hungary was politically the most liberal of the four countries studied, and its degree of freedom and standard of living for ordinary people were envied by the citizens of the less-fortunate Communist countries. The country's moderate prosperity, however, had no stable economic base, because it was driven partly by Western financial credits and partly by the shadow economy that served as an additional source of income for an increasing number of families. As Dessewffy and Hammer (1995) point out, in this system even party membership gradually lost much of its relevance, and most areas of culture, science, and art ceased to be controlled directly. "Trade" between the Communist leadership and the population seemed to work well.

In Poland, things were not so tranquil. Popular unrest over both economic performance and party politics erupted several times in waves of strikes and demonstrations. The most important were the student riots in Warsaw in 1968, the workers' unrest in the Baltic port cities of Gdansk, Gdynia, and Sopot in 1970, and the workers' strikes in Radom and Warsaw in 1976 (Cipkowski 1991). The Communist government reacted by both persecuting the protesters and voicing empty promises for change. Although the unrest in the early seventies did not lead to any real changes in the political situation, the political outcome of the 1976 strikes was extremely important—the Committee for the Defense of the Workers was established to give financial and legal help to those persecuted by the police, which marked a first step in building a real political opposition to the regime. Later, several other opposition groups also were established, the most important of which was the Confederation of Independent Poland, an anti-Communist dissident group founded in 1979 to fight for the establishment of an independent and democratic republic (Zuzowski 1991).

In Czechoslovakia, the seventies was a time of harsh persecution for any sort of opposition. This fact was made quite clear after the wave of arrests of Charta 77[19] activists in 1977 when they attempted to remind the state administration through a distributed manifesto that it ought to observe its own laws and follow the provisions for human rights based on the Helsinki Accords. A huge anti-Charta campaign in the media, combined with severe pressure from the party and security apparatus, persuaded millions of people to protest against the manifesto. Actually, an overwhelming majority of the protestors were aware of the manifesto only because of the campaign against it (it had never been officially published).

From an economic point of view, the situation was relatively stable in Czechoslovakia. Although the structure of the economy was becoming increasingly outdated, it was still effective enough to serve the basic needs of the inhabitants. Moreover, the Czechoslovak Communists, following a long tradition of tough fiscal and monetary policies, kept the budget balanced and refrained from asking for any financial credits from the West. In Slovakia, the economy continued to grow through subsidization by the federal budget.

The late seventies and early eighties saw the demise of all illusions about the viability of a command economy. The effects of the oil shock,[20] postponed by an agreement between the satellite countries and the Soviet Union that set the price of Soviet oil at the average of world market prices over the last five years, hit the region in the late seventies quite dramatically. Both the Hungarian and (especially) Polish economies suffered sharp declines in production and a rise in inflation, as well as serious financial problems arising from attempts to repay foreign debts. In Czechoslovakia, the growth of the gross domestic product (GDP) slowed and inflation increased (Jeffries 1993).

After the Polish government announced a general price increase in 1980, strikes spread throughout the country, and workers demanded wage increases in compensation. In the summer of 1980, a strike at the Gdansk shipyard, led by electrician Lech Wałęsa, quickly took on political overtones. Not only did the workers have their usual economic demands, but now they sought more civil liberties and independent trade unions. Faced with strong opposition, the regime backed down and signed an agreement with the strikers, which allowed them to establish a free trade union called Solidarity. Within several months, Solidarity became a sort of umbrella organization with ten million members. It gathered various types of organizations and movements, exercised free speech, and published several newspapers. The strength of Solidarity was secured by an alliance with the Catholic Church, which had never lost its extraordinary position in Polish society and which had greater freedom than any other church in the Communist bloc.

The period of limited freedoms did not last long, however. In December 1981, faced with the increasing threat of Soviet military action, the first secretary of the Communist Party, Gen. Wojciech Jaruzelski, announced the onset of martial law. Solidarity leaders were imprisoned, and street demonstrations were broken up by military forces. Yet the harassment of the opposition was not particularly severe, and most Solidarity leaders were released rather quickly. Meanwhile, the underground activities flourished, and illegal newspapers were printed regularly and read by tens of thousands of people. The Communist Party itself soon lost its confidence in vainly attempting to struggle against economic problems without the popular support it needed to back it up. As a result, the decline of Polish communism became more and more visible, especially after the turn in Soviet policy under Soviet leader Mikhail Gorbachev in the mid-1980s,[21] which gave more hope to the satellite countries that the Soviets would allow more independent development. In the late eighties, the Communist government was plainly not able to cope with both the economic and political problems, and rising inflation provoked a wave of unorganized strikes. The government, under the pressure of a worsening situation, finally decided to negotiate with the leader of the banned Solidarity, Lech Wałęsa, and offer him a trade: "If Wałęsa could persuade the strikers to go back to work, the regime would consider restoring Solidarity's legal status as an independent union" (Cipkowski 1991). Wałęsa halted the strikes, and the reborn Solidarity was invited to negotiate with the government about possible solutions to the crisis.

The negotiations, which began in February 1989, resulted in an agreement of which the most politically important elements were the legalization of Solidarity, the permission to publish independent newspapers, and a constitutional change—the introduction to Poland's parliament of an upper house whose members would be selected by free and open elections. The change also called for free elections for 35 percent of the 460 seats in the Sejm, the lower house of the parliament (the remaining seats were reserved for the Communist and the satellite parties). The way was paved for regime change.

As difficult as it may have been, the economic hardship of the early eighties in Hungary was not as dire as that befalling Poland. The more liberal Communist government in Hungary attempted to overcome the economic crisis by introducing several economic reforms that gave more autonomy and responsibility to the managers of state enterprises and allowed more freedom in private economic enterprises. But the gradual reforms, which tried to mix a command economy and a free market economy, were not particularly successful. Inflation rose and large social groups became impoverished.

Meanwhile, the appearance of Gorbachev and his reform agenda was a fortunate development for the Communist leadership of Hungary. The Hungarian type of *perestroika* closely followed events in the Soviet Union and shared the same goal: to reform society by political liberalization under the leadership of the Communist Party. The new electoral law of 1983 introduced some competitive features into the electoral contest. Even though all candidates had to be screened by Communist-dominated Patriotic Popular Front officials before the elections, the trivial fact that voters had a chance to choose from more than one candidate in the parliamentary elections represented a crucial departure from the classic Communist one-candidate "elections." Moreover, reformers within the Communist Party gained influence. The liberal Democratic Opposition, a clandestine group publishing underground newspapers, was becoming increasingly active and demanding that János Kádár resign from his position as party leader. When a group of dissenters founded the Hungarian Democratic Forum in 1987, officially a nonpolitical forum for debates on the most important problems in society, it received some support even from the reform Communists. Other opposition groups were encouraged by the fact that the regime did not pronounce such meetings illegal and that the press referred to them rather freely. In 1988, a group of students founded the Federation of Young Democrats. Officially, it was a youth organization that challenged the Communist Youth Organization monopoly, but, in fact, it was a kind of party. The Communist Party's reaction was atypical; instead of persecuting "the antisocialist forces," the party became preoccupied with the problem of internal division. Later in the year, historical parties such as the Independent Smallholders and the Social Democrats were reestablished, and the press became more open in its coverage of formerly taboo topics. Under such circumstances, the outcome of the work of the special Communist Party commission "studying" the circumstances of the year 1956 under the leadership of the reformer Imre Pozsgay represented a true disaster for the conservative apparatchiks. The commission deemed the events of 1956 a "popular uprising" instead of a *counterrevolution,* the term favored by regime propaganda.

In early 1989, when the Communist Party somewhat surprisingly committed itself to a multiparty system, the political change in Hungary was obvious. The spring of 1989 witnessed mass demonstrations in which people demanded free elections and the withdrawal of Soviet troops from the country. The government started roundtable negotiations with the leaders of the opposition about the major political issues of the day, including the electoral law and some constitutional changes. Under external pressure, the hard-liners among the Communist leadership were quickly losing power. Finally, at the party's extraordinary conference, János Kádár was pushed out of his post as general secretary and the reformers gained the majority of the leadership positions. The logical consequence of the reevaluation of the year 1956 was the reinterment of Imre Nagy and other victims of the revolution, which proved to be an extraordinarily good occasion for an immense anti-Communist rally. In September, the Hungarian government opened the former iron curtain border with Austria for East Germans who wished to emigrate to West Germany. In doing so, Hungary demonstrated that it was no longer only a satellite state waiting for instructions from Moscow. The process of reforms, started from within the Communist Party, was completed by the dissolution of the party, the adoption of a new name (the Socialist Party) and a new political program in October 1989, and the subsequent declaration of Hungary as "independent and legal." Free parliamentary elections were scheduled for March 1990.

In the eighties, only a few Communist regimes were more orthodox than the Czechoslovak one. The government consisted of old conservatives who had gained power after the Soviet invasion of 1968 and who were far from considering any political reforms. They observed both the disturbances and the reform attempts in neighboring Communist countries with the highest suspicion. For that reason, in 1980 the regime propaganda bitterly denounced the striking workers in Poland, suggesting that they were lazy people who did not want to work and blaming them for all the economic problems their country had at that time. Moreover, Poland's economic troubles were used as a prime example of how the life of ordinary people could get worse if the party did not follow Marxist-Leninist ideology strictly. When Solidarity was legalized, the Czechoslovak Communists almost closed the border with Poland, allowing only Czechs with a written invitation from some Polish citizen to visit. Martial law in Poland was welcomed with quiet relief and unconditional praise, but administrative measures complicating visits to Poland remained in effect until the end of decade.

The orthodoxy of the Czechoslovak Communist leadership became even more obvious after the start of *perestroika* in the Soviet Union. Shocked by the contents of some articles in the Soviet magazines which openly described the terror of the Stalinist era and the malpractice of the Leonid Brezhnev government and called for more freedom and openness in public life, Czechoslovak leaders cautiously attempted to restrict the circulation of the Czech editions and even used direct censorship to prevent Czech and Slovak readers from being influenced by what they perceived as deviation from true Marxism-Leninism.

As time marched on, it became increasingly obvious that even the key argument used for the legitimization of the regime—a relatively stable economic situation (especially when compared with that of the other Communist states)—was losing its persuasive power in the face of the growing obsolescence of the economy and the apparent delay in the adoption of the newest technologies. The most visible sign of the declining self-confidence of the ruling Communists was the program adopted at the seventeenth Party Congress in 1986 which somewhat defensively declared that the main goal of the economic strategy was "to maintain an already reached high standard of living." It spoke (in an almost postmaterialist way) about the need to consider the quality of life instead the quantity of material assets. Yet for everybody who was used to reading party officials' statements the message was clear: people should prepare for worse times.

Hopes for political changes from within the party were abandoned after the resignation of Gustáv Husák from the post of general secretary in 1987 and his replacement by the somewhat comical figure of Miloš Jakeš. Jakeš was well remembered as the chairman of the central control and auditing committee that had implemented and overseen the extensive purges of all reformist elements in the Communist Party after the Soviet invasion of 1968. Yet during the period of *perestroika* Jakes was unanimously elected the new party leader. Opposition to the regime, however, was neither numerous nor influential. In the Czech Lands, dissent was traditionally centered around Charta 77 and, more recently, around some environmentalist groups. In Slovakia, Catholic activists were the main source of opposition to the regime. On the whole, however, the contrast between the changes in neighboring Communist countries and the unchanged domestic politics in Czechoslovakia tended to provoke more popular dissatisfaction.

The first observable display of popular discontent was the "candle demonstration" of Catholic activists held in the Slovak capital, Bratislava, in 1988. The demonstrators demanded more religious freedom and urged the regime to follow its own laws. The reaction of the government was symptomatic: the peaceful demonstrators were harshly dispersed by trun-cheons, tear gas, and water cannons. Even the usual explanations for police action (such as the need to protect working people from hooligans) could not be used, because amateur radio operators had recorded the event.

The dialogues from police transmitters later broadcast by Radio Free Eu-rope made it more than clear that the only reason for police brutality was to show the participants and the general public that the regime would not tol-erate any opposition. The police attacks on the participants in the peaceful demonstrations, which were held in Prague at the time of the politically sen-sitive anniversaries,[22] persuaded a growing number of inhabitants that the government's only goal was to maintain power. Thus the government was quickly losing the last remnants of its popular support.

Events in East Germany, which led to the fall of the Berlin Wall in early November 1989, and especially the subsequent passivity of the Soviet lead-ership, proved to be the last nail in the regime's coffin. No longer able to de-pend on military backing from the Soviet army, the orthodox Czechoslovak Communists suddenly lost their firm grip on most of their power; it was only a matter of time before the regime collapsed. The actual fall of Communist rule came even sooner than anyone expected. When an authorized student demonstration in memory of Jan Opletal (a student who was killed by the Nazis at the pro-freedom demonstration in 1939) was dispersed by the riot police and by the special army forces using extraordinarily brutal means,[23] popular unrest spread throughout the country, starting with strikes in the theaters and in the universities, followed by mass rallies attended by hun-dreds of thousands of people and culminating in a one-hour general strike. The Communist government quickly gave up and opened negotiations with the leaders of the opposition Civic Forum and Public Against Violence, um-brella movements unifying all types of Czech and Slovak opposition groups. An article proclaiming the "leading role of the Communist Party in society" was removed from the constitution, a government with a majority of nongovernment members was established, and a candidate from the Civic Forum, playwright Václav Havel, was elected president by a unanimous vote of the still-Communist parliament. Revolutionary changes were com-pleted by the resignation of most of the members of the party from the par-liament and the co-optation of the new members of parliament nominated by the opposition. This revolutionary, multicolor parliament adopted an electoral law based on proportional representation with a 5 percent legal threshold and set the date for the first free election in roughly half a century.

2

A New Day: Parties in the
Post-Communist Period
(1990 to the Present)

The sudden collapse of the Communist regimes in 1989, followed by the collapse of Soviet Union itself, had far-reaching consequences. For both the East and the West, the early nineties was a time of great hope for the future. The era of a bipolar world was over, the arms races were over, and it was time to take advantage of the "peace dividend."

Soon, however, it became clear that the simple fact that the Soviet-type Communist regimes no longer existed in Europe did not necessarily mean that world was approaching the golden era of peace and prosperity. Not all Communist regimes ceased to exist. Many non-European ruling Communist Parties—such as those in China, North Korea, and Cuba—survived without much change. They watched the apparent demise of the Communist Parties in Europe with the highest suspicion and did not want to follow their example. When the transition of the countries formerly dominated by the Soviet Union proved to be more complicated than was expected in the pre-1989 revolutionary euphoria, Communist officials outside Europe gained arguments again reforms.

Indeed, the transformation of the state-planned economies into market economies was far from easy. The first stage of economic transformation was accompanied by a sharp rise in unemployment, the bankruptcy of large companies unable to compete on the world market, and a general decline in economic production. The political transition also was far from easy. In fact, the demise of the Communist ideology was followed by the rise of nationalism and ethnic conflicts in many countries, when many of the old tensions that had been suppressed by the unifying Communist ideology ex-

39

ploded abruptly. To the surprise of many Western observers, among various countries deep differences originating in the pre-Communist period were revealed.

Overall, the transformation process demonstrated the importance of the institutional framework of reforms as well as the significance of the cultural stereotypes and habits that had evolved under communism or earlier. This chapter describes in detail the development of the emerging party systems in the new democracies studied here so that readers are able to get a better picture of what happened in the political sphere in those countries.

Hungary

In both Poland and Czechoslovakia, the first free parliamentary elections were perceived as decisive battles between the old regime, represented by the Communists, and the opposition. The situation in Hungary resembled much more a standard electoral contest in which the victory of one party did not spell victory or catastrophe, but rather represented only a change in the policy of the government. Even the post-Communist Hungarian Socialist Party (MSZP), dominated by reform Communists, did not represent a direct threat to the economic and political reforms, because the most orthodox Communists had left the party, founded the Hungarian Socialist Workers Party (MSZMP), and declared themselves the heirs and legal successors of the one-party system of the past decades. Popular support for this party was limited almost exclusively to Communist Party members (Kéri and Levendel 1995).

The opposition to the still-ruling socialists consisted of both old and new parties. Among the "old" or historical parties (usually ones reestablished by the politicians who had been members of similar parties in the pre-Communist period), the most visible was the Independent Smallholders Party (FKGP). This party was the successor of the strongest political party in Hungary after World War II. It declared itself the defender of agricultural interests and pushed political programs for the radical reprivatization of the land and other properties collectivized or nationalized after 1947 (Lomax 1995). The Christian Democratic People's Party (KDNP), heir of the strongly anti-Communist Democratic People's Party, represented a moderate Christian democratic orientation in Hungarian politics. The Hungarian Social Democratic Party (MSZDP) prolonged the tradition of social-democratic political ideas.

The historical parties symbolized the return to political roots, and the new parties symbolized change. The Hungarian Democratic Forum (MDF), led by the conservative historian József Antall, was inspired by the German postwar model of economic development and stressed national character and the need to implement moral values into the life of society. Liberal democratic values and a radical economic transformation were promoted by the Alliance of Free Democrats (SZDSZ), a party rooted in the liberal anti-regime opposition of the 1980s. Its political fortune rose substantially during the campaign before the November 1989 referendum in which voters were to decide whether the president should be elected before or after the parliament. Unlike the socialists and the MDF, the SZDSZ campaigned for parliamentary elections to be held first. Its victory in the referendum became its entry point into high politics, where the party became well known and supported for its radical pro-free market and pro-Western attitudes. Finally, the Federation of Young Democrats (FIDESZ), which was an intellectual student movement rather than a political party at that time, represented a radical alternative to tradition for the younger generation.[1] FIDESZ was known for its liberal and pro-market political attitudes. The drop in popular support for the socialists, combined with the growing popularity of both the conservative and liberal opposition parties (which was repeatedly confirmed by different preelection opinion polls) placed the MDF and SZDSZ in the preelection spotlight.

The complicated parliamentary electoral system, which combined the system of proportional representation based on national and regional party lists with a two-round contest[2] of individual candidates from single-member districts, worked to the advantage of the Hungarian Democratic Forum in the 1990 parliamentary election (Table 6). Although the party received only 24.7 percent of the vote in the first round of the election (not much more than its main rival), its candidates were extraordinarily successful in the second round of individual contests, which gave the MDF more than 42 percent of parliamentary seats.

In 1990, only six parties were able to gain more than one seat in parliament under the existing electoral law.[3] Three of them—the MDF, FKGP, and KDNP—formed a government under the leadership of Jószef Antall. The new government, backed by a solid parliamentary majority, stressed its conservative and national character while committing itself to a program of economic reforms.[4] The implementation of such reforms, however, was far from easy. The Smallholders, who were the stronger of the two junior coalition partners, threatened the unity of the government by insisting on their controversial plan for the broad reprivatization of agriculture and thus a

Table 6

The 1990 Parliamentary Election Results, Hungary

Party	Percent of Votes (first round)	Seats Number	Percent
Hungarian Democratic Forum (MDF)	24.7	164	42.5
Alliance of Free Democrats (SZDSZ)	21.4	92	23.8
Independent Smallholders Party (FKGP)	11.7	44	11.4
Hungarian Socialist Party (MSZP)	10.9	33	8.6
Federation of Young Democrats (FIDESZ)	9.0	21	5.4
Christian Democratic People's Party (KDNP)	6.5	21	5.4
Hungarian Socialist Workers Party (MSZMP)	3.7	—	—
Hungarian Social Democratic Party (MSZDP)	3.6	—	—
Agrarian Alliance	3.1	1	0.3
Other parties and independents	5.5	—	—
Total	100.0	386	100.0

Source: Béla Király and András Bozóki, eds., *Lawful Revolution in Hungary* (New York: Columbia University Press, 1995).

restoration of the pre-Communist situation—a policy not considered "meaningful" by any other parliamentary party. Moreover, the rather radical economic reforms implemented by the MDF (it had promised painless, moderate reforms) were not very well accepted. As inflation grew and unemployment rose, the popularity of the governing party (as measured by the opinion polls) fell rapidly and was accompanied by increased popular support for FIDESZ and MSZP.

Facing external pressure and trying to cope with economic hardship, the government coalition increasingly turned its attention to more ideological and symbolic issues. Thus in 1991 issues such as the role of religion in society, the restitution of church property, and the relationship with the Hungarian minorities in neighboring countries were the ones most frequently discussed. The liberal opposition in parliament accused the government of preparing a return to the prewar "Christian-national" authoritarian regime. And, indeed, some indication of such a move was observed, such as the government's efforts to place the electronic media under its direct control, the rising activities of the populist-nationalists within the governing parties, the growing suspicion toward Western liberalism, the emphasis on the "Third Road" between capitalism and socialism, and the rising concern about the Hungarian minorities in neighboring countries.[5] The events that followed, however, did not support the gloomy forecasts.

In August 1992, István Csurka, the vice chairman of the governing MFD, published a pamphlet entitled "A Few Ideas on the Two Years of Political Change and the Hungarian Democratic Forum's New Program" that blamed a conspiracy of Communists, Jews, journalists, and international financiers for the country's troubles. Prime Minister Jószef Antall aggressively distanced himself from Csurka's ideas. Later, after they were expelled from the party, Csurka and his followers established their own far-right Hungarian Justice and Life Party (MIÉP). Csurka's expulsion, however, was not the only event weakening the government coalition. As the economic problems continued and the government forecasts of economic growth failed to materialize, the junior coalition partners increasingly attempted to distance themselves from the unpopular government.

In 1992, the Christian Democrats began to criticize the government's privatization policy. In response to the internal quarrels over economic policy, the Smallholder members of parliament split into four different factions (the most populist one even joined the opposition). The Smallholders who maintained their loyalty to the government and who guaranteed a slight majority in parliament for the government were later expelled from the Smallholders Party and formed separate parties. In the meantime, opinion polls consistently showed high support for FIDESZ, the leading party since the beginning of 1991, and a rise in the credibility of the post-Communist MSZP. The electoral chances of FIDESZ especially were extremely good: the party had popular leaders with proven abilities, they were connected neither with communism nor with the hardship of the transformation, and the party appeared capable of bringing breathing new life into Hungarian politics. The fortune of the Young Democrats, however, did not continue. At its congress in April 1993, the party sharply changed its style and its image: the age limit for new members was lifted and a centralized party structure was adopted. After the congress, the bitter battle over the chairmanship of the party, between the incumbent Vicktor Orbán and the popular Gábor Fodor, shattered the illusion that FIDESZ represented a type of politics different than that of all the other parties, and its support declined rapidly. In December 1993, Prime Minister Antall died and was replaced by the minister of the interior, Péter Boross. Because of the unpopularity of the government and the sharp decline in popular support for FIDESZ, the Hungarian Socialist Party took over first place in public support. Even so, when the votes were counted after the June 1994 parliamentary election, the scope of the MSZP victory was quite surprising (see Table 7).

The Socialists, led by Gyula Horn, the minister for foreign affairs in the

Table 7

The 1994 Parliamentary Election Results, Hungary

Party	Percent of Votes (first round)	Seats	
		Number	Percent
Hungarian Socialist Party (MSZP)	33.0	209	54.1
Alliance of Free Democrats (SZDSZ)	19.7	71	18.4
Hungarian Democratic Forum (MDF)	11.7	38	9.8
Independent Smallholders Party (FKGP)	8.8	26	6.7
Christian Democratic People's Party (KDNP)	7.0	22	5.7
Federation of Young Democrats (FIDESZ)	7.0	20	5.2
Other parties and independents	12.8	—	—
Total	100.0	386	100.0

Source: Béla Király and András Bozóki, eds., *Lawful Revolution in Hungary* (New York: Columbia University Press, 1995).

last Communist government, received 33 percent of the vote in the first round of the election and an overwhelming majority of seats in single-member districts. Only five other parties were able to exceed the 5 percent legal threshold and enter parliament. In fact, parliament consisted of the same parties as in the preelection period; only the strength of the individual parties changed. The Socialists may have improved their position dramatically and the Christian Democrats very slightly, but the other parties lost. The greatest losers were the MDF and the FKGP, because both were held responsible for the government's unsuccessful performance. The far-right Hungarian Justice and Life Party, led by the former MDF prominent Istvan Csurka, gained no more than 1.6 percent of the vote and the hard-liner Communists, under the Workers Party, received only 3.2 percent of the vote.

In an electoral system that disproportionally rewarded the biggest party, the MSZP gained an absolute majority of seats in the parliament. Nevertheless, it offered to form a coalition with the second strongest party, the Alliance of Free Democrats, and the offer was finally accepted on the condition that the government continue the reforms. Thus the Socialists gained a good rating as a pro-reform government from the business community while avoiding the danger of being labeled a pure ex-Communist government.

In following a pragmatic rather than an ideological course, the government agreed to give priority to its economic policy, proclaimed its Western orientation, and announced its intentions to improve relations with neighboring countries that harbored large Hungarian minorities. Indeed, employing an unpopular and painful program of economic reforms, the government stabilized the economic situation and continued to privatize and promote foreign investment. In the area of foreign policy, the government was able to negotiate basic treaties with both Romania and Slovakia and successfully bring the country into pre-accession negotiations with both the North Atlantic Treaty Organization (NATO) and the European Union. Because economic reforms continued to produce positive results over the next two years, the Socialists continued to be popular. Little able to criticize the government's poor economic performance, the opposition attacked the Socialists' alleged neglect of Hungarian national interests. Notably, the FIDESZ turned its politics substantially from liberal toward national and conservative and thus achieved a position as the strongest opposition party (under a slightly modified name, the Federation of Young Democrats–Hungarian Civic Party—FIDESZ-MPP). The main point of contention between the government and the opposition, then, was not economic policy but the concept of nation and state (Tóka 1998).

Although the Socialists ranked first in the first round of the 1998 parliamentary election (Table 8), the decisive battle for the majority in parliament was won by the FIDESZ-MPP and its ally the MDF in the second round by securing the majority of the seats in the single-member districts. The Independent Smallholders Party, under the leadership of József Torgyán, did surprisingly well and ranked third. The Alliance of Free Democrats lost much of its popular support, as did the coalition partners from the first post-Communist government—the Hungarian Democratic Forum and the Christian Democratic People's Party. The MDF was able to gain some seats in the par-

Table 8

The 1998 Parliamentary Election Results, Hungary

Party	Percent of Votes (first round)	Seats	
		Number	Percent
Hungarian Socialist Party (MSZP)	32.3	134	34.7
Federation of Young Democrats–Hungarian Civic Party (FIDESZ-MPP)	28.2	148	38.3
Independent Smallholders Party (FKGP)	13.8	48	12.4
Alliance of Free Democrats (SZDSZ)	7.9	24	6.2
Hungarian Justice and Life Party (MIÉP)	5.5	14	3.6
Hungarian Democratic Forum (MDF)	3.1	17	4.4
Other parties and independents	9.2	1	0.3
Total	100.0	386	100.0

Source: Report of the National Election Committee, Magyar Közlöny, 1998.

liament thanks to the support given to its candidates by the FIDESZ-MPP, but the KDNP failed miserably, not gaining a single seat. By contrast, the election witnessed the political rebirth of István Csurka whose extreme right-wing Hungarian Justice and Life Party exceeded the 5 percent legal threshold.

Because the two strongest parties were of comparable strength, the winner of the election—FIDESZ-MPP—was pressed to seek support from among the smaller parties in the parliament. The result was the establishment of a right-wing coalition between FIDESZ-MPP and the Smallholders. FIDESZ-MPP gained a majority of ministries in the government, and the Smallholders obtained the rest of them. Jószef Torgyán, the leader of the Smallholders, became minister of agriculture, an important post for the leader of a party that relies on the agricultural constituency. Moreover, the Smallholders were promised the support of the FIDESZ-MPP for nominating their own candidate for the next presidential election in 2000.

Although many commentators predicted that the new Hungarian government would move toward more populist policies under the influence of the Smallholders and feared the candidacy of Torgyan for the presidential post, the actual outcome proved less dramatic. In the spring of 1999, Hungary was accepted as a new member of NATO (together with Poland and the Czech Republic), but then it immediately became involved in a conflict with Serbia over Kosovo. Yet even in this potentially very conflicting situation, the Hungarian government remained stable. The government also continued to push the country toward the European Union; indeed, Hungary was repeatedly proclaimed to be one of the best-prepared candidate countries. Even the election of the president was managed by the governing parties without much political tension. Aware of his low popularity among the general population and the potential conflict with the coalition partners over his candidacy, Torgyán withdrew from contention for the presidential post, and his party supported instead the nomination of well-known law professor Ferenc Mádl, an expert on the European Union law. Mádl, the only candidate for president, was elected by the parliament in June 2000 without much political conflict.

Czechoslovakia, Slovak Republic, Czech Republic

The basic features of the political situation in Czechoslovakia prior to the first free post-Communist era election were somewhat similar to that in

Poland in 1989. The main actors on the political scene were the umbrella-type revolutionary movements—the Civic Forum (OF) in the Czech Lands and Public Against Violence (VPN) in Slovakia—and the former satellite parties—the Czechoslovak People's Party (ČSL), the Czechslovak Socialist Party (ČSS), and the Communist Party of Czechoslovakia (KSČ). The chief difference with the situation in Poland was that political development in the country was taking two paths. Indeed, from very beginning the country was faced the development of not one but two party systems, supported by the existing constitutional dualism. After 1968, when Czechoslovakia adopted a federal structure, the country was ruled by the federal government, which was exclusively responsible for foreign relations, the army, the country's finances, and general economic policy. In addition to the federal government, each part of the federation (the Czech and the Slovak republics) had its own government. These governments were responsible for the implementation of the federal government policies in the respective republics, but they acted to a great extent autonomously in some fields (such as education and health care). Similarly, in addition to the federal parliament each republic had its own parliament—the Czech and Slovak national councils, responsible for legislation specific to the individual republics. As a result of this arrangement, voters in each republic elected their representatives to both the federal parliament and their own national council.

Following tradition, all "Czechoslovak" parties were perceived in Slovakia as Czech, and thus "real Slovak" parties also were being established. Even the revolution itself was perceived as two parallel revolutions, because the Slovak opposition in Bratislava did not simply establish another local branch of the Civic Forum, but rather the specifically Slovak movement, Public Against Violence, even though the political programs of both movements were almost identical at the time. Internal disputes within the VPN between some Catholic dissidents and liberals in the leadership finally led to the Catholic dissidents to leave the movement and create the Christian Democratic Movement (KDH) under the leadership of Ján Čarnogurský. In fact, then, there were really no Czechoslovak political parties before the election; all the political parties and movements were either specifically Czech or Slovak. Even within the Communist Party itself, its Slovak republic organization acted quite independently.

The victory of the Civic Forum in the 1990 federal parliamentary elections was quite impressive; it received more than 50 percent of the vote (Table 9).[6] Although the defeat of the Communists was quite obvious, the party, in an unaltered form as the Communist Party of Czechoslovakia

Table 9

The 1990 Parliamentary (Federal) Election Results, Czech Republic

		Seats	
Party	Percent of Votes	Number	Percent
Civic Forum (OF)	51.6	118	67.0
Communist Party of Czechoslovakia (KSČ)	13.6	27	15.3
Movement for Self-Governing Democracy–			
Society for Moravia and Silesia (HSD-SMS)	8.5	16	9.1
Christian Democratic Union–Czechoslovak			
People's Party (KDU-ČSL)	8.7	15	8.5
Other parties	17.6	—	—
Total	100.0	176	100.0

Source: Federal Statistical Office, *Volby do Federálního shromáždění České a Slovenské Federativní Republiky v roce 1990* (Elections to the Federal Assembly of the Czech and Slovak Federative Republic in 1990) (Prague: FSÚ, 1991).

(KSC), was still doing rather well. Only two other parties entered the parliament, both supported mostly by Moravian voters, the easternmost of the two historic Czech Lands. The People's Party, running under the somewhat modified name of the Christian Democratic Union–Czechoslovak People's Party (KDU-ČSL), attracted Catholic voters by stressing its Christian orientation and moral values, and the politically unknown Movement for Self-Governing Democracy–Society for Moravia and Silesia (HSD-SMS) surprisingly attracted many voters with its program to restore the historic lands of Moravia and Silesia and return to them the status of autonomous administrative units.

Although the Slovak counterpart of the Civic Forum—Public Against Violence—won the electoral contest, it did not receive a majority of the Slovakian vote (Table 10). The reason was quite simple: the Christian Democratic Movement gained a substantial part of the vote. Except for the Communists (who ranked third), only two other parties—the Slovak National Party (SNS) and "Coexistencia," the coalition of Hungarian parties (called here simply the Hungarian Coalition)—exceeded the 5 percent legal threshold and were able to enter the federal parliament.

Soon after the elections, a center-right coalition government that mixed conservatives and liberals (OF, VPN) with Christian Democrats (KDU-ČSL, KDH) was formed and backed by a solid majority in both chambers of the federal parliament. The two main tasks of the new representation were to begin economic reforms and to create a new constitution. Although the

Table 10
The 1990 Parliamentary (Federal) Election Results, Slovakia

Party	Percent of Votes	Seats Number	Percent
Public Against Violence (VPN)	34.9	52	41.9
Christian Democratic Movement (KDH)	17.8	25	20.2
Communist Party of Czechoslovakia (KSČ)	13.6	20	16.1
Slovak National Party (SNS)	11.2	15	12.1
Hungarian Coalition	8.5	12	9.7
Other parties	14.0	—	—
Total	100.0	124	100.0

Source: Federal Statistical Office, *Volby do Federálního shromáždění České a Slovenské Federativní Republiky v roce 1990* (Elections to the Federal Assembly of the Czech and Slovak Federative Republic in 1990) (Prague: FSÚ, 1991).

government was strictly Czecho-Slovak and multipartisan, the economic reform strategy was created and conducted by a group of neoliberal Prague economists under the leadership of Václav Klaus. They prescribed more or less the same antidote as their Polish colleagues: a broad liberalization of both prices and trade, privatization, and devaluation of the currency, supplemented by a policy of tough fiscal and monetary restraints. As in Poland, radical reforms proved to be efficient in achieving their main goals. The negative side effects of this economic policy, however, proved to be a mirror image of the situation in Poland: the GDP fell, inflation and unemployment grew. Although the hardship accompanying the shock therapy was not as dramatic in Czechoslovakia as in Poland[7]—primarily because of the better state of the Czechoslovak economy before reforms and the willingness of the government to help the biggest companies—the government's economic policy quickly became the main political issue.

The disagreement among the various groups within the Civic Forum about the economic strategy, accompanied by varying views on the internal organization and structure of the movement, led to its split into three groups. The conservative Civic Democratic Party (ODS) of Václav Klaus stressed the need to build up a standard political party. The Civic Democratic Alliance (ODA) tried to be a kind of think-tank or an electoral type of political party without a big membership base. The third new party, the liberal Civic Movement (OH), favored a more cautious approach to the reforms and a greater role for the state in the economy. Although most of the former Civic Forum ministers and members of parliament became members of the

Civic Movement, the key economic positions of the government, as well as the economic policy, remained unchanged.

On the Slovak side of the Czechoslovak political scene, the situation was more complex. The political discourse between the supporters and opponents of the federal government's reform policy was complicated by the fact that all of the key economic ministers in the government were Czechs. Thus the economic troubles accompanying the reforms were largely perceived as a burden laid on Slovakia by the Prague government. The fact that unemployment rose far more rapidly in Slovakia than in the Czech Lands[8] especially provoked the growing dissatisfaction among both the Slovak population and some of the political elite. Moreover, it became increasingly obvious that Czech and Slovak members of parliament disagreed about the new constitution. Finally, the demands for both a change in economic policy and broader autonomy for the individual republics within the federation fused: Slovakia needed more power, because it needed different economic reforms. Although these ideas were shared by many Slovak politicians of different political backgrounds, they were most explicitly declared by the increasingly popular Vladimír Mečiar, prime minister of the government of the Slovak Republic.

The "Slovak question" not only was a matter of dispute between Czech and Slovak political representatives, but also played a divisive role within the Slovak political arena. The growing nationalism and populism of Prime Minister Mečiar, who was nominated to his position by the Public Against Violence, led to open conflict among the movement's leaders. When Mečiar was stripped of his seat by the parliament in April 1997, he left the movement (followed by a third of the VPN members of parliament) and established the Movement for a Democratic Slovakia (HZDS). The rest of the VPN (under the name of the Civic Democratic Union—ODÚ), although weaker, was able to maintain the basic direction of the reform policy. It was supported by the Christian-Democratic Movement, whose leader, Ján Čarnogurský, was to become the next Slovak prime minister.

Other Slovak political parties underwent similar developments. A group of more nationalistic deputies created their own party called the Slovak Christian Democratic Movement; several Green Party members of parliament established the more national Green Party in Slovakia, and some Democratic Party deputies[9] left their party and joined Mečiar's movement. The Communist Party of Slovakia also split, but because a division emerged between reformers and hard-liners and not because of the Slovak question. The reformers took over the party and established the social democratic-oriented

Party of the Democratic Left (SDL) under the leadership of Peter Weis, a lawyer who, despite his party membership, had gained respect as a legal defender of some dissidents in the late Communist period. The hard-liners left the party and later reestablished the Communist Party of Slovakia.

The removal of Mečiar and his followers from the government did not calm the situation. Quite the contrary, the popularity of Mečiar, who presented himself as a "victim of the Prague and its Slovak cooperators anti-Slovak conspiracy," rose dramatically, and political support for the governing parties began to slide. Slogans such as "Slovak sovereignty," however it was defined, became frequent in all public political discourse, and the share of voters who favored more power for the Slovak government continued to increase. In this atmosphere, even moderate Slovak politicians in positions of power demanded more power for the individual republics (and less power for the federation) than Czech political representatives were willing to offer. Thus, while the economic reforms proceeded more or less successfully, the second basic problem of the first post-Communist government—the adoption of a new constitution—remained unresolved and was left up to the political representatives who would emerge from the parliamentary election scheduled for the spring of 1992.

The results of the elections in the two republics were indeed different (see Tables 11 and 12).[10] In Slovakia, the right (the former VPN running under the name of the Civic Democratic Union), suffered quite a disaster; it did not win a single seat. Mečiar's HZDS, by contrast, attracted over 37 percent of the vote, even more than the VPN itself in 1990. The Party of the Democratic Left gained most of the former Communist Party votes, while

Table 11

The 1992 Parliamentary (Slovak National Council) Election Results, Slovakia

Party	Percent of Votes	Seats	
		Number	Percent
Movement for a Democratic Slovakia (HZDS)	37.3	74	49.3
Party of the Democratic Left (SDL)	14.7	29	19.3
Christian Democratic Movement (KDH)	8.9	18	12.0
Slovak National Party (SNS)	7.9	15	10.0
Hungarian Coalition	7.4	14	9.3
Other parties	23.8	—	—
Total	100.0	150	100.0

Source: Federal Statistical Office, *Volby 1992 ČSFR* (Elections 1992, ČSFR) (Prague: FSÚ, 1992).

Table 12

*The 1992 Parliamentary (Czech National Council) Election Results,
Czech Republic*

Party	Percent of Votes	Seats Number	Seats Percent
Civic Democratic Party (ODS)	29.7	76	38.0
Communist Party of Bohemia and Moravia (KSČM)	14.1	35	17.5
Czech Social Democratic Party (ČSSD)	6.5	16	8.0
Liberal Social Union (LSU)	6.5	16	8.0
Christian Democratic Union–Czechoslovak People's Party (KDU-ČSL)	6.3	15	7.5
Association for the Republic–Republican Party of Czechoslovakia (SPR-RSČ)	6.0	14	7.0
Civic Democratic Alliance (ODA)	5.9	14	7.0
Movement for Self-Governing Democracy– Society for Moravia and Silesia (HSD-SMS)	5.9	14	7.0
Other parties	19.1	—	—
Total	100.0	200	100.0

Source: Federal Statistical Office, *Volby 1992 ČSFR* (Elections 1992, ČSFR) (Prague: FSÚ, 1992).

the orthodox Communist Party of Slovakia failed. The Christian Democratic Movement lost some of the support of its more nationalist voters, and the Slovak National Party and the coalition of Hungarian parties maintained their positions. In the end, a coalition government of the HZDS and SNS was formed under Mečiar's leadership.

In the Czech Republic, the position of the right, originating from the Civic Forum, was strengthened. The clear winner of the election was the conservative Civic Democratic Party of Václav Klaus; the liberal Civic Movement failed to gain single seat. The second-place Communists maintained their position, and the other six parties entering parliament scored only a little bit over the 5 percent threshold. The presence in parliament of the Civic Democratic Alliance and the Christian Democrats under the name of the Christian Democratic Union–Czechoslovak People's Party allowed the establishment of a center-right coalition that was even more dedicated to a free-market economy and conservative political ideology than was the previous government. Of the opposition parties, three had no previous parliamentary representation: the historical Czech Social Democratic Party strengthened by several former Civic Forum deputies; the Association for the Republic–Republican Party of Czechoslovakia (SPR-RSČ), representing an extreme right and xenophobic stream within Czech politics; and the Liberal Social Union, an artificial amalgam of the Agrarian Party, the historical Czechoslovak Socialist Party, and the Green Party. Following the Slovak example, Václav Klaus, the leader of the strongest party, became prime minister of the Czech government.

Because the election produced such disparate results in the two republics, they faced the problem of how to create a federal government. After several weeks of difficult negotiations it became clear that no agreement about a common future of Czechs and Slovaks within a common state would be forthcoming. After a Declaration of Sovereignty was adopted by the Slovak national council in July 1992, Czechoslovak president Havel resigned, and negotiations shifted from how to forge a common country to how to divide Czechoslovakia peacefully. On December 8, 1992, the federal parliament approved the Constitutional Law about the Extinction of the Federation, which provided for full legislative power for the national councils of the two republics. The federation had dissolved itself. The independent Czech and Slovak Republics came into being on January 1, 1993.

Slovakia

In 1993, independent Slovakia experienced a series of economic troubles caused by the breakup of the common state. With the cessation of the monetary union with the Czech Republic, a new currency had to be introduced. The new Slovak currency was devalued about 10 percent, already high unemployment further increased, and a large deficit in the state budget emerged. Moreover, the political situation was far from stable. The first major political conflict swirled around the election of the first president of independent Slovakia.[11] Mečiar's attempt to nominate his favorite candidate even against the will of some other movement leaders failed. A compromise candidate from within the movement, economist Michal Kováč, was then elected with the partial support of the opposition. In response to their alleged disloyalty, Mečiar expelled the minister of foreign affairs and the minister of economy from the government. They were followed by several other deputies. Having lost its majority in the parliament, Mečiar's government survived only through the temporary support offered by the Party of the Democratic Left.

Less than one year later, in the spring of 1994, the situation was repeated, only now with different actors in the role of disloyal ministers. Once again, the government lost its majority and did not survive a no-confidence vote in parliament. A new coalition government was formed by the Christian Democrats, the SDL, and the Democratic Union (DU, the party created by former members of parliament representing the Movement for a Democratic Slovakia). The government, however, was perceived as provisional, and an early election was scheduled for late September. Although the political situation was more stable after the change of government and the economy was showing the first signs of a recovery, Mečiar once again triumphed in the election (Table 13).

In the 1994 election, the HZDS received almost as many votes as two years ago, but it could not restore the previous coalition because the overall share of "wasted votes" (given to parties not exceeding the 5 percent threshold) dropped from 23.8 percent in 1992 to only 13.0 percent in 1994. Moreover, the former junior coalition partner SNS lost some popular support. Thus the old two-party coalition would not even have had a simple majority. After months of negotiations, a tri-party coalition under Mečiar's leadership was formed, including a rather new party, the extremely left Association of Workers of Slovakia (ZRS), founded and led by a dissenter deputy from the SDL. The strongest force within the opposition became the coalition Common Choice, dominated by SDL, but also including the Social Democrats and some smaller parties. The rest of the opposition basically remained unchanged, because the Hungarian Coalition, KDH, and the Democratic Union all safely exceeded the 5 percent threshold.

Table 13

The 1994 Parliamentary Election Results, Slovakia

Party	Percent of Votes	Seats	
		Number	Percent
Movement for a Democratic Slovakia (HZDS)	35.0	61	40.7
Common Choice (Party of the Democratic Left, SDL)	10.4	18	12.0
Hungarian Coalition	10.2	17	11.3
Christian Democratic Movement (KDH)	10.1	17	11.3
Democratic Union of Slovakia (DÚ)	8.6	15	10.0
Association of Workers of Slovakia (ZRS)	7.3	13	8.7
Slovak National Party (SNS)	5.4	9	6.0
Other parties	13.0	—	—
Total	100.0	150	100.0

Source: Soňa Szomolányi and Grigorij Mesežnikov, eds., *Slovakia Parliamentary Elections 1994* (Bratislava: Slovak Political Science Association, 1995).

Although no one would have predicted a long life for the new Mečiar government, and even though the political situation after the 1994 election was far from quiet,[12] the party system and the coalition government remained surprisingly stable. The encouraging figures on the macroeconomic performance of the Slovak economy, together with the ability of HZDS leaders to maintain the loyalty of junior coalition partners through a combination of economic corruption and blackmail, were probably the factors chiefly responsible for stabilizing the power structure. Moreover, the political preferences of the population, measured by regular opinion polls, did not change dramatically until 1997, if one does not take into account the disappearance of the Association of Workers of Slovakia from the opinion polls' results. After all, almost all the party's deputies, who entered parliament intent on defeating all economic reforms, ended their crusade against capitalism once they became members of various management and supervisory boards or owners of formerly state-owned companies privatized by the government and placed in the hands of "predetermined owners."

Mečiar's government may have remained firm, backed by a solid parliamentary majority, but Slovakia's position on the international scene declined sharply. Objections to Mečiar's blatant disregard of the basic rules of democratic politics (such as misusing the secret service against the political opposition, banishing disloyal HZDS deputy František Gaulieder from the parliament, ignoring the decisions of the Constitutional Court, and thwarting a referendum on the presidential election by the ministry of the interior) adversely affected the relationships between Slovakia and the Western democracies and led to the exclusion of Slovakia from the first group of candidates seeking to join NATO and the European Union from among the former Communist countries. Dissatisfied with political developments and faced with a highly popular Mečiar and his HZDS, the opposition parties were willing to cooperate with one another more closely. The first example of such cooperation was the creation of the right-oriented Blue Coalition, consisting of the Christian-Democratic Movement, the liberal Democratic Union, and the conservative Democratic Party. Later, the coalition was joined by two other parties—the Slovak Social Democracy and the Green Party—and its ideological profile moved slightly toward the center. It adopted a new name—the Slovak Democratic Coalition (SDK)—and designated itself Mečiar's major rival in the parliamentary election scheduled for the fall of 1998. Indeed, judging by the SDK's rapid and stable popular support, this idea was accepted by many Slovak voters.

At the beginning of 1998, the political situation seemed to be unambiguous and stable. There were two major contestants, the party in power (HZDS) and the major opposition (SDK). The three smaller political parties—the Slovak nationalists (Slovak National Party), the moderate socialists and social democrats (Party of the Democratic Left), and the party of the Hungarian population (the Hungarian Coalition)—had distinct political agendas. In the spring, however, a new actor entered the political scene. Supported by the influential private TV Markíza, Rudolf Schuster, the popular mayor of the second largest city in Slovakia, Košice, decided to establish the Party of Civil Understanding (SOP). He claimed it was an option for those who were tired of the deep political conflicts between Mečiar and his opposition, and he promised to move politics from the hate and quarrels of politicians toward "the daily problems of citizens." Although rather vague in its political program, SOP immediately attracted a high degree of popular support (mostly from former opposition supporters), allowing it to safely secure the third position in the voting pools. Facing the danger of electoral defeat, Mečiar and his allies, who still dominated the parliament, changed the electoral laws to complicate the situation of the opposition. Of all the changes made, the most serious was a new rule that required each party in the electoral coalition to exceed the 5 percent legal threshold. In response to this new electoral rule, the Slovak Democratic Coalition and the coalition of Hungarian parties transformed themselves into political parties.

Although in a tight contest with the Slovak Democratic Coalition, Mečiar's Movement for a Democratic Slovakia was able to defend its position as the strongest political party in Slovakia. The overall showing of the opposition parties, however, made the 1998 elections a breakthrough. Together, they gained a solid majority of seats, 93 out of 150 (Table 14). As a result, they were not only able to form a coalition government with a solid parliamentary backing, but also able to change the constitution because they had more than a three-fifths majority in the parliament. The newly established majority then used its new influence to introduce the direct election of the president (which required at least a three-fifths majority), and the presidential election of 1999 was expected to be the last step in the complete defeat of Vladimír Mečiar by his opponents (Table 15).

Mečiar's good showing in the preelection polls frightened many voters who strongly opposed his political style. Fearing Mečiar's possible victory and his return to power, most of his opponents declared their support for Rudolf Schuster, the leading presidential candidate in many opinion polls. As a result, the popular support for the other candidates remained marginal, and the election turned out to be a battle over Mečiar's political future. Ul-

Table 14
The 1998 Parliamentary Election Results, Slovakia

Party	Percent of Votes	Seats	
		Number	Percent
Movement for a Democratic Slovakia (HZDS)	27.0	43	28.7
Slovak Democratic Coalition (SDK)	26.3	42	28.0
Party of the Democratic Left (SDL)	14.7	23	15.3
Hungarian Coalition	9.1	15	10.0
Slovak National Party (SNS)	9.1	14	9.3
Party of Civil Understanding (SOP)	8.0	13	8.7
Other parties	5.8	—	—
Total	100.0	150	100.0

Source: Central Election Commission (online at: volby.statistics.sk).

timately, Rudolf Schuster, the official joint candidate of the governing parties, defeated Mečiar in the second round of the contest and became the president of the Slovak Republic.

The presidential election, however, became Mečiar's comeback rather than his final defeat, because he was able to mobilize the support of over one-third of all participating voters in the first round of the election and almost 43 percent of voters in the second round. The economic and political circumstances under which the new government operated even worked to increase the political strength of Mečiar's HZDS. As unemployment rose and the governing parties proved unable to fulfill their own unrealistic pre-

Table 15
The 1999 Presidential Election Results, Slovakia

Candidate	Votes, First Round (percent)	Votes, Second Round (percent)
Rudolf Schuster	47.4	57.2
Vladimír Mečiar	37.2	42.8
Magda Vašáryová	6.6	—
Ivan Mjartan	3.6	—
Ján Slota	2.5	—
Boris Zala	1.0	—
Juraj Švec	0.8	—
Juraj Lazarčík	0.5	—
Ján Demikát	0.2	—

Source: Central Election Commission (online at: volby.statistics.sk).

election promises to rapidly improve the economy, the government's popularity plummeted. Under the pressure of public criticism, the governing
coalition began to come apart.

The frequency of conflicts increased not only among the individual coalition parties but within the parties themselves. From the very beginning, the
internal pressures were evident within the Slovak Democratic Coalition. Although under law, the SDK became a unified party, in practice it continued
to function as a coalition of five individual parties. The ideological differences, personal animosities, and divergent opinions toward SDK's organization had to be forgotten before the election could become part of the
political agenda. The unresolved question of SDK's identity and organizational future was complicated by the fact that Prime Minister Mikuláš
Dzurinda, who was nominated to his post by the Christian Democratic
Movement, had not succeeded in leading his own party. Thus the prime minister, who was at least formally the leader of the Slovak Democratic Coalition, was not even the leader of one of the parties who nominated him to his
post. Although the leadership of the KDH insisted that the creation of the
Slovak Democratic Coalition and its transformation into a party were just a
tactical necessity in order to avoid the threat of Mečiar's electoral law,
Prime Minister Dzurinda pushed the idea that the SDK could serve as a platform for the unification of the political parties involved and should become
one unified party in the near future.

The conflict over the SDK's future gradually intensified and finally led
to the establishment in 2000 of a new party called the Slovak Christian and
Democratic Union (SDKÚ) under the direction of Dzurinda and a group of
his adherents. This development seemed to gain the acceptance of many voters, and SDKÚ received relatively high support in the opinion polls. Later,
however, the popularity of the original parties constituting the SDK dropped
substantially, and most found themselves around or below the 5 percent legal threshold. Meanwhile, the second strongest party in the government
coalition, the SDL, underwent a similar period of internal tensions, resulting in the departure of the most popular SDL deputy, Róbert Fico, from the
party and the creation of a new party called Smer (The Direction). Smer
turned out to be something of a rerun of the story of SOP and Rudolf Schuster. The one-man party defined itself as pragmatic and neither right wing nor
left wing; it just wanted "order, justice, and stability." And like SOP, Smer
quickly reached a high level of popular support in opinion polls (over 20
percent), but it remained something of a puzzle policy-wise. More broadly,

more than ten years after the breakdown of the Communist regime in Slovakia, the situation on the party scene continued to be unclear.

Czech Republic

Compared with politics in Slovakia, politics in the Czech Republic was far from dramatic during the first two years of independence. In January 1993, former Czechoslovak president Václav Havel was elected president of the new Czech Republic by a solid majority of deputies in the parliament. As the economy improved, the position of the coalition parties became even stronger as measured by opinion polls, and most of opposition parties underwent a period of instability.[13] The Liberal Social Union dropped off very quickly after the political differences among its members proved that common political action was not possible. Similarly, the Movement for Self-Governing Democracy–Society for Moravia and Silesia, facing a drop in popular support and ongoing internal struggles, underwent several party splits and name changes before practically disappearing from the political scene. Within the parliamentary caucus of the Communist Party of Bohemia and Moravia, the conflict between the more and less orthodox[14] members of parliament resulted in a split. Because the group of less-orthodox members did not find any political support within the party, it established its own party called the Left Bloc. The more orthodox group of Communist deputies, backed by an overwhelming majority of members, maintained control of the party and become more dogmatic. The only opposition party that fortune smiled on was the Czech Social Democratic Party. The election in early 1993 of Miloš Zeman as prime minister (Zeman was a charismatic speaker and author of the Civic Forum electoral program) proved to be an important impetus for increased party support, and the Social Democrats began to collect votes from the other opposition parties and build a viable non-Communist alternative to the government's politics.

Although the economic performance in 1995 was the best of all those in the post-Communist years, the situation worsened for the governing parties in 1996 after the deputy prime minister and the chairman of one of the junior coalition parties accused the Security Information Service of spying on politicians for the benefit of the senior coalition party. This accusation was never proved, but the scandal damaged relations within the coalition. As the parliamentary elections scheduled for June 1996 neared, political quarreling among the coalition parties became increasingly visible. There were many areas of conflict: restitution of church property, the role of the non-governmental sector, and the electoral system for Senate elections.[15] Over time, the popularity of the governing politicians and the credibility of the governing institutions fell. Later in the year, some economic problems emerged—the trade deficit grew and several small banks went bankrupt. Although opinion polls revealed that the popularity of the Social Democrats was on the rise, the supremacy of the governing parties seemed beyond doubt. In this respect, the results of the 1996 parliamentary election were quite surprising (see Table 16).

In the election, Václav Klaus's Civic Democratic Party basically maintained a voting pattern similar to that of the previous election and the junior coalition parties together received an even slightly higher proportion of the vote, but the governing coalition lost the majority of parliamentary seats. Apparently, the Czech Social Democratic Party collected an overwhelming majority of votes from the former voters for the smaller parties that could not enter parliament in 1992 because they did not meet the 5 percent threshold.

After the election and several years of political stability, the situation on the Czech political scene changed dramatically. A minority government from the current coalition parties was established under Klaus's leadership, and the chairman of the Social Democratic Party, Zeman, was elected

Table 16

The 1996 Parliamentary (Lower Chamber) Election Results, Czech Republic

Party	Percent of Votes	Seats	
		Number	Percent
Civic Democratic Party (ODS)	29.6	68	34.0
Czech Social Democratic Party (ČSSD)	26.4	61	30.5
Communist Party of Bohemia and Moravia (KSČM)	10.3	22	11.0
Christian Democratic Union–Czechoslovak People's Party (KDU-ČSL)	8.1	18	9.0
Association for the Republic–Republican Party of Czechoslovakia (SPR-RSČ)	8.0	18	9.0
Civic Democratic Alliance (ODA)	6.4	13	6.5
Other parties	11.2	—	—
Total	100.0	200	100.0

Source: Czech Statistical Office, *Volby do Poslanecke Sněmovny Parlamentu České Republiky v roce 1996* (Elections to the lower chamber of the Parliament of the Czech Republic in 1996) (Prague: ČSÚ, 1997).

Speaker of the parliament. However, the coexistence of a right-oriented government and an opposition-dominated parliament proved too complicated and led to political tension. In the November Senate election, one of the most important messages the electorate sent to politicians was its extreme disillusionment with politics; only 36 percent of voters participated in the first round of the election, compared with 96 percent, 86 percent, and 75 percent in 1990, 1992, and June 1996. The very low turnout, however, cannot be attributed only to the fact that voters were tired of the never-ending political quarrels. Many people believed that the Senate (the upper chamber of parliament) served only to increase the number of well-paid jobs for generally unpopular politicians.

The 1996 Senate election, organized as a two-round contest in eighty-one single-member constituencies, led to a clear victory by the coalition (Table 17). Yet the election revealed increasing problems between ODS and one of its junior coalition parties, the Christian Democratic Union–Czechoslovak People's Party. One of the telling signs of the conflict was the fact that many KDU-ČSL candidates unsuccessful in the first round of the election advised their voters to vote against an ODS candidate in the second round, asserting that the dominance of one party in the Senate constituted a danger for democracy and for pluralism.

In the spring of 1997, the Czech Republic was hit by serious economic problems. GDP growth dropped from 5 percent to almost zero, the currency was devalued, inflation increased, and interest rates multiplied. Klaus's gov-

Table 17

The 1996 Parliamentary (Senate) Election Results, Czech Republic

Party	Percent of Votes (first round)	Seats (total)	
		Number	Percent
Civic Democratic Party (ODS)	36.5	32	39.5
Czech Social Democratic Party (ČSSD)	20.3	25	30.9
Christian Democratic Union–Czechoslovak People's Party (KDU-ČSL)	9.9	13	16.0
Civic Democratic Alliance (ODA)	8.1	7	8.6
Communist Party of Bohemia and Moravia (KSČM)	14.3	2	2.5
Other parties and independents	10.9	2	2.5
Total	100.0	81	100.0

Source: "Senátní volby 96'" (Senate elections 1996), *Lidové noviny,* November 25, 1996.
Note: All eighty-one senators were elected in 1996.

ernment was pressed to reduce budget expenditures sharply and to adopt a tight, restrictive economic policy. The shock from the unexpected end of the "Czech economic miracle" provoked great popular discontent, and the popularity of the government plummeted. The ensuing questions about the worthiness of the economic policy of the Klaus government culminated in an open debate about suspicious privatization cases. Voter confidence in the parties in power was nearly destroyed when the media revealed information about the dirty side of party financing. At the same time, a group within ODS led by Jan Ruml, a former dissident and minister of the interior in Klaus's government, publicly requested Klaus's resignation from the party leadership and a police investigation of the party's financial scandals. That was a signal for both junior coalition partners to leave the government. Although Klaus had to resign from the post of prime minister, he dismissed the accusations as "virtual reality" created by the media, responded to the internal dissent as a sign of little more than political opportunism, and immediately began his campaign for reelection as party leader. This tactic proved successful, and in the early spring of 1998 Klaus was reelected leader of the ODS by a clear majority of the delegates to an extraordinary congress of the party.

Klaus's defeated challenger, Jan Ruml, and his supporters left ODS and created the Union of Freedom (US). The new party embraced the right side of the political spectrum, announcing its openness to people wishing to be involved in politics and stressing the importance of both the rule of law and decentralization. In the meantime, negotiations about the formation of a new government opened under the supervision of President Havel. Because the ODS refused to enter the government, the negotiations produced a provisional government that mixed the rest of the former coalition with nonpartisan experts under the leadership of the chairman of the Czech National Bank, who resigned from his post to assume the premiership.

The main task of the new government was to stabilize the economic situation and to prepare for early elections to the lower chamber in June 1998 (Senate elections were held the following November). During the long and unusually bitter electoral campaign, the leader of the Social Democratic Party spoke about the "burned land" created by the six years of Klaus's government of "defrauders and liars," and Klaus warned voters against the "leftist coup" being prepared by the Social Democrats and encouraged all people "to defend freedom" by voting for the ODS.

The results of the 1998 election for the lower chamber were somewhat surprising (Table 18). The victory of the Social Democrats was foreseen,

Table 18

The 1998 Parliamentary (Lower Chamber) Election Results, Czech Republic

Party	Percent of Votes (first round)	Seats Number	Seats Percent
Czech Social Democratic Party (ČSSD)	32.3	74	37.0
Civic Democratic Party (ODS)	27.7	64	32.0
Communist Party of Bohemia and Moravia (KSČM)	11.0	25	12.5
Christian Democratic Union–Czechoslovak People's Party (KDU-ČSL)	9.0	19	9.5
Union of Freedom (US)	8.6	18	9.0
Association for the Republic–Republican Party of Czechoslovakia (SPR-RSČ)	3.9	—	—
Pensioners for Social Securities	3.1	—	—
Other parties	4.4	—	—
Total	100.0	200	100.0

Source: Czech Statistical Office, *Volby do Poslanecke Sněmovny Parlamentu České Republiky v roce 1998* (Elections to the lower chamber of the Parliament of the Czech Republic in 1998) (Prague: ČSÚ, 1998).

but the large percentage of votes obtained by Klaus's ODS had not been forecast—either by the political commentators or by any public opinion research before the election. On the other hand, despite the general belief that the extremists had the best chance for success in a time of economic uncertainty and political instability, Czech voters sent the racist and xenophobic Republicans (SPR-RSČ) out of the parliament and rejected the pure leftist populism of the Pensioners for Social Securities. Even the Communists did not improve their position, and, although they gained some seats in the parliament, they remained politically isolated.

After the election, then, the situation seemed promising. Either right-center or left-center majority governments (with either the ODS or the ČSSD as the senior coalition partners and both the KDU-ČSL and US as junior partners) could be established. But the negotiations among parties quickly revealed that the interpersonal relations were worse and the ideological differences greater than anticipated. Finally, to the great surprise of most voters, the two largest parties decided to sign what they called "The Opposition Agreement between the Czech Social Democratic Party and the Civic Democratic Party on the Creation of a Stable Political Environment," which enabled the Social Democrats to establish their own minority government "tolerated" by the ODS. The Social Democrats agreed to offer the

ODS chairmanship posts in both the lower and upper chambers of parliament. The parties agreed that long-term political stability would require changing the constitution in order to diminish the power of the president and changing the electoral system for the lower chamber of parliament from one of proportional representation to some form of majority system in order to reduce the negotiating power of the smaller parties.

The opposition agreement sharply divided public opinion. Indeed, even the opposition to the agreement was divided. On one side were some ODS supporters who felt deceived by a party that had claimed to be the only barrier against the danger of a potentially leftist government before the election but that helped the Social Democrats to gain power after the election. On the other side were the voters attached to the smaller parties; they perceived the planned changes in the electoral laws as an attack on their parties. A substantial part of the public, however, accepted the arguments of the parties involved in the opposition agreement and praised the party leaders for what they saw as a solution to potential political instability.

The first election in which the strength of both camps could be tested was the Senate contest, scheduled for several months after the signing of the opposition agreement, in November 1998. Because the ČSSD and ODS did not have enough time before the election to implement the proposed constitutional changes, voters did not react to the individual changes but rather reacted only generally to the idea of the opposition agreement. And, because senators were elected under the two-round majority system, the Senate election also would serve as a test of the possible effects of introducing the majority system into the election for the lower chamber of the parliament. Facing the majoritarian effects of the Senate electoral law, the four smaller parties—the Union of Freedom, Christian Democratic Union–Czechoslovak People's Party, Civic Democratic Alliance (ODA), and Democratic Union (DEU)—repeated those tactics that proved successful in the first election to the Senate in 1996. These four parties agreed on a unified candidate list and participated in the electoral race as one political party called the Four-Party Coalition.

The results of the election, summarized in Table 19, present a somewhat ambiguous picture of citizens' political opinions. On the one hand, the parties connected by the opposition agreement did not lose too much of their public support as measured by the percentage of votes obtained. Interestingly, the ČSSD, which was holding all the ministerial posts, lost more supporters than the ODS. After the election, the ODS and ČSSD maintained the three-fifths majority necessary for any constitutional change by the least

Table 19

The 1998 Parliamentary (Senate) By-election Results, Czech Republic

Party	Percent of Votes (first round)	Seats (total)	
		Number	Percent
Four-Party Coalition (KDU-ČSL, US, ODA, DEU)	26.3	13	48.2
Civic Democratic Party (ODS)	27.8	9	33.3
Czech Social Democratic Party (ČSSD)	21.8	3	11.1
Communist Party of Bohemia and Moravia (KSČM)	16.6	2	7.4
Other parties and independents	7.5	—	—
Total	100.0	27	100.0

Source: Czech Statistical Office (online at: www.volby.cz).
Note: Since 1998, one-third of senators (twenty-seventy of total eighty-one) are elected every two years.

possible margin—a single seat. On the other hand, the Four-Party Coalition was the clear winner of the election. In most electoral districts where the candidates of the Four-Party Coalition had managed to come in first or second in the first round and participate in the runoff, the second round of the election proved successful as well. (When voters had to decide in the second round between a candidate of the Four-Party Coalition and a candidate of one of the parties connected by the opposition agreement, they voted as a rule for the candidate of the Four-Party Coalition). The victory of the Four-Party Coalition, however, was overshadowed by the low turnout; the 42 percent turnout in the first round dropped to only 20 percent in the second round. The election, then, proved to be more a manifestation of voters' dissatisfaction with politics than an event that politically mobilized the opponents of the opposition agreement.

In 1999, the general population seemed to be even unhappier with politics. Now more familiar with the way the opposition agreement worked in practice (that is, it called for the appointment of either ČSSD or ODS party members to well-paid or influential posts under state control), many voters were looking for a way to express their own dissatisfaction with those currently ruling. They got their chance when one ODS senator died. The by-election, organized by chance in a downtown electoral district of Prague, was scheduled for August 1999. In fact, it was a very crucial one for the ODS and ČSSD, because they needed that seat to maintain the three-fifths majority they needed to pass the planned changes in the constitution. Trying to avoid the potentially negative consequences of voters' unhappiness with the excessive role of political parties in all spheres of public life, the most important parties nominated well-known nonpartisan sympathizers as candidates. Their efforts were foiled, however, when Václav Fischer, owner of a popular travel agency, decided to participate in the election as an independent candidate. In response, voters used the election as a way of expressing their disgust with the established political elite. Fischer, who only stressed that he was not dependent on any political party and that he would vote against the constitutional changes prepared by the ODS and ČSSD, decisively beat all party candidates in the first round by receiving over 71 percent of the votes. The ODS candidate, a popular actress, received only about 12 percent of the votes in the electoral district that used to be an ODS stronghold and where her predecessor obtained almost 40 percent of the votes over three years ago. With this loss and the loss of the three-fifths majority in the Senate, the plans for constitutional changes became more complicated. Today, however, the possibility of changes in other laws (such as those governing elections) that could strengthen the ruling parties remains open and is one of the main topics of political discourse in the Czech Republic.

Poland

Poland was the first Communist country in which the Communists were pressed to partially give up their privilege of having their parliamentary seats for life and to join the fray in elections by trying to persuade voters that they were a better alternative than the opposition. Yet for the party the results of the 1989 parliamentary election were devastating. Of the seats being contested, all but one went to candidates of the Citizens Committee, an organization dominated by the trade union Solidarity, and the only remaining seat went to an independent candidate. In the districts where the Communist candidates had no opponents, no one was elected, and the seats were declared vacant because of the extremely low turnout. In spite of its bitter electoral defeat, the Communist Party held, together with the satellite parties, a majority in the Sejm, because those seats were not contested and went directly to candidates nominated by the Communists and their satellite parties. As a result, the Sejm was able to elect Gen. Wojciech Jaruzelski, the general secretary of the Communist Party, as Polish president.

Forming the government, however, was more complicated. The former minister of the interior, Czeslaw Kiszczak, who was appointed prime minister by the president, was not able to form a government supported by a majority of deputies. In view of this situation, Lech Wałęsa, the leader of Solidarity, invited the United Peasants Party and the Democratic Party to join Solidarity. The former satellite parties then broke their ties with the Communists and, together with Solidarity, formed a new non-Communist majority in the parliament. A grand coalition government was then formed under the leadership of the Catholic dissident Tadeusz Mazowiecki. This loss of governmental power was yet another shock for the Communist Party and led ultimately to its demise and the birth of a new party, the Social Democratic Party of Poland, under the leadership of Aleksander Kwaśniewski.

In the meantime, faced with severe economic problems inherited from the Communist era,[16] the Mazowiecki government adopted a program of economic stabilization aimed at halting the danger of hyperinflation. It consisted of restrictive fiscal and monetary policies and the microeconomic liberalization and deep restructuring of institutions. Although the policy achieved its main goals, it had some important detrimental side effects such as a sharp drop in actual incomes, a decline in industrial output, and a rapid rise in unemployment.

Faced with the hardships accompanying the economic transformation, Poles rapidly became disillusioned with the government. The result was greater diversity on the political scene as Solidarity leader Wałęsa, who was not a member of the government, more and more openly criticized the government for both the real and alleged shortcomings of its economic policy and the tolerant attitudes it displayed toward the former Communists in various posts throughout the state administration. Mutual controversies were intensified after a group of Solidarity activists associated with Wałęsa formed the Center Alliance (PC), which called for an early presidential election and the speeding up of reforms. In response, the Citizen's Movement–Democratic Action (later renamed the Democratic Union, UD) was established by the supporters of Prime Minister Mazowiecki. At the same time, political parties were developing both outside the Solidarity movement, such as the Confederation of Independent Poland and the Christian National Union (ZChN), and inside Solidarity, such as the Liberal Democratic Congress (KLD). Moreover, the former satellite Agrarian Party changed its name to the United Peasants Party and demanded a return to the pre-Communist tradition. Two other parties claimed to be successors of the pre-Communist Agrarians: the Polish Peasants Party (PSL) and the Polish Peasants Party "Solidarity."

The fact that the era of the unified opposition was over was particularly obvious during the campaign leading up to the presidential election in October 1990. Not only was it characterized by ad hominem attacks, it also revealed deep differences over basic issues such as church-state relations, individual versus collective rights, and the definition of citizenship (Tworzecki 1996). Although six candidates were able to collect the necessary endorsement of 100,000 signatures, the presidential contest was expected to have two favorites—Wałęsa and Mazowiecki.

Although the Wałęsa victory was expected, the election results were surprising (see Table 20). The politically unknown populist expatriate businessman, Stan Tyminski, running as an independent candidate, was able to gain almost a quarter of the vote and thus end Mazowiecki's chances of participating in the second ballot. In the second ballot, Wałęsa was able to secure a clear victory and replace Jaruzelski in his post. Mazowiecki resigned as prime minister after his electoral failure and was replaced by the leader of the Liberal Democratic Congress, Jan Krzysztof Bielecki.[17] The political parties then began to prepare for the upcoming parliamentary election. New parties mushroomed, others split, and many electoral alliances and coalitions were established and dissolved. In the 1991 election, the highly proportional electoral system helped twenty-nine political parties gain representation in the Sejm (the ten most successful parties are listed in Table 21).

In the extremely fragmented postelection Sejm, the strongest party (Mazowiecki's Democratic Union) obtained only 12.3 percent of the vote, and a coalition of at least the five biggest parties was necessary to constitute any simple parliamentary majority. The fragmentation of political parties also was observable in the Senate, although senators were elected on the basis of the "first and second past the post" system in the individual provinces.[18] In spite of the Senate's different electoral system, which theoretically should have helped the biggest parties and eliminated the smallest ones, thirteen nationwide parties were able to secure at least one seat out of one hundred. Fourteen seats went to independent candidates and candidates of regional parties.

The political situation in the parliament after the election was indeed confusing. The process of government building was long and difficult. All parties, including the smallest ones, were trying to use their presence in the parliament more to enhance their public image than for anything else. Under these circumstances, the minority government, which consisted of the Christian National Union (the strongest party in Catholic Electoral Action),

Table 20
The 1990 Presidential Election Results, Poland

Candidate	Number of Votes (first round)	Percent of Votes (total)
Lech Wałęsa (Center Alliance)	6,569,889	40.0
Stan Tyminski (Independent)	3,797,605	23.1
Tadeusz Mazowiecki (Solidarity)	2,973,264	18.1
Włodziemierz Cimoszewicz (Left)	1,514,025	9.2
Roman Bartoszcze (Peasants)	1,176,175	7.2
Leszek Moczulski (KPN)	411,516	2.5

Source: Frances Millard, *The Anatomy of New Poland: Post-Communist Politics in Its First Phase* (Aldershot, Hants, England: Edward Elgar, 1994).

the Center Alliance, and the Peasants Alliance and was led by Jan Olszewski from the Center Alliance, fell after only six months in office. The main reason for the government's downfall was not its poor economic performance (in fact, it had showed the first signs of a solid recovery in 1992), but the attempt of the interior minister to reveal certain files containing the names of persons who had allegedly cooperated with the Communist secret police.

Table 21
The 1991 Parliamentary (Sejm) Election Results, Poland

		Seats	
Party or Group	Percent of Votes	Number	Percent
Democratic Union (UD)	12.3	62	13.5
Alliance of the Democratic Left (SLD)	12.0	60	13.0
Catholic Electoral Action (including Christian National Union, ZChN)	8.7	49	10.7
Polish Peasants Party (PSL)	8.7	48	10.4
Confederation for an Independent Poland (KPN)	7.5	46	10.0
Center Alliance (PC)	8.7	44	9.6
Liberal Democratic Congress (KLD)	7.5	37	8.0
Peasants Alliance (post-Solidarity Polish Peasants Party "Solidarity")	5.5	28	6.1
Solidarity (trade union)	5.1	27	5.9
Beer Lovers Party	3.3	16	3.5
Other parties	20.8	43	9.4
Total	100.00	460	100.0

Source: Larry L. Wade, Alexander J. Groth, and Peter Lavelle, "Estimating Participation and Party Voting in Poland: The 1991 Parliamentary Elections," *East European Politics and Societies* 8 (winter 1994): 94–121.

After Jan Olszewski lost his position as prime minister, he established the clearly anti-Communist Movement for the Republic (ROP, later called the Movement for Poland's Reconstruction) which attracted some deputies from the Center Alliance. Meanwhile, Wałęsa appointed Waldemar Pawlak, the leader of the Polish Peasants Party, as prime minister, but Pawlak was not able to obtain the necessary support for his government in the Sejm. Finally, Hanna Suchocka from the Democratic Union successfully formed a government of seven parties, of which the Democratic Union, the Liberal Democratic Congress, the Christian National Union, and the Center Alliance were the most influential. The government proved to be surprisingly effective in avoiding big interparty disputes and in continuing the reform policy of the first post-Communist governments. In the meantime, the most remarkable move on the political scene was the establishment of the Union of Labor (UP), a social democratic party that originated in the left wing of Solidarity.

Although the economic performance of Poland under the Suchocka government was generally more encouraging,[19] many problems remained such as a high level of unemployment and a decrease in the real wages of state employees. When the government refused to raise the wages of teachers and health care workers, it came under attack in the parliament and was defeated in a no-confidence vote. Because an alternative government was not proposed, Wałęsa dissolved the parliament and called for an early election.

The 1993 parliamentary elections were held under a new electoral law that introduced a 5 percent legal threshold (8 percent for coalitions)[20] intended to prevent future parliaments from extensive fragmentation (see Table 22 for the election results). And the electoral law truly worked—only six parties entered the parliament. The Alliance of the Democratic Left (SLD, a coalition dominated by Kwaśniewski's Social Democratic Party of Poland) was the clear winner, followed by the Polish Peasants Party, the successor of its former satellite. Besides those two parties, only the liberal Democratic Union, the post-Solidarity social democratic Union of Labor, the nationalist Confederation for an Independent Poland (KPN), and the Non-Party Bloc for the Support of Reforms (BBWR, a nonparty alternative that came into existence, promoted but not directly led by President Wałęsa) were represented. Among the parties left out of parliament were the conservative Catholic parties and Solidarity. President Wałęsa appointed the leader of the Polish Peasants Party, Pawlak, as prime minister. In his second attempt to form the government, Pawlak, backed by a solid majority of a coalition of the SLD and PSL, proved successful. Surprisingly, the new

Table 22

The 1993 Parliamentary (Sejm) Early Election Results, Poland

Party	Percent of Votes	Seats	
		Number	Percent
Alliance of the Democratic Left (SLD)	20.4	171	37.2
Polish Peasants Party (PSL)	15.4	132	28.7
Democratic Union (UD)	10.6	74	16.1
Union of Labor (UP)	7.3	41	8.9
Catholic Electoral Committee "Fatherland"	6.4	—	—
Confederation for an Independent Poland (KPN)	5.8	22	4.8
Non-Party Bloc for the Support of Reforms (BBWR)	5.4	16	3.5
German minority	0.6	4	0.9
Other parties	28.2	—	—
Total	100.0	460	100.0

Source: Hubert Tworzecki, *Parties and Politics in Post-1989 Poland* (Boulder: Westview Press, 1996).

government, based on a post-Communist party and on its former satellite, committed itself to a policy of Western orientation, as well as to the continuation of economic reforms. Although some commentators claim that under Pawlak's leadership reforms in agriculture practically halted because of pressure from the peasant lobbies, the overall macroeconomic results of the 1993–1995 period were impressive: Poland enjoyed the highest GDP growth of all post-Communist countries in the region (with the exception of Albania), the Warsaw stock market rose substantially, and foreign investment grew. Small political parties with similar political programs began to cooperate more closely because of the requirements of the electoral law, giving rise to the Covenant for Poland, a coalition that incorporated the Christian National Union, Center Alliance, and Peasants Alliance. The Liberal Democratic Congress also merged with the Democratic Union to become the Union of Freedom (UW).

The year 1995 was very active politically. The conflict between President Wałęsa and the Pawlak government about the alleged inability of the latter to govern was resolved by the formation of a new government made up of the same coalition partners but under the leadership of Józef Oleksy, a long-time Communist Party employee nominated to the post by the SLD. However, the key event of the year was the presidential election scheduled in November. Even though most political parties with similar political programs were unable to agree on one candidate to back, there were two favorites: the incumbent president, Wałęsa, and the candidate of the SLD, Kwasniewski. As the preelection campaign continued, the contest became increasingly symbolic, with Kwasniewski seen as representing the old times of communism and Wałęsa the reforms. Thus those who believed that Kwasniewski meant the return of communism had no choice but to vote for Wałęsa (after all, nobody else could defeat Kwaśniewski). And those who were not benefiting from the economic reforms, or who were afraid of the rising power of the Catholic Church, or who were dissatisfied with Wałęsa had only one option—to vote for Kwaśniewski (after all, who else could defeat Wałęsa?).

In the 1995 election, the two leading candidates, whose popular support was almost the same, did not give the other candidates much of a chance (Table 23). Although the incumbent president was declared the probable winner by most of commentators and journalists before the second round, the actual results were somewhat different—Kwaśniewski received 52.7 percent of the vote and became president, thereby rounding out the success of the Alliance of the Democratic Left. The victory of Kwaśniewski as well as the replacement of Prime Minister Józef Oleksy (who was accused of having cooperated secretly with the KGB) by the other SLD candidate, Włodziemierz Cimoszewicz, in early 1996 did not substantially change either the country's foreign policy orientation or the domestic socioeconomic policies of the government.

In the parliamentary elections of 1997, six main political actors had a real chance to exceed the 5 percent threshold and enter the parliament (Jasiewicz 1997). Four of the six political actors were represented in parliament before the election: the Democratic Left Alliance, the social democratic party headed by President Kwaśniewski; the liberal democratic Union of Freedom under the leadership of Leszek Balcerowicz; the post-Solidarity socialist Union of Labor led by Tadeus Zieliński; and the populist Polish Peasants Party of Pawlak. The other two political actors with a good chance for future parliamentary representation were the Movement for Poland's Reconstruction, the party of former prime minister Olszewski which embraced both Christian democratic and populist elements, and the Christian democratic-oriented Solidarity Electoral Action (AWS), the coalition dominated by the Solidarity trade union under Marian Krzaklewski's leadership. The results of the 1997 parliamentary election are summarized in Tables 24 and 25.

The actual electoral results for the Sejm varied only slightly from Jasiewicz's (1997) preelection estimation (Table 24). Only the Union of Labor did not manage to overcome the 5 percent legal threshold in the Sejm

Table 23
The 1995 Presidential Election Results, Poland

Candidate	Percent of Votes (first round)
Aleksander Kwaśniewski	35.1
Lech Wałęsa	33.1
Jacek Kuroń	9.2
Jan Olszewski	6.9
Waldemar Pawlak	4.3
Tadeus Zieliński	3.5
Hanna Gronkiewicz-Walz	2.8

Source: Hubert Tworzecki, *Parties and Politics in Post-1989 Poland* (Boulder: Westview Press, 1996).

contest. The share of wasted votes—that is, those given to parties without any chance of gaining any seats in the Sejm—dropped substantially, from almost 35 percent in 1993 to about 13 percent in 1997. This factor was one of the reasons why the election turned out to hail the return of the conservative right united under the umbrella of Solidarity Electoral Action. Although the Alliance of the Democratic Left gained even more votes than four years earlier, it lost several seats in the Sejm.

The shift in popular support toward the right was even more visible in the Senate election results (Table 25). The electoral success of the right and the substantial loss of the Polish Peasants Party enabled Solidarity to form

Table 24
The 1997 Parliamentary (Sejm) Election Results, Poland

Party	Percent of Votes	Seats Number	Percent
Solidarity Electoral Action (AWS)	33.8	201	43.7
Alliance of the Democratic Left (SLD)	27.1	164	35.7
Union of Freedom (UW)	13.4	60	13.0
Polish Peasant Party (PSL)	7.3	27	5.9
Movement for Poland's Reconstruction (ROP)	5.6	6	1.3
Union of Labor (UP)	4.7	—	—
German Social and Cultural Society Opole Silesia (MN Opole)	0.6	2	0.4
Other parties	7.5	—	—
Total	100.0	460	100.0

Source: Polish Press Agency, 1997.

Table 25

The 1997 Parliamentary (Senate) Election Results, Poland

Party	Number of Seats	Percent of Seats
Solidarity Electoral Action (AWS)	51	56.7
Alliance of the Democratic Left (SLD)	28	20.0
Union of Freedom (UW)	8	8.9
Independent candidates	5	5.6
Movement for Poland's Reconstruction (ROP)	5	5.6
Polish Peasants Party (PSL)	3	3.3
Total	90	100.0

Source: Polish Press Agency, 1997.

a coalition government with Balcerowicz's Union of Freedom. Prof. Jerzy Buzek, backed by a solid majority in the parliament, served as prime minister. Buzek's government committed itself to the politics of continuing economic reforms, decentralization, and Western orientation.

The Factors Underlying Party Development

This chapter has described the evolution of political parties in East-Central Europe since 1989. Although the transformation process in the region was not without its problems, it was rather successful. In contrast to the post-1989 situation in the Balkans or in some post-Soviet republics, there were no wars in the East-Central Europe. The newly established democratic regimes proved their capacity to solve ethnic and social conflicts peacefully. Although many new political leaders were sometimes tempted to use the same tactics as the old Communist governments, they generally respected democratic principles either because they believed in them or simply because they had to. Free elections were held regularly, the results of elections were respected, and the defeated parties peacefully transferred power into the hands of the winners. Politicians also learned the limits of their power. They learned to respect the decisions of independent courts and to live under the criticism of media. Moreover, the once highly centralized power typical of Communist regimes of Soviet type was eroded by the devolution of the power of the central government to regional and local governments.

On the economic front, after several years of deep economic troubles the economic reforms began to bear fruit. Companies were gradually restructured, foreign investment was promoted, the rise of unemployment was tempered by an increase in the number of new jobs, and GDPs began to grow.

One of the most striking features of economic development was the almost total reorientation of foreign trade and integration into the international economic structures of the developed world. In the 1990s, all four countries studied become member states of the Organization for Economic Cooperation and Development (OECD) and Council of Europe and signed association agreements with the European Union. Poland, the Czech Republic, and Hungary also joined NATO in 1999.

Anyone studying party development in the post-Communist era will probably sooner or later raise questions about the events described here. Was the process of political party development chaotic and unpredictable, or were there some general tendencies and common features? Are political parties simply institutions created and used by ambitious, power-seeking individuals as tools to fulfill their desires, or do they also reflect existing deep social cleavages by giving political expression to the various interests of different social groups? What factors—historical, cultural, social, economic, and legal—shape party systems? Why are party systems in neighboring countries so different, and are they really so different? Chapters 3–5 discuss the factors that influence political party development. In doing so, they explicitly suggest that something outside politics itself has been influencing party development in East-Central Europe—that is, the political parties in the post-Communist countries are not isolated from the society. Of the many factors underlying party development, these chapters will concentrate on three: the history and culture of a country (Chapter 3), social cleavages (Chapter 4), and the legal context (Chapter 5).

3

The Party System: A Product of a Country's History and Culture?

As Chapters 1 and 2 reveal, the political parties that emerged after the fall of communism did not emerge from nowhere; at the very least, they were influenced by the history of their respective countries. History, however, can play two different roles. In studying the development of political parties after the fall of Communist rule, either one can search for some signs of historical continuity or one can interpret some features of party development in the post-Communist era as a reaction to the history of the country. Historical continuity can take several forms: of political parties as institutions, of the relative strength of the individual parties, of party allegiances, of political traditions and symbols, of political ideas and ideologies, of a "national mentality," of cultural stereotypes and political culture.[1] Some of these forms, as found in the countries studied, are discussed in this chapter.

Historical Continuity of Political Parties as Institutions

In all four of the countries studied, the historical continuity of political parties as institutions is similar. On the basis of institutional continuity and links with the past, five types of political parties or movements can be distinguished: (1) the Communist and post–Communist era parties; (2) the former satellite parties that existed legally during the Communist period; (3) the historical pre-Communist parties banned by the Communists and reestablished after the fall of their regime; (4) the parties that emerged out of the dissident movements; and (5) quite new parties with no political history (Cipkowski 1991; Körösényi 1991; Kostelecký and Kroupa 1996).

The Communist Parties enjoyed the longest organizational continuity, because after 1989 no former ruling party was officially banned in any of the studied countries. Although the Communists were pressed by the new regimes to give up some or most of their property and suffered a rapid decline in membership, the party infrastructure (which still included a large membership and a network with local and regional organizations) was not destroyed, allowing the parties to undertake effective grassroots political work. Moreover, the peaceful regime changes, driven by political strategies of reconciliation, avoided any extensive persecution of Communist Party leaders or of ordinary members.[2] Such a tactic helped to stabilize the party's position in the new atmosphere. Continuity, however, was not always to the advantage of the Communist Parties in the region. On the contrary, they were trying hard to disassociate themselves from their totalitarian past.

Eventually, the Hungarian, Slovak, and Polish reform Communists overtook the leadership of their parties and transformed them into socialist or social democratic parties of the Western European type. This maneuver enabled new leaders to promote the "double image" of the reform parties. In other words, when speaking to the voters afraid of reforms or nostalgic for the "good old days," they could stress the socialist welfare state provisions, job protection, stability, political experience, and managerial professionalism inherited from the old party, and when speaking to voters seeking an alternative to the policies of conservative governments, they could stress the party's new image—a commitment to democracy, human rights, a social market economy inspired by the postwar German economic model, and the European political left. The new Communist leaders further built on this new image by reminding voters that the most orthodox of the Communist leaders had been expelled from the party or had established their own "true Communist" parties on the political periphery. In this way, the mainstream post-Communists were able to distance themselves from the extremists.

The story of the Czech Communists is somewhat different, however. Although most of the discredited leaders were expelled from the party quickly after the regime change and the party officially declared its commitment to democratic rules, reformists in the new leadership made several attempts to redirect the Communist Party's political program toward a more social democratic orientation. These attempts failed, however, when several party congresses proved that the supporters of orthodox Communist politics were much stronger than the reformists. The explanation is clearly historical: in the early seventies the party had systematically destroyed all reformist elements within its ranks, and twenty years proved to be an insufficient period of time for the development of any new reformist movement within a party whose orthodoxy in the 1970s and 1980s was notorious. Moreover, the fact that Czechoslovakia's economic performance prior to the reforms was relatively better than Poland's or Hungary's supported the argument than no radical change in the party's program was needed. The Czech Communists, then, were the only Communist Party in the region not to undergo any substantial programmatic reform. The fact that it even refused to remove the word *Communist* from its party name bears witness to the party's continuity.

After the fall of communism, the former satellite parties that had legally coexisted within the Communist states as a part of the umbrella front organizations but under the supervision of the Communists found themselves in a delicate situation.[3] On the one hand, they could use their organizational structures, relatively large memberships and new political freedoms to develop independent politics. On the other hand, they had to defend themselves against accusations of collaboration with the old regime. Like the Communist Parties themselves, then, the satellite parties tried to combine the advantages of continuity with those of a new image. The first step in this direction usually consisted of breaking of ties with the Communists, accompanied or followed by a change in the party's leadership. Parties found, however, that having an organization, property, and a membership did not necessarily guarantee a long-term political future. Rather, time proved that only parties with close links to certain social groups were assured of success. For example, the Polish Democratic Party, traditionally an exponent of the interests of the non-Marxist intelligentsia and the urban middle strata, tried to present itself as a liberal party with a nationwide appeal (Grzybowski 1991b). The party subsequently failed, however. Similarly, the Czech Socialist Party, traditionally associated with the urban middle class, presented itself as a representative of the non-Communist variant of socialism, national democracy, and liberalism, but it did not attract any substantial popular support, despite a well-developed territorial organization, sufficient funding, a nationwide newspaper, and several ministers in the first post-Communist coalition government. The Slovak Freedom Party and the Party of National Revival, both rather artificial, Communist-inspired organizations established after World War II (without either a pre-Communist historical tradition or a clear constituency), disappeared from national politics rather early. On the other hand, the United Peasant Party, which "had returned to the traditions of the prewar and early postwar period and organized under the banner of the Polish Peasant Party Reborn," was able not only to survive politically, but within a few years to become the main representative of the peasantry and a member of several coalition governments (Grzybowski 1991b). Similarly, the Czechoslovak Peoples Party,[4] intentionally designed to represent the Czech Catholic population, changed its leadership and its name to the Christian Democratic Union–Czechoslovak Peoples Party. This strategy proved to be very successful, because the party, backed by a stable electorate, was a junior coalition partner in all post-Communist governments in the Czech Republic until 1998. With their networks of local organizations and large memberships, the former satellite parties proved even more successful in the local elections (Surazska 1993; Kostelecký and Kroupa 1996; Vajdová 1996; Vajdová and Kostelecký 1997).

The situation of political parties that had at least some pre-Communist historical traditions but had been banned by the Communists was the opposite of that of the satellite parties. Immediately after the fall of the regime, the reborn pre-Communist parties had no local organizations, no property and only a few members, yet they generally projected a good image as democratic institutions and as victims of the former regime. The path back to democratic politics, however, was far from easy. The fact that the parties had a history often enforced a perception that they were old-fashioned. The manner in which these parties were reestablished (usually by a group of former party activists), as well as the political programs they tended to adopt (very often calling for the restoration of the pre-Communist situation), supported the widespread image of the parties as clubs of old men dreaming about their youth. But not all of the reestablished parties had dark political futures. Both the Hungarian Independent Smallholders Party and the Christian Democratic People's Party were able to overcome periods of internal struggle (during which the younger and more pragmatic politicians ousted the older guards), were able to define a clear relationship with their constituencies (peasants and Catholics), and were represented in the post-Communist parliaments. Both parties also reported an increase of activities on the local level and a rise in membership (Lomax 1995).

The best example of the successful reestablishment of a party is the political development of the Czechoslovak (later Czech) Social Democratic Party, which had long been on the Czech political scene. Reestablished by the joint efforts of its former members and social democratic emigrants, the party failed to gain any parliamentary seats in the 1990 election and did not exceed the 5 percent legal threshold. Soon after a new generation of leaders from the former left wing of the Civic Forum took power, the popular support of the party rose, as did the number of members and local organizations. The reborn Social Democrats also benefited from the orthodoxy of the Communist Party. Because of the Communists' rigidity, generally un-accepted by a majority of the population, most opponents of the conservative government had no option but to vote for the Social Democrats. Moreover, the Social Democrats' refusal to cooperate with the Communists helped them to overcome public fear that the Social Democrats were only Communists in disguise.[5]

The political parties and movements with roots in the dissident movements were, politically speaking, in the most favorable position immediately after the fall of the Communist regime. Their leaders were perceived as the heroes of the revolution and their political programs promised alternative reforms. Moreover, having no institutional history became an advantage. The idea of nonpolitical politics was rather popular, and partisanship was generally discredited. In such a climate, the results of the first free election was a triumph of parties or movements based on a dissident tradition, despite the fact that most of them did not have effective organizations and were rather broad movements led by a group of popular leaders rather than by political parties.[6]

Many political parties without any links to the institutions of either the pre-Communist or the Communist period also emerged in the post-Communist political scene. Some of them proved to reflect the needs of various social groups; others seemed to be individual attempts to enter politics. The length of their "political lives" varied, but some managed to become a stable part of their country's political system.

Historical Continuity in Political Culture

The fact that some political parties lacked institutional continuity or a historical predecessor does not mean that, for them, history is irrelevant. Indeed, quite the opposite is true, as the works of many scholars have shown: history is always a factor in the politics of the post-Communist era.

Regional Continuity

One of the most fascinating pieces of evidence for this statement is the surprising level of regional continuity in political culture, especially in the continuity of well-documented voting patterns in all of the studied countries. For example, big regional differences in both voter turnout and political preferences were noticed immediately after the Polish presidential election in 1990 (see, among others, Parysek, Adamczyk, and Grobelny 1991). Matykowski and Tobolska (1994), who studied the 1991 and the 1993 parliamentary elections in Poland from the regional perspective, concluded that "in Poland's regional structure we can distinguish voivodships with a permanently high and a permanently low voter turnout. The first cover mid-Western and south-Eastern Poland." Tworzecki (1996) devoted a whole chapter of his book to parties and politics in post-1989 Poland and focused on the regional cleavages from the political and geographic viewpoints. He not only confirmed the previous findings, including the substantial continuity of voting patterns, but also concluded that "at the regional level, at least, the party system effectively 'froze' into its present shape within a year or two of the 1989 elections."

Even more interesting than the existence of persistent regional political patterns is the fact that voting patterns are not easily explained by factors such as differences in unemployment levels, demographic differences, or differences in the economic structure of individual regions. Rather, they reflect profound cultural or historical differences. Tworzecki takes into account the differences in the development of particular historical regions in Poland with the goal of explaining their contemporary political character. For example, the population of Galicia, formerly under the relatively liberal rule of the Austrian Monarchy, which strongly resisted the pressures to impose Communist agricultural collectivization, has, in accordance with its historical tradition, tended to have a higher voter turnout and to vote more anti-Communist and more conservatively. The western provinces of Poland have remained a Communist stronghold. They are characterized by more urbanization, a high level of collectivization, and a lower level of social integration, because they were resettled by Poles after the expulsion of the Germans at the end of World War II. The lowest electoral turnout can be found in the provinces that were under the absolutist rule of the Russian czar the longest.

Poland, however, may not be a typical country, because the country's more than one hundred years of lasting division and the divisions among it and its powerful neighbors have created various conditions for the development of political traditions. Yet similar studies concentrating on the other three countries support the idea of persistent regional variances in voting behavior. Kostelecký and Jehlička (1991) noticed differences in the electoral results between western, eastern, and southern Slovakia in the 1990 parliamentary elections that resembled those found in the pre-Communist elections. Krivý (1995) and his colleagues (1994, 1996), working extensively on the problem of the delineation of political regions in Slovakia and using data from both the 1992 and the 1994 parliamentary elections in Slovakia, confirmed the findings of Kostelecký and Jehlička. Krivý et al. (1994) concluded that there are many signs that past voting patterns have persisted. Not only does southern Slovakia, populated by a Hungarian minority, differ from the rest of the country, but there are also differences within regions among the exclusively Slovak population. Vladimír Mečiar's Movement for a Democratic Slovakia (HZDS) and the Slovak National Party (SNS) were much stronger than other parties in northwestern Slovakia, while eastern Slovakia became a stronghold of Mečiar's opponents. The research by Krivý et al. (1994) clearly shows that the revealed regional differences are based on cultural and historical factors rather than on social and economic factors. In fact, their regression analyses aimed at explaining the percentage of votes for individual parties in districts without a Hungarian population showed that purely economic indicators such as the unemployment rate were among the least important.[7] The most interesting finding is the fact that the voting pattern for Mečiar's Movement for a Democratic Slovakia was very similar to that for Hlinka's prewar Slovak People's Party (HSLS). Krivý et al. point out that the historically rooted political culture of the different regions is a very important factor in the explanation of contemporary voting patterns in Slovakia. Studying the results of the parliamentary election in 1998, Krivý (1999) came to the conclusion that the relation between the strongholds of the prewar HSLS, Mečiar's HZDS, and the Slovak National Party's 1998 strongholds was even tighter than in any previous elections. Simply put, the regional differences in value orientations as reflected in electoral preferences have proved to be one of the most stable factors in Slovak politics. Although it is not quite clear why the inhabitants of some regions tend to support nationalist populism and authoritarian policies far more than voters living in other regions, the fact is that, once identified, the regional pattern tends to repeat.

The Czech case seems to project the same story. Jehlička and Sýkora (1991) first noticed a similarity between the voting patterns in the 1990 parliamentary elections and the prewar elections. It was later repeatedly proven that the spatial continuity of voting patterns and the regional differences in political culture remain important features of post-Communist politics in the Czech Republic (Kostelecký 1993a, 1995a, 1995b). And once again it was shown that persistent differences in the political orientation of different regions are not simply the consequence of the social and economic characteristics of the regions and their populations, but rather historical and cultural factors. Thus several clearly different political regions can be identified in the Czech Republic. The contemporary Communist Party strongholds copy the prewar ones, including not only the traditional mining regions, but also the traditional "areas of red peasants" in Western Bohemia. For that reason, the Christian Democratic Union–Czechoslovak People's Party is doing well in the exactly same regions of South Moravia that its predecessor was most successful. Both the Prague region and the regions in eastern Bohemia have become the strongholds of pro-market and right-oriented civic parties, a circumstance similar to the prewar situation. On the other side, northwestern Bohemia has repeatedly proven to be a stronghold of extremist parties.

At first glance, the Hungarian example seems to diverge from the observations about the persistence of political regionalism. The winner of the first free parliamentary election, the Hungarian Democratic Forum, reportedly had small regional differences in its electoral support (Körösényi 1991). This pattern, however, does not mean that there are no links with the pre-Communist situation. Z. Kovács (1993), for example, refers to the long-term differences between the country's western and eastern parts in electoral turnout, political orientation, and historical continuity of pro-Communist votes. Similarly, Körösényi (1991), who analyzed the links between past and present contemporary Hungarian politics, concluded that "there is a remarkable continuity between pre- and post-Communist Hungarian politics" and within regional political preferences themselves. Körösényi also has shown that closer links with history are evident (not surprisingly) for the so-called historical parties: the Smallholders were doing disproportionately well in the Protestant-rural east both in 1947 and in 1990; the Christian Democratic People's Party was the most successful in the same regions in western Hungary in 1990 as was its forerunner in 1947; and the Communists were the strongest in the industrial northeast in both the 1947 and 1990 elections.

In fact, the time–space continuity of political preferences is not so surprising for parties with close links to some specific electorate, such as the Catholics or the peasants. Despite the huge economic and social changes introduced by the Communists during their forty years of rule, some regional differences remained more or less untouched: the traditionally more pro-Catholic regions remained more pro-Catholic than the others, and the traditionally agricultural regions usually remained more agricultural than the others, despite industrialization. However, why should Slovak voters in eastern Slovakia constantly reject a vote for nationalist parties? Why should voters in eastern Bohemia continually vote for pro-market parties[8] when the region's wealth is well below average (and, moreover, was not improved during the economic transformation conducted by these parties)? And why should voters in western Hungary have a consistently higher electoral turnout than the voters in eastern Hungary? Examples of regions preserving their traditional political orientations, even when no structural reason for this is obvious, are many.[9] Thus in East-Central Europe political culture is importantly influencing politics, much in the same way that this phenomenon has occurred in Western Europe (Inglehardt 1988).

Continuity in Ideology, Political Issues, and Symbols

The concept of political culture helps to explain why some post-Communist political parties continue to exploit tradition, even when they have no institutional history and are not historical in any real sense of the word. Indeed, contemporary post-Communist politics echoes old ideological cleavages, traditional political issues, and old symbols. When the Hungarian Democratic Forum won the 1990 parliamentary election, the new prime minister, Jószef Antall (a historian by profession), interpreted the electoral results as a return to the pre-Communist era: "After having gone through the last 45 years, the Hungarian people have cast votes more or less the same way. This means that after several decades of dictatorship, their historical and political reflexes are not different. We are still alive" (quoted in Cipkowski 1991). And, indeed, the fact that old political reflexes are still alive was well represented by the reappearance of old ideological cleavages. On one side, the governing coalition often used the Christian-national image, stressed national issues, expressed suspicions about Western liberalism, and appeared less than devoted to the country's pro-Western orientation. On the other side, the leading opposition party, the Alliance of Free Democrats, was from the beginning perceived as representative of liberalism, cosmopolitanism, and the Jewish urban intelligentsia. Indeed, often in post-Communist Hungarian politics old ideological divisions play at least some role (Lomax 1995; Bigler 1996). Especially the "Jewish question," which comes up from time to time in current politics, seems to be clearly ideological and not structural, because Jews constitute only about 1 percent of the country's population (Bigler 1996). Political debates about the relationship of the Hungarian state to its neighbors (especially to Hungarian minorities in neighboring states) and the conflict over the government's attempt to take control of the media also have followed prewar ideological patterns. Indeed, Schöpflin (1993) believes that Soviet-type systems preserved a variety of "pre-modern" values and beliefs that are so evident in contemporary politics that they serve as one of the most important obstacles to the development of Western European-type politics. After all, as Schöpflin argues, values and beliefs are not negotiable.

In Czechoslovakia, the reintroduction of a free political game after the fall of communism quickly revealed many traditional political issues. Among them, the most visible was the unresolved relationship between the Czechs and the Slovaks within a common state. Most of the political debates on this topic within the federal parliament faithfully imitated the political discourse from the interwar period. During both periods, the Slovak nationalists initiated the dialogue with the accusation that the Czechs were exploiting Slovakia economically and were incapable of understanding the Slovaks' specificity. They argued, therefore, that Slovakia needed more autonomy. As the conflict deepened, Slovak representatives demanded the independence of Slovakia, because independence was considered the only possible solution to the thorny Czech-Slovak relations. Although this scenario is not unique to Czechoslovakia or Slovakia, as nationalist movements elsewhere have proven,[10] the resemblance of their demands in the early 1990s to their demands in the early 1920s (and even the similarity of some of the slogans used during parliamentary debates) is astonishing.[11]

From the very beginning in the post-Communist period, political debates within the federal parliament were very much about symbols. In the spring of 1990 there were passionate quarrels that lasted for weeks about the name and state symbols of the post-Communist state. Slovak politicians did not agree with the new name of the state suggested by the Czechs (Czechoslovak Republic, later Czechoslovak Federative Republic). They insisted that only a hyphenated country name would make explicit the separate and equal identity of the two nations (Czecho-Slovak Federative Republic). They also pointed out that the first documents issued in the name of the state at its inception in 1918 had used the hyphenated form, and thousands of Slovaks demonstrated in Bratislava, the Slovak capital, against the omission of the hyphen. A month later, the federal parliament finally came up with the compromise solution and named the country the Czech and Slovak Federative Republic.[12]

Within Czech politics, the traditional difference between the political representatives elected in the historical Czech Lands of Bohemia and Moravia was evident from the very beginning. The distinction between Moravian politics and Bohemian politics was manifested best by the regionally specific Society for Moravia and Silesia. Its political program calling for the restoration of their historical lands with their own diets and their own governments was clearly based on historical and ideological arguments.[13] Even Václav Klaus's Civic Democratic Party, declaring itself to be a modern European party offering the voters reforms, referred to the history of Czechoslovakia in its successful electoral campaign before the 1992 parliamentary election. The party's TV spots repeatedly showed old cinema pictures and stressed the glory of Czechoslovakia's interwar industry, while party leaders hammered home the message "Look at the fame of our history! Vote for us and you will have pride in our presence!"

Slovakia also serves as another good example of the continuity of old ideological cleavages. As described briefly in Chapter 1, the key issues of Slovak politics were national sovereignty and independence. During the Hungarian rule, a broad, umbrella-type "national" party was seeking to defend the interests of Slovaks against oppression, while at the same time other political activists were playing an active role in Hungarian parties. Similarly, in the interwar period Hlinka's Slovak People's Party presented itself as a kind of broad organization that was serving the interests of the entire Slovak nation by bringing together those desiring more Slovak sovereignty. Slovaks who were not supporters of Hlinka worked in the Slovak branches of Czechoslovak parties and were not considered "true Slovaks."

The same scheme evolved quickly after the fall of communism when most "national politicians" were unified under Mečiar's broad and ideologically fuzzy Movement for a Democratic Slovakia (the rest of the "true national politicians" had already established the Slovak National Party). Other politicians, often accused of being federalists (that is, not real Slovaks), served in a whole range of parties resembling their classical Western European counterparts. Surprisingly, this traditional ideological division in the Slovak political scene did not disappear after the establishment of an independent Slovakia in 1993, when the main strategic reasons for the existence of broad, all-national parties disappeared. Indeed, Szomolányi (1995) notes in her study of the results of the 1994 parliamentary election in Slovakia that the governing coalition was composed of parties with vague political programs, while the opposition represented the classical political spectrum of the Western European type. Moreover, the governing parties declared themselves to represent the interests of the entire nation and not narrow interests as the opposition parties did. The traditional arguments, then, may be summarized by two points: first, whoever is against all-national movements is against the nation itself, and, second, opposition parties are not in fact "truly Slovak"—indeed, they are often "anti-Slovak."

In Poland, political traditions and historically developed political cultures also have played a big role in contemporary politics. The Catholic Church, which has held a traditionally strong position in Polish society and has served as the primary institution for preserving Polish national identity during the country's frequent periods of foreign oppression, is only one well-known example mentioned by nearly all students of Polish politics (for example, Zarnowski 1990; Sabbat-Swidlicka 1993; Zuzovski 1993; Tworzecki 1996). Other historical factors also have shaped Polish politics. As Davies (1981) points out, the historical traditions of old Poland, marked by a prominent position for the nobility and a preference for autonomous territorial units resembling a federation-type organization rather than a centrally ruled body, were reproduced even in the organizational structure of the Solidarity movement in the early 1980s. Zuzowski (1993) also mentions that Poles have a long tradition of not recognizing the supremacy of the authority's rights over human rights, which may explain why Poland's dissidents' movement during the Communist era was much greater in scope than those in neighboring countries. The existence of these traditions of independence and autonomy help to explain why the Polish post-Communist political scene is so fragmented and Polish political parties are so organizationally unstable. It also could help to interpret the strength of the labor movement in both the Communist and the post-Communist periods.[14]

And in Poland, as elsewhere, politicians were intentionally working with historical symbols. For example, when President Wałęsa spearheaded the formation of the Non-Party Bloc for the Support of Reforms as a nonparty alternative to partisan politics before the 1993 parliamentary elections, he intentionally selected a name that would use the same acronym, BBWR, as the movement established by Józef Piłsudski in 1927. When asked about his intentions, Walesa insisted he would not repeat Piłsudski's error, referring to the military coup in 1926, but pleaded (like Piłsudski sixty years earlier) for stronger executive power and against excessive power for political parties (Vinton 1993).

A Country's Historical Development

Some features of party development in the post-Communist era can be interpreted as a reaction to the historical development of the country or even to individual events in a country's history. In fact, history can play the role of a textbook from which current politicians try to learn how to avoid repeating some notorious political mistakes. For example, when lawmakers amended the electoral laws prior to Czechoslovakia's 1990 parliamentary election, they abandoned the traditional concept in which the parliamentary seat was considered to be a possession of the political party and not that of the elected individual (in that way, party leaders could expel disloyal members of parliament from the party and then from parliament). Those arguing for change pointed to the bad historical experiences with power-hungry party secretariats. The introduction of the 5 percent legal threshold (which discriminated against small parties and prevented excessive fragmentation of parliament) was defended in a similar fashion.

Each nation's historical experiences strongly shapes its politics. Szomolányi (1995) and Musil (1995), who provide some very interesting historical explanations for the present political differences among the four countries studied, note that the Czech Lands reached the peak of its modernization process earlier than the other three countries and so the Czech experience with modernization was not connected with the Communist era in any way. Indeed, in many aspects development during the Communist era went against global trends[15] and thus can be considered a kind of demodernization. According to the opinion polls, most Czechs agree that the golden days of the Czech economy preceded the Communist era, during which the Czech economy experienced a deep, overall decline.

Because the Polish, Slovak, and Hungarian periods of industrialization occurred later than those of the Czech Lands and certain other Western European nations (Table 26), a change of lifestyles and improvements in standards of living are connected in some people's minds with the Communist

Table 26

The Industrial Era in Selected Countries

Country	First Year	Last Year
England	1841	1932
France	1869	1974
Germany	1876	1981
Austria	1884	1980
Czech Lands	1900	1991
Slovakia	1950	1991
Hungary	1951	1980
Poland	1957	1980

Source: Jiří Musil, ed., *The End of Czechoslovakia* (Budapest: Central European University Press, 1995).
Note: "First year" refers to the year the share of industry exceeded the share of agriculture in the economy; "last year" refers to the year the share of industry was exceeded by the share of services.

period. From the political point of view, it does not matter that the overlap of the industrialization and modernization periods with the early Communist period was merely a coincidence in timing. It is even less important that modernization without communism would surely have been more successful than it was with the advent of communism. Szomolányi (1995) even argues that because of the different timing in Poland, Hungary, and Slovakia of modernization, the "crucial momentum . . . is not the contest between left and right, but the struggle between traditionalism and modernity." Regardless of this explanation, which will be proven or disproven by future political developments in the observed countries, it seems clear that historical and cultural factors really matter and must be taken seriously.

4

The Party System:
A Reflection of Social Cleavages?

Traditionally, the development of European political parties has been studied in relation to the development of social structures. The concept of *cleavages,* the divisive lines among various groups within society around which political conflicts evolve, is one of the most useful notions in political sociology. But which cleavages play what role in the process of party formation? Or, more generally, what kinds of divisions within society should be considered cleavages—that is, are politically significant? The situation is further complicated because the relationship of social divisions to politics is mediated by the whole realm of political culture, popular political perceptions, and independent political activity of parties as institutions (Inglehardt 1988; Almond and Verba 1989; Sartori 1990; Tworzecki 1996).

Discussions attempting to determine which of the many possible approaches (political sociology, political culture, institutionalism) provides the best explanation of party system development seem to be never-ending. This study, however, will not join that general discussion. The objective here is more modest and addresses the following basic questions: What social cleavages can be identified in the studied countries? What general trends can be observed in the development of social cleavages? Do political parties reflect social cleavages? What is the link between social development and party development?

Lipset and Rokkan: Four Societal Cleavages

The starting point for any study of the origins of party systems is Lipset and Rokkan's 1967 work on the development of party systems in Western Europe. This chapter will follow this tradition, even though some readers may ask whether the theoretical framework developed to explain the origin of party systems in Western Europe can be applied to party development in the post-Communist countries of East-Central Europe. The answer is that the many connections between contemporary post-Communist politics and the political histories of the four countries studied (all of which are described in Chapter 3) justify this approach.

Lipset and Rokkan maintain that the deciding factors in the formation of party systems in Western Europe were the social cleavages that originated in history. The authors, studying the nation-building processes from their very beginning, distinguish four different basic societal cleavages. During a historical period of so-called national revolutions in the eighteenth and nineteenth centuries, *center–periphery cleavages* and *state–church cleavages* emerged. The center–periphery cleavage (sometimes referred to as the dominant versus subjected culture cleavage) was the conflict between the centers unifying the national states and the peripheries, which often opposed this effort. The state–church cleavage was the struggle between the increasingly secularized states and the church, which attempted to maintain its position in society through economic power, educational institutions, and its leading role within the state administration. The second pair of cleavages—*agriculture–industry cleavages* and *class cleavages*—is connected with the industrial revolutions. The agriculture–industry cleavage evolved from the changing influence of and rising conflict between agriculture and industry. Tensions between employees and employers gave birth to the classical class-based cleavage. This section looks at whether the basic societal cleavages mentioned by Lipset and Rokkan exist in the post-Communist states studied here and, if so, how they are related to the development of party structures.

The Center–Periphery Cleavage

The effect of the center–periphery cleavage in Hungary is ambiguous. Because of the loss of peripheral territories with ethnically mixed populations, Hungary is, on the one hand, a prime example of a well-integrated state. Indeed, at least 91.4 percent of its population is Hungarian, and the ethnic minorities that are present are scattered throughout the country.[1] Of the five biggest ethnic minorities—Roma (3.9 percent), Germans (1.7 percent), Slovaks (1.1 percent), Jews (0.8 percent), and Croats (0.8 percent)—only the Slovaks and Croats are minorities that could theoretically be backed by neighboring countries.

Although the rights of minorities within Hungary is not a major point of contention, either domestically or internationally, and no significant political party declaring itself to be an advocate of minority interests has emerged, nation-building kinds of political questions are being asked in Hungarian politics about the many Hungarian minorities living in neighboring countries. For some Hungarian politicians, relations with Hungarians living outside of Hungary raise questions of statehood and legitimacy (especially the Treaty of Trianon, which determined Hungary's big territorial losses). National revisionism, however, has not gained support among either mainstream politicians or the population. The Hungarian Justice and Life Party (MIÉP) of Istvan Csurka, the former deputy chairman of the Hungarian Democratic Forum (MDF) and the most visible proponent of these ideas, failed to gain single parliamentary seat in the 1994 election and only a few seats in the 1998 election.

The center–periphery conflict is not limited to a conflict between the national state and its minorities; it also can take the form of a struggle between economic, political, and cultural center(s) and peripheral regions, even if no ethnic question is present. In fact, Hungary has a strong predisposition toward this kind of conflict.[2] Although the traditional regional division was highlighted by the consequences of economic reforms (which fell hardest on the northeast periphery where the unemployment rate was as high as 17–19 percent, compared with the acceptable 6 percent in the Budapest area—see Ehrlich and Revesz 1995), regional economic differences have not produced any significant political outcome—that is, no political parties seeking to defend the periphery against the center have emerged. The fact that in the 1990 parliamentary election the Independent Smallholders Party (FKGP) was supported much more in the villages than in Budapest and other cities can be attributed to its agrarian appeal rather than to a peripheral character.[3]

Poland's situation is somewhat similar to Hungary's. Because of events after World War II, Poland became almost entirely homogeneous ethnically; 97.8 percent of its inhabitants in 1992 were ethnic Poles. The ethnic minorities included Ukrainians (0.8 percent), Belorussians (0.5 percent), and Germans (0.5 percent). Although the German minority is represented in parliament,[4] political conflict between the predominantly Polish parties and the politically marginal minority representation does not in fact exist. The main enemy of the Polish nationalist parties such as the Confederation of Independent Poland and the Christian National Union (see Bugajski 1994) are the domestic Communists and neighboring Russia. That said, because of Poland's history, political struggles based on the internal division of the country into several territories with different cultures and histories could emerge. And, indeed, the feeling of regional distinctiveness among the several million Polish Silesians in both Upper and Lower Silesia has found political expression in the existence of the Movement for Silesian Autonomy (Bugajski 1994). This political movement, however, has not gained massive political support even within Silesia itself and has remained politically marginal. In the economic realm, Tworzecki (1996) has pointed out that parties representing agrarian populism as opposed to market liberalism are stronger in the peripheral and rural eastern provinces, but that difference probably has more to do with the history and political culture of these regions than with the center–periphery relationship, because the above-average support for market liberalism in the regions on the western periphery is clearly evident.

The center–periphery cleavage may not be a significant dividing line within post-Communist politics in both Hungary and Poland, but it is in Czechoslovakia. Although the events connected with World War II (the slaughter of Czechoslovak Jews and the postwar expulsion of Germans) led to a growing homogeneity within the population, the country has remained a multinational state. According to the 1991 population census, the population of Czechoslovakia consisted of Czechs (63.2 percent),[5] Slovaks (31.0 percent), Hungarians (3.8 percent), Roma (0.8 percent),[6] Germans (0.4 percent), Poles (0.4 percent), and other minorities (0.4 percent). The more major ethnic groups lived in clearly delineated territories. Of the Slovaks and Czechs, the two largest groups, Slovaks made up only 3.0 percent of the population of the Czech part of the federation, and Czechs made up only 1.1 percent of the population of Slovakia. Practically all Hungarians lived in southern Slovakia, where they substantially outnumbered Slovaks, and almost all Poles lived in the region of Těšín in the Czech Republic. Both the Hungarian and the Polish minorities resided in regions adjacent to the neighboring states that became part of Czechoslovakia after World War I. Although the German minority tended to live in the border regions, it did not constitute a majority in any territory. Finally, the Roma were scattered throughout the country.

In the early 1990s, the center–periphery cleavage in Czechoslovak politics had three different dimensions according to the different centers and peripheries that can be identified. The most important dimension was the division between Czech and Slovak politics, which finally led to the country's split in the beginning of 1993. This division was a good example of a political struggle based on tensions between the integrating tendencies of the center (Czech politics) and the disintegration tendencies of the periphery (Slovak politics), manifested, among other things, in the quite different approaches the representatives of the individual republics took toward their roles within the common state. For example, during the negotiations between the Czech and Slovak national councils about the division of duties between the federal government and the governments of the individual republics, the leaders of the Czech national council favored concentrating more power in the federal parliament and the federal government than in the republics, even if the institution they represented would gain more power and influence under the Slovaks' proposal. Because the basic features of the Czecho-Slovak political split were described in earlier chapters, this chapter will concentrate on two other dimensions of the center–periphery cleavage: the ethnic minority versus majority and the city versus the countryside.

In both the Czech Republic and Slovakia, centers and peripheries emerged. Shortly after the fall of communism, several Hungarian political parties based on ethnic principles were established in Slovakia, covering the entire political spectrum. Fearful that they would not be able to attract enough votes to exceed the 5 percent legal threshold in the federal parliament, the individual Hungarian parties pressed began to think about possible coalitions.[7] Yet except for the small right-oriented Hungarian Civic Party, whose candidates ran on the Public Against Violence (VPN) list, no other Hungarian party created any coalition with their Slovak ideological counterparts. Instead, they established the ideologically broad movement "Coexistencia," which in theory was intended to unify the political representatives of all minorities, but actually was a kind of grand Hungarian coalition. Electorally, this tactic proved to be successful, because the movement entered parliament in 1990 having well exceeded the 5 percent threshold (it picked up votes exclusively in Hungarian-dominated southern Slovakia).

The Slovak–Hungarian political cleavage was even more visible later when the future of Czechoslovakia was under discussion (Hungarian parties strongly opposed the division of the country), and particularly after the split. Although Hungary (wisely) did not often directly interfere in the relationship between the Slovak government and its Hungarian minority (especially not after the Socialists' victory in the 1994 election), the political relationship between these two ethnic groups remained cold. The strains were manifested not only in the controversial politics of Vladimír Mečiar's government toward the Hungarian minority, but also in the lack of Hungarian representatives in even the broad government coalition that replaced

Mečiar's group after the 1994 no-confidence vote (although the coalition was supported by Hungarian deputies in the parliament). Moreover, in both the 1992 and the 1994 parliamentary elections no Slovak-Hungarian political coalition existed. In short, as Krivý (1995) has noted, the ethnic division of the contemporary political scene in Slovakia is the most important one and the most stable one.

Although the Czech Republic is more ethnically homogeneous than Slovakia and thus no explicit minority party exists, the center–periphery cleavage has found its expression in Moravian regionalism. The surprisingly good electoral results in 1992 of the totally unknown Movement for Self-Governing Democracy–Society for Moravia and Silesia (HSD-SMS), established by a group of former employees of the southern Moravia regional administration and of several academics in Brno,[8] catapulted the formerly neglected topic of the administrative division of the Czech Republic close to the top of the political agenda. The feeling of regional distinctiveness resulted in unexpected electoral support for a single-issue party demanding the restoration of historical Moravian and Silesian lands with their own diet and government. Although the movement proclaimed itself to represent both Moravian and Silesian interests, it remained a mainly southern Moravia regionalist movement and has attracted almost no popular support in either Silesia or northern Moravia (Kostelecký, Jehlička, and Sýkora 1993). The HSD-SMS achieved its greatest political success in its campaign, conducted before the 1991 population census, that resulted in the inclusion of Moravian and Silesian ethnicity among the census options. As a result, around 13 percent of the inhabitants of the Czech Republic (about 34 percent of Moravia itself) declared itself to be ethnically Moravian. The movement later floundered, however, because the concept of Moravian autonomy gained support neither among politicians nor among the majority of the Moravian population. After the split of Czechoslovakia, Moravian autonomists were rejected by most of their former supporters, who feared further divisions in an already divided country.

The third dimension of the center–periphery cleavage observable in the Czech political scene was a cleavage between the cities and the countryside. For example, the bigger the city, the higher was the probability of voting for the reformist Civic Forum (OF) in the 1990 election and for the Civic Democratic Party (ODS) and Civic Democratic Alliance (ODA) in the 1992 and 1996 elections. Although some overlap exists between the center–periphery cleavage, the effects of the agriculture–industry cleavage, and the social and economic status of voters (city dwellers generally tend to be more

educated), some center–periphery effects remain in effect even if one controls for the structural characteristics (Kostelecký 1993b). The pattern of
support for parties that in the 1990 and 1992 elections stressed the need for
vast reforms resembled patterns observable in studies on the mechanisms
for spreading innovation. In this respect, the political ideas spread by re-
form-oriented parties may be viewed as a kind of political or cultural innovation that is accepted in centers and opposed in peripheries.

The State–Church Cleavage

The second classical Rokkan and Lipset cleavage is the one between church
and state. As noted in Chapter 1, the tensions between church and state during the period of increasing state secularization in the late nineteenth century found their political expression in the establishment of political parties
defending the interests of the church. The role played by the church in social and political developments, however, varied from country to country.

Because they lie east of the line dividing the Catholic West and the Orthodox East, all four of the countries studied here are firmly within the
sphere of Western Christianity. Yet centuries earlier, the Protestant Reformation rocked East-Central Europe, and a substantial proportion of its population joined the non-Catholic churches of both domestic (Utraquists,
Czech Bretheren) and foreign (Lutherans, Calvinists) origin that emerged
in the region.[9] In both the Czech Lands and Hungary, it is estimated that a
majority of the population became non-Catholic in the sixteenth century
(Kann and David 1984; Pungur 1992). The formal and informal pressures
that accompanied the Counter-Reformation, however, led to a substantial
drop in the number of Protestants in the population, and soon all four countries became, once again, predominantly Catholic. The course of the
Counter-Reformation differed in the four countries. In the Czech Lands, the
non-Catholic churches were persecuted and the Catholic Church was proclaimed the only legal church soon after the Battle on White Mountain in
1620. Rulers in Hungary (which at the time included Slovakia) were more
tolerant.

An assessment of the role of individual churches in the Rokkan and
Lipset period of "national revolutions" is further complicated by the fact
that the development of various religious movements was often connected
with national questions. Thus the rather scarce manifestations of Czech
Protestantism were broadly perceived by many leaders of the National Revival movement[10] in the nineteenth century as indigenous because of the

domestic Hussite and Bretheren traditions, while widespread Catholicism was often denounced as a tool used by Austrian rulers for national oppression. These reservations toward the historical role of Catholicism ended in a rather massive outflow of members from the Catholic Church after the founding of Czechoslovakia in 1918 and later in an attempt to establish a kind of national church in the form of the Czechoslovak Hussite Church. The consequence of the anti-Catholic campaign in the 1920s was ambiguous, however. The Catholic Church lost much of its membership, yet the Czechoslovak Hussite Church did not become a national church, because many former Catholics, proclaiming themselves to be atheists, did not join any church. As a result, the Czech Lands became one of the most secularized territories in Europe.

In Hungary, the Protestant churches became national churches by providing spiritual leadership to those living under Turkish or Habsburg rule in the sixteenth and seventeenth centuries. At the same time, they were perceived as the guardians of national identity, language, and culture (Pungur 1992). Later, the Catholics became more numerous, yet the re-Catholicization process was more gradual and less dramatic both in Hungary and in Slovakia than in the Czech Lands, and Protestants were able to maintain some influence.

Although the majority of Slovaks have always been Catholic, Protestants have played an important role in the country's history. With their Czech counterparts, the Protestants helped to maintain the national identity[11] of Slovaks under Hungarian rule in the sixteenth and seventeenth centuries and later participated substantially in the development of the Slovak language, education, and culture. After the founding of Czechoslovakia in 1918, however, the position of Slovak Protestants, who had always represented a kind of link between the Slovak and Czech nations, became more problematic. The more conservative Slovak Catholics' concerns about the influence of Czech atheism, liberalism, and materialism, together with the somewhat privileged position of Slovak Protestants within both the state administration and the political representation of the new state, found its political expression in the growing nationalism and the anti-Czechoslovak bent of political Catholicism. In short, only Catholics were true Slovaks.

This period ended in the creation of an independent Slovakia, led by the president and Catholic priest Jozef Tiso, who was under the tutelage of Nazi Germany. Under President Tiso, Slovakia became a war ally of Germany, declared a state of war against the enemies of Adolf Hitler, and participated in the persecution of Jews and Roma. Although the Czechoslovak exile government in London managed to reunify prewar Czechoslovakia (and thus helped Slovakia to avoid the status of a defeated Nazi ally), the events of the war badly damaged the image of the Slovak Catholic Church in the eyes of the Czech political elite. Thus immediately after World War II, Czech politicians, supported by Slovak Communists, banned all political parties perceived as "cleri-fascist." Soon after the Communists came to power in 1948, they began to heavily persecute not only proponents of Tiso's puppet regime but also clergymen and laymen who had nothing in common with the fascist regime. This persecution, organized mainly by the Czech-dominated Czechoslovak Communist government, was not perceived positively by much of the Slovak population. As a result, the Catholic Church in Slovakia, cast now as the victim of Czech communism and the defender of the true Slovak values, was able to revive its positive image. Later, in the 1970s and 1980s, the Catholic Church helped the large dissident movement in Slovakia, but other groups in the society remained somewhat suspicious toward the Catholic Church.

The role of Catholicism in Poland was very specific. The Catholic Church was not only accepted by an overwhelming majority of the population, but also traditionally played an important role in politics and served as a symbol of national identity (Zuzowski 1993). Its role as a national institution was strengthened during the period that Poland was divided between (Lutheran) Prussia and (Orthodox) Russia and, later, in the constitution of the modern Polish state after the First World War. The Communist takeovers, however, dramatically interfered with the relations between church and state. The openly atheistic new Communist rulers declared the churches to be remnants of the old system and enemies of the people. Church property was nationalized; Catholic priests, members of religious orders, and Protestant ministers were persecuted; and attendance at religious services was perceived as a mark of faithlessness toward the new regime. All church institutions that were not directly abolished were subjected to state (and secret police) control. Under such pressure, church membership quickly declined, and the role of the church in society (except in Poland) was substantially diminished.[12]

A look at all four countries in the late 1980s and early 1990s reveals that Poles are almost totally Catholic (Table 27). The Czechs, in contrast, continue to be one of the most secular nations in the region. In both Slovakia and Hungary, the Catholic population prevails, but Hungary has a high proportion of Protestants. The figures in Table 27 about religious affiliation should be read very cautiously, however. The official figures are usually

Table 27

Religious Affiliation of the Population of the Czech Republic, Slovakia, Poland, and Hungary (percent)

Country	Year	Catholics	Protestants	Others and Nonreligious
Czech Republic	1991	39.1	4.8	56.1
Slovakia	1991	63.8	8.0	28.2
Poland	1988	95.8	0.3	3.9
Hungary	1988	64.7	23.0	12.3

Sources: Paul Bock, "Czechoslovakia and Poland," in *Protestantism and Politics in Eastern Europe and Russia,* ed. Sabrina Ramet (Durham: Duke University Press, 1992); Joseph Pungur, "Protestantism in Hungary: The Communist Era," in *Protestantism and Politics in Eastern Europe and Russia,* ed. Sabrina Ramet (Durham: Duke University Press, 1992); *Catholic Almanac 1996* (Huntington: Our Sunday Visitor, 1996).

based on the declarations of religious affiliation made by census respondents or on the internal documentation of individual churches. But it is difficult to determine what in fact censuses measure. Different sociological surveys have shown repeatedly that church membership figures correspond neither with the data on attendance at religious services nor with respondents' real opinions and attitudes about religious questions. There is, of course, some relationship between the characteristics of the respondents. The people declaring themselves to be atheists neither attend religious services nor believe in God. But the people declaring themselves to be Catholics or Protestants may or may not attend any religious services. And some people declaring themselves to be Catholic or Protestant even reject the existence of God. Thus the declaration of some religious affiliation indicates either a religious belief connected with a commitment to some church or represents only an indirect answer to an (unasked) question about the religion in which the respondent was raised or baptized. This hypothesis seems to be supported by the difference between the statistics on service attendance and the statistics on membership compiled by the churches themselves. This difference can be attributed to the fact that the Catholic churches and the largest traditional Protestant churches in the region keep all who were baptized in the church on their membership registers, but only some of those baptized remain active in the church into their adulthood. It is logical to assume, then, that the numbers of devoted Catholics and Protestants are lower than the figures seem to show.

How have religious cleavages and church-state relations influenced politics in the post-Communist era? In all of the countries studied, parties claiming to be explicitly Christian emerged immediately after the fall of the

Communist regimes. Among the most influential were the Christian Democratic Union–Czechoslovak People's Party (KDU-ČSL) in the Czech
Lands, the Christian Democratic Movement (KDH) in Slovakia, and the
Christian Democratic People's Party (KDNP) in Hungary. In Poland, the situation was complicated by the enormous number of political parties competing for parliamentary seats. In the 1991 parliamentary election, an electoral coalition was created under the common banner of the Catholic
Electoral Action. It consisted of the Christian National Union (ZChN), the
Christian People's Party, the Party of Christian Democrats, and the Christian Democracy. All these parties were able to gain seats in the parliament,
and most of them participated in the government, yet their electoral gains
had been lower than was expected prior to the elections.

Meanwhile it became clear that Christians (Catholics) were not necessarily voting for the Christian party. In East-Central Europe after the fall of
communism, many Catholics voted for broad anti-Communist movements—the Civic Forum in the Czech Republic and the Public Against Violence in Slovakia—or for conservative parties—the Civic Democratic
Party in the Czech Republic and the Hungarian Democratic Forum. In almost all-Catholic Poland, the Catholic vote was spread out among a variety
of parties, many of which stressed their commitment to Christian or
Catholic values in their programs, while not declaring themselves to be
Christian (Catholic) parties.

Although most of the Christian parties claimed to be ecumenical in character, all were in fact Catholic. Because no Protestant parties were formed,
there was no political struggle between different confessional parties. Instead, most political issues related to religion were linked to the ideological cleavage between the Catholic Church and the secular state, which
raised a whole series of practical questions about the role of the Catholic
Church within the state. As Jasiewicz (1993) points out, there was "much
more at stake than just the right to abortion or religion as a subject in public schools." Indeed, the basic question was: Should Catholic social doctrine
and ethical norms serve as a basis for the state legislature and administration, or should religion be only a private matter?

Were these questions really important for the voters during the period of
huge economic and social change that accompanied the post-Communist
transformation? Scholars who have studied the political development of the
region say they were. Both Jasiewicz (1993) and Wiatr (1993) found the religious–secular cleavage to be one of the most important factors shaping the
political scene in Poland. Indeed, the existence of a relationship between re-

ligious affiliation, religious activity, and voting preferences has been proven empirically on both an individual and an aggregate level. Using regression analysis, Wade, Groth, and Lavelle (1994) estimated the party vote in the 1991 parliamentary election on the aggregate level of each electoral district and proved that independent variables measuring both the percentage of residents in each district engaging in religious practice and the number of priests in each district per 10,000 inhabitants were among the most valuable predictors of voting trends in Poland. Not only was the percentage of votes for the Catholic Electoral Action higher in districts with a more religiously active population, but also for the Center Alliance of Jaroslaw Kaczynski and for the Democratic Union of Tadeusz Mazowiecki. On the other side, both the post-Communist Alliance of the Democratic Left (SLD) and the former satellite Polish Peasants Party (PSL) were supported more often in districts with smaller religious populations. Moreover, data presented in the "Bulletin of Electoral Statistics" (1994) show a negative correlation between church activities and a preference for SLD. The ideological conflict between supporters and opponents of the strong antiabortion legislation adopted in early 1993 is cited among the most important factors for the victory of the post-Communist left in the 1993 parliamentary election (Wiatr 1993). Marody (1995) notes that from about 1993 on, SLD was mentioned by respondents as a party they considered capable of putting a stop to the growing power of the Catholic Church. Finally, religious affiliation influenced voting participation—believers were significantly more likely to participate in elections than nonbelievers. In short, the state–church cleavage is well represented in post-Communist Polish politics.

It is not very surprising that in Poland, a nation with a long tradition of mixing religion and politics, some effects of the state–church cleavage have been identified. The similar interconnections found in Hungary are even more interesting. Angresano (1992) notes that the church versus secularism has been one of the main ideological differences dividing Hungarian politics since the 1991 parliamentary election. Körösényi (1991) even used the traditional religious differences between areas of Hungary in delineating political regions. Tóka (1995a), who thoroughly studied the impact of religious issues on electoral preferences in Hungary between 1990 and 1994, stresses the fact that during that period the most important political cleavage in the Hungarian political scene was the "traditionalist-collectivist" versus the "modernist-individualist" conflict, which defined two opposing political camps: nationalists and Christians on the one side and free-marketeers and liberals on the other.[13] This basic political cleavage is multifaceted, with economic (state redistribution versus free-market), clerical-secular, and national-cosmopolitan faces. Using survey data, Tóka demonstrated that the different attitudes about the role of the church in social and political life were (together with age) the strongest determinants of voters' decisions in the 1990 and 1992 elections. The strong correlation between party choice and respondents' church-going habits also remained in effect during the 1994 election (Tóka 1995b).

Even in the Czech Republic, usually the only post-Communist country in which the socioeconomic left–right cleavage dominated politics (Krause 1996; Vlachová 1997), the role of the state–church cleavage in forming the political spectrum was undeniable. When the economic, social, and historical factors underlying voting patterns in both the 1990 and 1992 parliamentary elections were studied at the district level, religious factors, even when measured by aggregate census data, were among the most valuable predictors of electoral results (Kostelecký 1994). Not only was there an obvious correlation between the share of Catholics in the population and support for the explicitly Christian KDU-ČSL, religious independent variables also proved useful for predicting the popular support for Václav Klaus's ODS (the more Protestants in the population, the higher the electoral support) and for Social Democracy (the more Catholics in the population, the lower the electoral support). Moreover, religious traditions and the religious composition of the population in individual districts were among the factors able to explain the stable differences in the political behavior of the various regions of the Czech Republic (Kostelecký 1995b). Thus regions whose citizens repeatedly tended to vote for parties representing more traditionalist views on different political problems were characterized by a higher share of nonurban Catholics. The regions whose citizens repeatedly voted for more pro-market political parties tended to have a higher level of education and a higher share of Protestants in the population.[14]

In Slovakia, some signs of church–state cleavages can be identified, but they are not as relevant to Slovak politics as they are in the politics of neighboring countries. Yet at the very least links between electoral support for the Christian Democratic Movement and the share of Catholics in the population are evident (Kostelecký, Jehlička, and Sýkora 1993). Krivý (1999), who studied the results of Slovakian parliamentary elections from 1992 to 1998, also concluded that in municipalities with the relatively highest share of Catholics the electoral support for both the KDH and Mečiar's Movement for a Democratic Slovakia (HZDS) was well above the national average. Interestingly, as the voting patterns for the KDH, which explicitly claimed to be a Christian party, became linked less and less with the municipalities and regions with the highest shares of Catholics, the relationship between HZDS voting patterns and the population's share of Catholics became closer and closer. Similarly, the data on an aggregate level reveal that the former Communist Party, the Democratic Left, gained relatively more votes in regions with a traditionally higher share of atheists. The higher the share of Protestants in the population, the lower was the probability of support for the KDH.

The Agriculture–Industry Cleavage

The agriculture–industry cleavage evolved as a political reaction to the changing role and power of individual sectors of the economy during the Industrial Revolution. Indeed, in all of the countries studied agrarian parties operating under different names emerged when universal suffrage was introduced, and soon became among the most influential parties. Although there were ideological differences among individual agrarian parties, one feature remained common to all of them: they relied almost exclusively on support from the agrarian population. The decline in the importance of agriculture for national economies in the first half of the twentieth century and the rising strength of the socialist, social democratic, and Communist Parties, backed by the growing numbers of industrial workers, gradually narrowed the political space of agrarian parties and led to the adoption of a defensive strategy in which the agrarian parties gradually became more traditionalist and known as defenders of the agricultural and rural interests.

The constituencies of agrarian parties differed substantially from country to country. Agriculture was weakest—as measured by its share of the gross national product (GNP)—in the Czech Lands. Indeed, during the whole interwar period the share of the agricultural sector of Czechoslovakia, which included the less-industrialized Slovakia and Ruthenia, was relatively low—between 22 and 26 percent—and comparable to that of some Western European countries (Mitchell 1975). At the beginning of the 1950s, the agricultural share of GNP was around 14 percent in Czechoslovakia, while the same figures ranged between 20 percent and 34 percent in Hungary and between 30 percent and 41 percent in Poland. But as industrialization continued during the Communist period, differences among the countries began to diminish. According to the *Transition Report on Economic Transition in Eastern Europe and the Soviet Union* (European Bank for Reconstruction and Development 1994), there was only a slight differ-

Table 28

Agricultural Sector Employment in the Czech Republic, Slovakia, Hungary, and Poland, 1970–1989 (percent of total employment)

Country	1970	1980	1989
Czech Republic	14.6	10.9	9.4
Slovakia	23.5	14.8	12.2
Hungary	24.7	22.0	19.6
Poland	38.6	30.5	27.8

Sources: Václav Průcha, "Economic Development and Relations, 1918–89," in *The End of Czechoslovakia,* ed. J. Musil (Budapest: Central European University Press, 1995); Eva Ehrlich and Gábor Revesz, *Hungary and Its Prospects, 1985–2005* (Budapest: Akademiai Kiado, 1995).

ence among the countries in 1992—6.0 percent, the Czech Republic; 6.3 percent, Slovakia; 7.3 percent, Hungary; and 8.3 percent, Poland. Clearly, then, the importance of agriculture to the economy is minimal in the countries studied and more or less equivalent. For the purposes of this chapter, however, the figures showing employment in agriculture as a percentage of total employment are even more valuable (see Table 28), because they are more directly related to the potential constituencies of the agrarian parties.

At the end of 1980s, employment in agriculture was three times higher in Poland and twice as high in Hungary as in the Czech Republic. The employment rates in the Czech Republic and Slovakia in 1989 were remarkably similar, however. The decrease in agricultural employment during the last twenty years of Communist rule in Slovakia was the most rapid in the entire region. Yet soon after the fall of communism, specific agrarian parties reemerged on the political scene.

In Poland, the former satellite United Peasants Party broke its ties with the Communists, changed its name slightly (to the Polish Peasants Party), turned its political program toward the needs of the peasants, and received considerable support. Several other agrarian parties also were established in Poland, the most important of which was the Peasants Alliance, which originated in the Rural Solidarity movement. Although both of these parties received support predominantly from the peasants, they differed in the level of religious affiliation of their peasant supporters (Millard 1994a; Wade, Groth, and Lavelle 1994). The post-Solidarity Peasants Alliance was supported mainly by the more religious peasants, while the former Communist ally, the Polish Peasants Party, gained support from those who were less religious (Tworzecki 1996). Although the peasants parties differed in their origins and ideological orientations, their common interest in protecting the agricultural sector from their common enemy (radical economic reformers) pulled them closer together. This process culminated in the virtual disappearance of the Peasants Alliance and the elevation of the PSL, which became the dominant agrarian party after the 1993 parliamentary election when it received the majority of the peasant votes (Tworzecki 1996).

The situation in Hungary was somewhat similar. Soon after the fall of communism, the agrarian Independent Smallholders Party, claiming to be heirs to the pre-Communist party, was reestablished. The Agrarian Alliance, a modern agrarian party with a liberal political program closely geared to the managers of cooperative farms, also was founded. From the very beginning, it was clear that the Smallholders would aim its program at small private farmers and attempt to revive the past. But because the number of private peasants was much lower in Hungary than in Poland, it could be said (with some exaggeration) that the Smallholders adopted a political strategy designed to help the party create its own electorate as it strongly pushed a program of land restitution to former small landowners and their heirs. After this tactic proved to be somewhat successful, the Smallholders entered parliament and later became part of the governing coalition. The Agrarian Alliance, however, did not exceed the 5 percent legal threshold and was kept out of parliament.

Among the supporters of both parties, voters employed in agriculture were heavily overrepresented (Tóka 1995a). Because the Agrarian Alliance practically disappeared from the political scene after its failure in the 1990 parliamentary election, the Smallholders remained the only politically influential party claiming to defend the interests of the agrarian population. Indeed, it was the only party relying on the peasants' support that managed to gain parliamentary seats in all subsequent elections. After four years spent in the opposition, the party returned to the government as a junior partner in a coalition with the Federation of Young Democrats–Hungarian Civic Party (FIDESZ-MPP) in 1998. The link between agricultural voters and the Smallholders was rewarding for both sides: the party obtained several ministerial posts and the party leader, József Torgyán, who was appointed minister of agriculture, used the power of the party to increase subsidies for agricultural producers.

In the Czech Republic and Slovakia, where the agricultural population was smaller than those in Poland and Hungary, agrarian parties were less successful. In spite of its long history, the prewar Agrarian Party was not reestablished. Instead, a group of collective farm managers established a new Agrarian Party, composed solely of Czechs even though the party was officially Czechoslovak. No specific Slovak agrarian party was established (a professional agrarian organization was founded, but it never succeeded in obtaining much popular support).

The Czechoslovak Agrarian Party adopted a strategy similar to that of its counterparts in the neighboring countries; it stressed the need to protect the agricultural sector and warned against too many quick changes and excessive liberalism. Thus the prewar Agrarians had defended free-market principles against socialism, and the post-Communist Agrarians defended cooperative farming against the free-market ideology. In a sense, it was a continuation of old traditions. Then as now, the main task was to protect the peasants from the threat of the "novelties" from the cities. As a result, voter support for the post-Communist Agrarians closely corresponded with prewar patterns, even though the two parties stood on opposite sides of the political spectrum ideologically (Kostelecký 1995a). Both the prewar and the post-Communist Agrarians were supported predominantly by the peasants living in regions with a relatively low percentage of Catholics. Because Catholic peasants tended to vote for Catholic parties, the Agrarian Party did not exceed the 5 percent threshold in the 1990 election and, consequently, did not gain any seats in the parliament. The rapid decline (by 50 percent between 1989 and 1993) in agricultural employment generated by the ongoing economic transformation further decreased the chances for success of any political party focusing on the support of the agricultural population (Machonin et al. 1996). Aware of this fact and even more of the 5 percent legal threshold for political parties entering parliament, the Agrarian Party formed a coalition, the Liberal Social Union (LSU), with the Greens and the Socialists. Although the coalition gained a few parliamentary seats in 1992, the Agrarian Party, now affiliated with some ideologically different parties, quickly lost support among the peasants and soon disappeared from the political scene.

The Class Cleavage

The last of Rokkan and Lipset's cleavages is that of class, but how does one define class in societies ruled for forty years by Communists whose main goal was to create a "classless society"?[15] The widespread nationalization and the systematic destruction of the entire social strata (including private employers and the self-employed) succeeded in eliminating classical class cleavages by the end of the Communist period. Yet the societies ruled by the Communists were not really "classless." Indeed, the first step toward a classless society was the introduction of a "working class government." Although the workers did not really govern society, they enjoyed some privileges (higher occupational prestige and higher wages), especially when compared with the blue- and white-collar workers in countries with market economies. The economic reforms adopted by the post-Communist governments, including both extensive privatization of state assets and restitution of some formerly nationalized property, significantly changed the situation. Matějů and Řeháková (1997) believe that, because of the gradual creation of a new class of owners and entrepreneurs and the loss of traditional privileges granted to the workers, the development of a classical class cleavage in Rokkan and Lipset's sense was to be expected.

Marx's approach to class, with its emphasis on ownership, is not, however, the only one. A whole stream within sociology, following the ideas of Max Weber, has evolved, and it stresses the importance of the power of different social groups (which may or may not be connected with ownership). Moreover, there is the concept of social stratification, in which the position of various social status groups is defined more specifically, usually taking into account several different dimensions: level of education, employment status, power, income, property, private consumption, and lifestyle (Machonin et al. 1996). Although the approaches to class are often different, there is something common to all of them—they assume that society is not the sum of equal individuals but that some people or groups of people, however defined, are on the top, while others are on the bottom. Yet this arrangement is not a dichotomy; the whole spectrum between the "top" and the "bottom" can be identified. Although the Communists practically destroyed class divisions in the classical Marxist sense, they did not eliminate the differences between the positions of various social groups. The question today, then, is how can one measure class or status in post-Communist societies? And how similar or how different are the situations in the four countries studied?

The most useful approach to answering these questions is the concept of multidimensional social status (Lenski 1954; Kolosi 1984; Machonin et al. 1996). It not only distinguishes different dimensions of social status, but also takes into account that individual dimensions may not necessarily be mutually consistent. It is crucial to emphasize here that, especially in the Communist countries, inconsistency in the dimensions of individual status was widespread. In Western societies, the relationships among education, employment, income, property, and lifestyle used to be more or less in accord (for example, higher education levels were equated with higher income), but the situation in Communist societies was often different. There, almost every combination of status dimensions could be found. Poor and poorly paid people might have high levels of education and job qualifications; poorly educated but well-paid people might have high rates of personal consumption but little property; poorly educated people might hold well-paid managerial posts. This inconsistency in status also presents another complication. Voters' political behavior is influenced by their subjective perception of their social position as well as by their actual position (Matějů and Řeháková 1997), or in Brokl's words (1996), "If people think that something is real, even if it is not, it becomes real in its consequences, since people act as if it were real." The higher the level of status inconsistency, however, the weaker and more volatile the link between the subjective and objective position of the individual in society. Anyone studying the connections between class or social status and voting preferences therefore cannot rely simply on the individual characteristics of social status.

Because data on education and income are the most commonly used, the most widely available, and the best-defined objective indicators of social status, these two indicators are used in this discussion of class cleavages and voting preferences. Nevertheless, this discussion also distinguishes carefully between subjective and objective social status. It begins by concentrating on the objective social status of voters and then looks at the mutual relations among subjective status, objective status, and electoral preferences.

In spite of the fact that differences between the rich and poor were persistently present in Communist countries, Communist societies were in general more egalitarian than Western societies. And, although one of the visible effects of the post-Communist economic reforms was a wider discrepancy in incomes (Ehrlich and Revesz 1995; Machonin et al. 1996; Večerník 1996;), the differences between the highest and lowest incomes were still smaller than in Western societies (see Table 29 for differences in the 1992 household income structure per capita among the four countries studied).[16]

In 1992, incomes in the Czech Republic were the most equal. Not only did the Czech Republic have the smallest share of inhabitants who could be considered poor (that is, earned less than 50 percent of the average income), but it also had the highest share of households with average incomes. The highest level of income inequalities was observed in Poland, where households of unskilled workers and peasants were strongly overrepresented among the poorest people and were largely not present within the group with average incomes. Of the four countries, Slovakia and Hungary occupied the middle positions in income distribution (Machonin et al. 1996).

Table 29

Income Differences in the Czech Republic, Hungary, Poland, and Slovakia, 1992 (percent)

Country	1	2	3	4	5	6	7	Total
Czech Republic	1.1	5.6	24.6	50.6	8.2	4.3	5.6	100.0
Hungary	2.2	11.2	24.6	37.9	9.8	6.0	8.3	100.0
Poland	4.1	15.1	25.2	34.9	7.2	4.6	8.9	100.0
Slovakia	1.7	10.4	20.4	44.6	9.6	5.7	7.6	100.0

Source: Pavel Machonin et al., *Česká společnost v transformaci* (Czech society in transformation) (Prague: Sociologické nakladatelství, 1996).
Note: 1—less than 25 percent of the average income per one household member; 2—25–50 percent; 3—50–75 percent; 4—75–125 percent; 5—125–150 percent; 6—150–175 percent; 7—more than 175 percent of the average income per one household member.

As for educational levels, the four countries are quite different (Table 30). Among other things, in 1993 the Czech Republic had the lowest share of citizens without a complete primary education and the highest share of those with vocational training. In Slovakia and especially Hungary, relatively high shares of the population had an incomplete elementary education. And Poland had the highest share of people who had completed a secondary education.

Machonin et al. (1996) note that the differences in educational structure reflect the fact that the Czech Republic underwent industrialization and urbanization earlier than the other three countries. Since 1993, the differences

Table 30

Educational Structure of the Czech Republic, Hungary, Poland, and Slovakia, 1993 (percent)

Country	Incomplete Primary	Primary	Vocational	Secondary	University
Czech Republic	1.2	24.0	39.2	26.8	8.8
Hungary	14.1	23.9	29.9	22.9	9.2
Poland	3.5	24.9	30.0	33.6	8.0
Slovakia	8.9	21.4	30.0	30.0	9.7

Source: Pavel Machonin et al., *Česká společnost v transformaci* (Czech society in transformation) (Prague: Sociologické nakladatelství, 1996).
Note: Table represents the 20–69 age group. In these countries, after completing eight to nine years of primary education, students had the option of continuing their education in a vocational school or secondary school. A vocational school, which was nonacademic, trained students for jobs or trades to be pursued as a career. A secondary education prepared students for clerical jobs, supervisory jobs, and the lowest-level managerial jobs. Completion of a secondary education was mandatory to enter a university.

among countries (which were even higher one generation ago) have gradually decreased. One effect of the nonparallel courses taken by the industrialization and urbanization processes in the countries observed is the rather divergent educational level among different generations. The oldest Czech generations tend to have a substantially higher level of education than their counterpart generations in the other three countries. On the other hand, the younger generations of Poles, Slovaks, and Hungarians are, on average, better educated than their Czech counterparts, mainly because of the rigidity of Czech Communist planners who purposely sent a substantial portion of potential high school and college students to vocational schools.

Educational structure not only is an outcome of historical development, but also to some extent reflects the ethnic structure of the population. The Roma minority, which for centuries has been designated as the group with the lowest social status and the least formal education and has often been the target of open discrimination, is heavily overrepresented among the people with an incomplete primary education. The relatively high shares of the Roma population in both Hungary and Slovakia may partially explain the higher shares of people with an incomplete primary education in those countries.

Machonin et al. (1996) have also put forth a general indicator of social status that combines five individual dimensions: education, income, complexity of work, position within management, and cultural activities (Table 31). The table shows the distribution of each country's population among different social strata, based on relative measures of social status in relation to the respective country's average social status. It is not possible to compare two different countries directly, because it is not possible to say, for example, that the social status of Slovaks is higher than that of Poles. However, it is possible to compare, based on the shape of the distribution, the social inequalities within each society. Thus in 1993 the Czech Republic had a large middle social strata, whereas in Hungary and especially in Poland the scope of inequalities in social status was substantially higher than in the Czech Republic and the lower social strata were the most numerous. Slovakia was somewhere in between. The individual status dimensions were the most consistent in Hungary (for example, income was the dimension most closely linked with education), while the lowest degree of consistency was observed in the Czech Republic. Theoretically, then, social status should play a more important role in relation to voting preferences in Hungary and Poland, because in these countries status differences are larger and individual status dimensions more consistent, while the opposite should

Table 31

General Social Status Differences among the Economically Active
Populations of the Czech Republic, Hungary, Poland, and Slovakia, 1993

Status	Czech Republic	Hungary	Poland	Slovakia
Highest	II	II	I	I
	IIII	IIII	III	IIIIII
	IIIIIIII	IIIIII	IIIIII	IIIIIIII
	IIIIIIIIIIIIIII	IIIIIIIIIIII	IIIIIIIIIII	IIIIIIIIIIIIII
	IIIIIIIIIII	IIIIIIIIIIIIIII	IIIIIIIIIIIIIIIIII	IIIIIIIIIIIII
Lowest	IIIIIIII	IIIIIIII	IIIIIIIII	IIIIIII

Source: Pavel Machonin et al., *Česká společnost v transformaci* (Czech society in transformation) (Prague: Sociologické nakladatelství, 1996).

Note: This table shows the distribution of each country's population among different social strata in relation to its average social status. Social status is measured by education, income, complexity of work, position within management, and cultural activities. It is not possible to compare two different countries directly, because it is not possible to say, for example, that the social status of Slovaks is higher than that of the Poles. However, it is possible to compare, based on the shape of the distribution, the social inequalities within each society.

be true for Slovakia and the Czech Republic, where the differences are smaller and complicated by a higher level of inconsistency between individual status dimensions. Yet what do the situations in these countries look like in practice?

For Hungary, several investigators of voting behavior have pointed out, quite surprisingly, that the effect of class on party preference was minimal in the 1990 parliamentary election (Körösényi 1991; Kolosi et al. 1992; Tóka 1995a). It is true that among the Smallholders and the Christian Democratic voters the poorer and less educated were overrepresented, while among supporters of the Alliance of Free Democrats (SZDSZ), the Hungarian Democratic Forum, and even the post-Communist Hungarian Socialist Party (MSZP) the more educated and the relatively well-to-do were overrepresented (Körösényi 1991). Nevertheless, social class had a smaller influence on voting decisions than other factors. Moreover, what relationship social class did have was very much influenced by the voter's age. According to Tóka (1995b), the "strength of the correlation between votes for liberal parties and educational level diminishes from generation to generation as we move from the younger to the older." For example, in the 1994 election the Socialists received relatively more votes from the more educated in the generation over fifty, but no such relationship existed for voters under fifty. Thus the Socialists did not recruit voters from among the lowest social strata but rather from people whose professional careers were connected with the Communist era. Yet the importance of social class to the electoral process should not be denied. Indeed, class characteristics have proven to be a robust factor in explaining the differences in electoral participation. The finding that class participation is more prevalent than class voting is, however, in striking contrast to the post–World War II trend in Western European electoral politics (Kolosi et al. 1992). In this respect, the situation in Hungary is more akin to the situation in the United States than in Western Europe.[17]

A study of the connections between education, income, and voting decisions in the 1991 Polish parliamentary election revealed that support for Mazowiecki's Democratic Union (DU) and the Liberal Democratic Congress (KLD), both of which were the strongest proponents of free-market principles in the economy, was higher among the more educated voters (Tworzecki 1996). Quite the opposite was true for both agrarian parties, the former satellite Polish Peasants Party and the post-Solidarity Peasants Alliance; they attracted the less educated. The same pattern held when looking at voters' incomes—among voters for the peasant parties, the poor were overrepresented. The typical voter for the post-Communist Alliance of Democratic Left was not uneducated, although the SLD presented itself as a protector of the lower classes' interests. The electoral support for other parties did not seem to be very much affected by voters' social positions. Similar results are presented by Millard (1994a) and by Wade, Groth, and Lavelle (1994) who studied the electoral results on the aggregate level of districts. Interestingly, the electoral support for the SLD was higher in regions with higher rates of unemployment. Based on this finding and the previous one that SLD voters were among the more educated citizens, one can conclude that the SLD was supported predominantly by the middle and higher strata living in the regions hardest hit by the problems accompanying the transformation process. In other words, supporters of the post-Communist SLD were not the poorest and the most underprivileged but rather people who were relatively well-to-do in both the old and new regimes but were afraid of the future. Because most of the people who found themselves in the lowest social strata after the onset of economic reforms (for example, small farmers and pensioners) had already been among the poorest during the Communist period, their dissatisfaction with the economic reforms may not have channeled into votes for post-Communist parties. As for voting participation in Poland, like in Hungary it was related to class; the less educated and the lower strata were overrepresented among nonvoters. All of these findings were more or less repeated in the 1993 elections in Poland

(Millard 1994b). Among the new parties entering parliament, the Union of Labor (UP) gained more support from the more educated, while the "presidential" BBWR was slightly more popular among the members of the population with higher incomes ("Bulletin of Electoral Statistics" 1994).

In the Czech Republic over the period 1980–1998, well-educated voters tended to vote for the Civic Forum and consequently for its right-oriented successors—Klaus's Civic Democratic Party and the ideologically similar Civic Democratic Alliance (ODA)—which pushed free-market-oriented economic reforms. The population with a lower level of education was overrepresented among the voters for the extreme-right SPR-RSČ, attracted by the party's simple solutions, and among the supporters of the Christian Democratic Union–Czechoslovak People's Party. The share of workers among the voters for the Czech Social Democratic Party (ČSSD) gradually increased from one election to the next (Matějů and Řeháková 1997). Because of the inconsistency in the dimensions of individual social status (for example, households of workers were not the poorest ones), the typical ČSSD voter was not the opposite of the ODS and ODA voter. Rather, both kinds of voters tended to be from the middle class. The social status of voters was not, however, among the most important determinants of voting decisions at both the individual level (Machonin et al. 1996) and the aggregate level of the districts (Kostelecký 1994; Pacek 1994). Although these findings for the Czech Republic agree with those for Hungary and Poland, that agreement does not extend to voters for the Communist Party. A typical Communist supporter in the Czech Republic was neither more well educated nor more well-to-do than average, but rather tended to be less educated, with below-average income.

The situation in Slovakia was far more complicated than that in the other three countries. Szomolányi and Mesežnikov (1995), who studied the connections between political party development and social structure development, concluded that the asynchrony of these two processes is a typical feature of Slovakia. Because in Slovakia the ideological profiles and the organizational structures of the parties changed more rapidly than the social structures, only a tenuous link remained between the two. Indeed, it is difficult to discover any relationship between incomes and party preferences. On the other side, it is true that the most significant sociodemographic cleavage between the adherents of the ruling coalition—the Movement for a Democratic Slovakia, the Slovak National Party (SNS), and the Association of Workers of Slovakia (ZRS)—and the opposition parties remained education (Bútorová, Gyarfásová, and Kúska 1996). Similar to the situation in the other three countries, the highest level of education could be found among the voters for pro-market, right-oriented parties, the Democratic Party (DS) and the Democratic Union (DÚ). And like in Poland and Hungary, the post-Communist Party of the Democratic Left (SDL) was not a party of the less educated. Even the opposition, the Christian Democratic Movement (KDH), was more popular among the better educated, unlike the situation in the other three countries. People with the lowest level of education tended to support parties in the government, especially the extreme left Association of Workers of Slovakia (but also Mečiar's HZDS).

Generational Cleavages

In addition to the social cleavages defined by Rokkan and Lipset, the age of voters is often mentioned in the literature as a factor, or cleavage, that shapes voters' political preferences, and this is not surprising. After all, in times of great change, such as a change of regime, both the formal and informal rules that a society follows can be rather quickly replaced by new rules, age-old habits that were relevant for many years can easily be found irrelevant, some life-long careers can be abruptly terminated, and quite new opportunities can arise. It is understandable, then, that different reactions to the vast scope of social change can be observed among the different age groups. But any look at the empirical data showing the mutual links between age and political preferences must be prefaced by consideration of the role that age played in a person's position within Communist societies. Although a positive relationship between age and social status is normally observed in any society, in Communist countries the lack of market criteria for evaluating working standards, the excessive state wage and salary controls, and the already noted weak influence of education on salaries led to the formation of a society clearly favoring the older generations over the younger ones (Machonin et al. 1996).[18] This "principle of seniority" influenced not only salaries and access to managerial or political positions, but also access to other benefits such as municipal housing. In an economy in which the distribution of some goods and benefits was not based on market allocation but rather on a lengthy waiting list, the position of the elders was better simply because they had been waiting for a longer period of time. Age says even more about different groups and in turn their political attitudes if the contrast between various historical periods and events occurring in East-Central Europe is taken into account (Možný 1991).

The fall of the Communist regimes led to many changes. The introduction of a market economy essentially changed the labor market: many old customs were abandoned, the importance of education rose, entrepreneurial opportunities emerged, firms were divided or privatized and some went bankrupt, jobs ceased to be secure and unemployment increased, and foreign investors introduced a new business culture. Although people generally found it difficult to adjust to all these changes, the perceptions of changes were age-specific: the older generations tended to perceive them as a threat, the younger generations most probably believed them to be an opportunity for success (Machonin et al. 1996). The reality proved to be even more complex than was expected. Some young people, especially those with a university education living in the cities, benefited from the new situation. Other young people—that is, the less educated and the freshly graduated—could easily have found themselves among the unemployed. Some older people lost their jobs and did not find new ones; other elders benefited from their higher managerial positions and became the new owners of privatized enterprises.

What do the data show about the influence of age on voting decisions? The most remarkable example of generational voting can be found in Hungary, where the Federation of Young Democrats (FIDESZ) programmatically pronounced itself to be the reform party of the young for the young. Not surprisingly, the party performed well within the youngest age group (18–33), members of which were twice as likely as the average voter to vote for the party in the 1990 election (Körösényi 1991). The supporters of the Alliance of Free Democrats also were younger than average. By contrast, the oldest people were heavily overrepresented among the Christian Democratic voters, because Christians are generally older than the average population, and slightly overrepresented among the supporters of the Hungarian Democratic Forum and the Smallholders. The decision to vote for a socialist party was not very much influenced by voter age. The same empirical findings were repeated in the 1994 election (Tóka 1995b).

In Poland, the age of the voters seemed to be less important than other factors in the 1991 parliamentary election, because only popular support for the Catholic Electoral Action increased significantly with age (Grzybowski 1991b). Both Mazowiecki's Democratic Union and the Liberal Democratic Congress received the most support from the middle-aged generation. The vote for the other parties was not determined by age. In the 1993 election, the relations between age and voting preference was even less clear and had even less impact (Millard 1994a).

In the Czech Republic, Klaus's ODS and one of its junior coalition partners, ODA, were repeatedly more popular among the younger generation of voters, but the ODS, surprisingly, received disproportional support from the very oldest generation as well. Disproportionately high popularity among the young, however, was also typical for the extreme-right Republicans. The supporters of the Communist Party and the Christian Democratic Union–Czechslovak People's Party tended to be older, and the Social Democrats received the most support from middle-aged voters.

In Slovakia, the positions of the pro-market Democratic Union and the conservative Democratic Party appealed most to the young. Soon after the regime change, the Christian Democratic Movement became popular predominantly among the older generation, but after the KDH led the opposition against Mečiar's HZDS, elderly voters were no longer typical supporters of the KDH (Bútorová, Gyarfásova, and Kúska 1996). After the departure of Mečiar and his followers from the Public Against Violence movement, the newly established HZDS became more popular among the younger generation. Later, however, the situation changed. The electoral results in 1994 and the opinion polls in 1995 and in 1996 repeatedly showed that the bulk of HZDS voters were the elderly (Bútorová, Gyarfásová, and Kúska 1996). Two junior coalition partners in the government—the nationalist Slovak National Party and the extreme-left Association of Workers of Slovakia—were somewhat more successful among the younger voters.

In summary, in the countries studied the age of voters has had a remarkable influence on voting decisions, and the empirical findings support to some extent the hypothesis that the post-Communist transformation was perceived as a threat by the older generation rather than a chance for improvement for the younger generation. Indeed, the parties pushing for reforms were more likely to be supported by younger people, but the younger voters who were not satisfied with the direction of the reforms tended to turn to extreme parties (nationalist, extreme left, or extreme right). And, not surprisingly, the new parties were usually more popular among the younger generations, while the historical or "established" ones appealed to the older voters. The interesting exception to this general tendency was the substantial support that older Czech voters gave to Klaus's ODS, a party committed to economic reforms. This phenomenon was unique to the Czech Republic. Although this support can be explained partially by the relatively cautious social policy of Klaus's government, which did not allow pensioners' incomes to drop substantially, the historical experience of different generations also must be taken into account. No matter how radical and new the reform pushed by the Klaus government seemed after forty years of communism, it was really nothing more than an attempt to return to the successful tradition of the liberal, democratic, and market oriented pre-Communist Czechoslovakia. Thus the pro-market orientation could just as well be attributed to traditionalism as to modernism. Indeed, empirical analyses of the relationships among voting, economic, and demographic behavior after the fall of communism reveal that the combination of traditional social and demographic behavior and modern pro-market economic behavior is typical in those regions where ODS was the strongest (Kostelecký 1995b).

Gender-based Cleavages

The last but not the least significant structural factor influencing post-Communist politics is that of gender. Gender-related political issues have been among those at the top of the political agendas of many Western countries for the last two or three decades. The debate has centered on the broadly defined topic of equality for women, which includes equality of opportunity and equality of outcome (Heitlinger 1993). In the Western countries, specific policies have been aimed at assuring women equal access to education and equal treatment in the labor market, banning all forms of discrimination against women, and promoting the participation of women in politics. Also over the last few decades, several very contentious women's rights issues such as abortion and sexual harassment have been publicly debated, articulated by various political movements and pressure groups, and added to the political agendas of established political parties. In short, gender-related political issues have gained substantial significance in Western politics. This was not the case in East-Central Europe, however, and especially not in the last two decades under the Communists.

Women in the Labor Force

When the Communists came to power in the region in the late forties, the issue of women's rights was included in their political agenda. Although the emancipation of women was not considered the highest-priority issue, the newly established Communist governments believed that it would be one of the welcomed byproducts of the revolution. Inspired by German socialist Friedrich Engels's notion that the emancipation of women would be achieved through the abolition of private property, the engagement of women in paid employment, and the socialization of homework and child care, Communist regimes adopted a set of policies meant to define women's place in society (Heitlinger 1995). They especially promoted women's participation in the labor market, because it would also help to solve the labor force shortage that accompanied the extensive postwar economic growth. To better enable women to participate full time in the labor force, governments established a network of subsidized child care centers and kindergartens, liberalized abortion laws, and publicly campaigned against the notion of female homemakers, depicting them as remnants of the obsolete, petty bourgeois lifestyle and as almost suspicious antiregime elements. Simultaneously, the wages and salaries set by planning offices for practically all sectors of the economy were so low that women's active participation in the paid labor force was an economic necessity for the economic survival of most families. Because the combination of push and pull incentives proved to be extraordinary successful, women's participation in the labor force of the Communist countries increased quickly and far exceeded that in the rest of the Europe (see Table 32).

Women in Communist countries not only participated in the paid labor force in much greater numbers than their Western counterparts, but also differed substantially in the sectors in which they worked and in the fact that almost all employed women were working in full-time positions. In Czechoslovakia, for example, only 7 percent of women worked part time in

Table 32

Labor Force Participation of Women between the Ages of Forty and Forty-four in Selected Communist Countries and Regions of Europe, 1950–1985 (percent)

Country	1950	1960	1970	1980	1985
Czechoslovakia	52.3	67.3	79.9	91.3	92.4
Hungary	29.0	51.8	69.4	83.2	86.1
Poland	66.4	69.1	79.5	83.2	84.7
Northern Europe	30.9	39.9	53.8	69.9	71.1
Western Europe	34.5	39.5	46.4	55.1	55.6
Southern Europe	22.4	25.3	29.7	35.7	37.1

Source: Nicole Kozera, "Czech Women in the Labor Market. Work and Family in a Transition Economy," Working Paper No. 6, Institute of Sociology, Prague, 1997.

Note: Northern Europe includes Sweden, Finland, Norway, Denmark, and Iceland; Western Europe includes Ireland, United Kingdom, France, Belgium, the Netherlands, Luxembourg, France, Germany, Austria, and Switzerland; and Southern Europe includes Portugal, Spain, Italy, and Greece.

the mid-1980s. The comparable figures elsewhere were 35 percent in Canada, 44 percent in United Kingdom, 53 percent in the Netherlands, and 30 percent in West Germany (Heitlinger 1993). In both Poland and Hungary, the norm was also full-time work (United Nations 1992). The East-West difference in the share of women in individual professions and occupations was notable as well. According to Čermáková (1997), the structure of female employment in the Czech Republic, Slovakia, Poland, and Hungary in the Communist era was typified by the high penetration of women into sectors traditionally considered to be the domain of men such as mining, electric power production, and transport. And women dominated some parts of the tertiary sector—education, health care, and social services. The spectacular growth of female employment in some high-skill professions was enabled by the rapid rise in women's educational levels, which rather closely followed the increase in the education of men (see Table 33, which describes the situation in the Czech Lands for the years 1950–1991).

Table 33 not only documents the general increase in the educational level of women (which is comparable with that of men), but also the existence of gender-related patterns of educational structure. Although men's domination of university degrees substantially declined from 1950 to 1991, still more men than women received a university diploma over that period. Similarly, more men than women received a lower secondary education—that is, in the Central European context they attended preparatory vocational schools. Women prevailed among the graduates of the higher secondary schools (both general and technical), but they were still overrepresented among those with only a primary education. Although the overall educational level of women was somewhat lower in Hungary and Poland than in the Czech Lands (the major difference was the higher share of poorly educated women among the oldest generations), the general trend was the same. This situation was a direct consequence of the system of central planning, which oversaw the level and the structure of education of the population. Thus if university graduates are not taken into account, the majority of men were trained to be manual workers, and the majority of women were prepared for nonmanual, routine jobs. Overall, the share of both young men and women expected to work as unqualified workers decreased drastically from 1961 to 1991.

The rising educational levels of women did not automatically lead to the equality of wages and salaries. During the Communist period, women generally received about two-thirds of the average income of men (Čermáková 1995a; Večerník 1996; Kozera 1997). In the early decades of communism,

Table 33

Educational Levels of Men and Women between the Ages of Twenty-five and Twenty-nine, Czech Lands, 1950–1991 (percent)

Year	Primary	Lower Secondary	Higher Secondary	University
Men				
1950	69.9	13.8	13.1	2.3
1961	67.7	10.7	13.4	6.7
1970	21.3	47.6	22.3	8.0
1980	16.0	52.7	19.4	10.0
1991	9.2	49.0	26.7	13.7
Women				
1950	78.5	14.0	5.8	0.4
1961	71.9	11.4	13.0	2.7
1970	43.6	20.7	27.4	7.1
1980	30.1	33.5	27.9	7.1
1991	12.1	34.9	40.6	11.3

Source: Pavel Machonin et al., *Česká společnost v transformaci* (Czech society in transformation) (Prague: Sociologické nakladatelství, 1996).
Note: "Lower secondary" refers to vocational training; "higher secondary" refers to a traditional secondary education. Categories "uncompleted primary" and "unknown" are not included in the table.

this discrepancy could be explained in part by the somewhat lower educational level of women. But what factors explain the persistent wage discrepancy later, when the general level of education of women rose substantially? One of the most important factors was the unequal placement of women in executive positions. For example, Šiklová (1993) reports that women held only 5 percent of leadership positions in Czechoslovakia in 1987. The other reason for the lower incomes of women in the Communist countries stemmed from the Communist ideology itself. Exaltation of the revolutionary role of the working class led to a low evaluation of education and a preference for heavy physical labor over "easy" nonmanual labor (Večerník 1996; Kozera 1997). As a result, manual laborers, mostly men, tended to be better paid than "officials," mostly women, in positions requiring no manual labor, despite the higher educational level required for the nonmanual jobs.

Although the Communist regimes fulfilled most of conditions considered necessary by Engels for the "emancipation of women," Communist societies did not get very far in reducing the work associated with running a household, either by introducing home appliances or by replacing housemaker tasks with easily accessible, cheap services (that is, restaurants versus food preparation in the home). Thus Engels's hypothesis that such changes would substantially save time for women and would lead to their expanded participation in public activities could not even be tested in practice (Heitlinger 1995). Lobodzinska (1995) points out that large refrigerators and freezers were rare in Polish urban dwellings, even in late eighties. In the Czech Lands, one of the most developed parts of the Communist world, about half of all households owned a private car from the late seventies on and about 15 percent owned a cottage for family recreation, but the share of households with an automatic washing machine was rather low—24.7 percent in 1978 and 45.5 percent in 1984—and the ownership of freezers was rare—2.0 percent in 1978 and 16.6 percent in 1984 (Machonin et al. 1996). This lack of labor- and time-saving devices was accompanied by a general shortage of the goods and food needed daily, forcing people (mostly women) to spend much of their time in shopping lines. Forced to deal with these shortages, and the traditional prejudices that prevented many husbands from participating in some home activities (such as washing clothes and dishes, cooking, and cleaning floors), many women led extremely demanding and exhausting lives as they carried what Western scholars aptly labeled the "double burden" (see Corrin 1992). In other words, a "second shift" of unpaid work at home was typically imposed on employed women under the Communist regime (see Table 34). The figures in Table 34 clearly prove that to speak about the "second shift" was not an exaggeration but rather a precise description of the situation.

Working mothers' lack of free time (most women of productive age were working mothers) was also considered one of the main explanations for women's low participation in the public sphere during the Communist era. It is true that the share of women deputies in national parliaments was

Table 34

Time Spent by Men and Women in Selected Activities, Czechoslovakia, Hungary, and Poland, 1965 (hours per week)

	Paid Activity		Unpaid Household Labor/Child Care	
Country	Women	Men	Women	Men
Czechoslovakia	29.8	44.4	40.7	15.1
Hungary	34.0	56.6	41.0	7.9
Poland	30.5	52.2	38.9	12.4

Source: Elaine Weiner, "Assessing the Implications of Political and Economic Reform in the Post-Socialist Era: The Case of Czech and Slovak Women," *East European Quarterly,* vol. 31, no. 3 (1997): 473–502.

high—24.6–29.3 percent in Czechoslovakia, 19.7–30.1 percent in Hungary, and 13.5–24.5 percent in Poland during 1970–1985—in comparison with the 6 percent share found in the United States, France, and the United Kingdom (Weiner 1997). But the national parliaments in Communist countries were not places where anyone made real decisions about anything really important—the Communist Parties were the institutions of real importance. Indeed, women in positions of true power were rare during the Communist era. For example, of the some twenty ministers in the Czechoslovak cabinet, only one or two were women during the whole Communist period, and only about 18 percent of women held nomenclature posts (that is, directly appointed managerial and supervisory posts) in the Czechoslovak Communist Party (Šiklová 1993). Of those holding political office, only 12.7 percent were women in 1987 (United Nations 1992). Moreover, only 17 percent of women were members of the Communist Party, compared with 33 percent of men (Castle-Kanerová 1992). In the 1970s, there was only one woman at most in the Polish government and in the Central Committee of Polish United Workers Party (Fuszara 1993). In 1986, only 11 percent of the Central Committee and only 5 percent of the members of President Wojciech Jaruzelski's consultative board were women (Titkow 1993). Similarly, only 12 percent of the Central Committee of the ruling party in Hungary were women, and only two women were reported to be members or candidates of the Politburo (Einhorn 1993). Thus the Communist model of full employment for women combined with a second shift at home coexisted with the traditional understanding of a division of labor between the public sphere, which belonged to men, and the private sphere, which was believed to be the realm of women.

Since the Communist regimes were swept out office at the end of the 1980s, there have been changes—some dramatic. Many social scientists from both within and outside of the region have studied the gender issues under transformation, but their opinions about what has happened to women during the post-Communist transformation have varied substantially. Indeed, there are more conflicts about the interpretation of the facts than about the facts themselves, but even an agreement over the facts is not so easy to reach. On the one side, some scholars claim the post-Communist transformations seriously influenced gender relations. Watson (1993), for example, believes that gender "is present in the very tissue of this change" and sees the process of transformation as intrinsically unfavorable for women. Funk believes the outcomes of the transformations have been so unfavorable for women that she even declares, "Women's interests are being sacrificed to transformation" (Funk and Mueller 1993). But other scholars claim that gender relations in the post-Communist societies have not changed very much, even though the economic and political systems in those societies have undergone a complete overhaul since 1989 (Čermáková 1997). Čermáková explains her conclusion by pointing to the historical inertia of value orientations and social norms, which delays the political and economic changes. Similarly, after Tuček et al. (1998) analyzed social changes in the Czech Republic in the post-Communist era from the gender point of view, they concluded that the historically developed specific model of social structure, including the division of labor between men and women, remains basically unchanged. Because of the stability of Czech social structures over time, which are supported by most of society itself, Tuček et al. did not predict any quick changes either favoring or disfavoring women in the near future. Regardless of the different opinions about how the transformation process affected the scope and direction of changes in the position of men and women in the society, most students of the issue would agree that reforms were not gender-neutral. The transformations, however, did not affect all aspects of life in the same ways.

Although there were some predictions that the restructuring of the economy, accompanied by a sharp reduction in overemployment in the big state-owned enterprises, "pressure from the traditionalists, and the overburdened women's desire to take a rest at home, would have ended in the reintroduction of the traditional model of the working husband and the housewife," nothing of the sort happened. The proportion of homemakers increased only marginally and remained well under the Western European level (Fodor 1997; Kuchařová 1999). The overwhelming majority of women simply continued the double-burdened life. Čermáková (1997) clearly documented that the 1990s did not mean a turning-point in the overall employment of women. After all, in the Czech Republic over 44–45 percent of the total labor force continues to be women. Similar figures are presented by Plakwicz (1992) for Poland, where women continued to make up about 45 percent of the total labor force at the beginning of the 1990s, and Corrin (1992) established that in 1990 women made up 44 percent of all the active wage earners in Hungary. Continuation of the transformations did not substantially reduce the share of women in total employment either in Poland (Lobodzinska 1995) or in Hungary (Koncz 1995), and there are no signs that this situation will change in the near future. Simply put, the forty-year-old tradition of practically full employment for women will not disappear within a few years. One of the reasons is quite pragmatic: most men and women consider the woman's additional income necessary for their family's well-being. In a survey conducted in 1992 in the Czech Republic and Slovakia, 12 percent of women declared themselves to be the sole breadwinners in the family, while an additional 48 percent considered themselves to be co-providers of the family income (Čermáková 1995b). But it is not all about the money. Čermáková (1995b) also notes that employment has become an inseparable part of the social status of both Czech and Slovak women. Yet even though most women who can afford to stay at home would continue working, some of them would prefer part-time jobs (Toth 1993).

Although the overall level of female employment did not change in the 1990s, several gender-related changes did affect the sphere of work. The increase in unemployment was especially sharp between 1990, at the beginning of the reforms, and 1993, after the first, most painful phase (see Table 35). The figures in Table 35 do not particularly support the generally expressed claim that unemployment affected women much more than men (Einhorn 1993; Funk and Mueller 1993; Lobodzinska 1995). In Slovakia, there was no substantial difference in the level of unemployment between men and women at least in terms of statistical significance. In Hungary, the unemployment of men was higher than that of women. The countries that fulfilled expectations were the Czech Republic and, explicitly, Poland. In Poland, unemployment among women significantly exceeded that of men, but also "in Poland women's disadvantage could be directly attributed to

Table 35

Unemployment Rates of Women and Men in the Czech Republic, Slovakia, Poland, and Hungary, 1990 and 1993 (percent)

Country	1990			1993		
	Women	Men	Total	Women	Men	Total
Czech Republic	0.8	0.7	0.7	4.3	2.9	3.5
Slovakia	0.6	0.6	0.6	13.0	12.7	12.9
Poland	3.8	3.2	3.5	17.3	14.3	15.7
Hungary	1.4	1.8	1.7	10.1	14.2	12.1

Sources: International Labor Office, *Yearbook of Labor Statistics,* as cited in Eva Fodor, "Gender in Transition: Unemployment in Hungary, Poland and Slovakia," *East European Politics and Societies* 11 (fall 1997): 470–500; *Statistical Yearbook of the Czech Republic* (Prague: Czech Statistical Office, 1994); *Statistical Yearbook of the Czech and Slovak Federative Republic* (Prague: Czech Statistical Office, 1992); Lubica Gajdošová et al., *Vývoj nezamestnanosti a jej struktury v SR v r. 1990–1995* (The development of unemployment and its structure in the Slovak Republic in 1990–1995) (Bratislava: Ministry of Labor, Social Affairs and Family, 1996).

discrimination based on gender" (Fodor 1997, 496).[19] Female heads of single-parent families, women with small children, and older women are definitely the targets of discrimination in the labor market (Heitlinger 1995). And once women become unemployed, they have lower chances of getting another job (Einhorn 1993; Lobodzinska 1995; Zajicek and Calasanti 1995). The fact that people with only a primary education generally occupy the least-favorable position in the labor market could put female job seekers at risk in Hungary and Poland, where the proportion of poorly educated women is still relatively high.

As for other features of the post-Communist labor market that are not gender-neutral, the proportion of women in leadership positions in the economy remains low (Kuchařová 1999), and a disproportionately higher number of men than women run private businesses. Although the general educational level of women continues to grow (young women are even better educated that young men—see Lobodzinska 1995; *Second Periodical Report* 1999), the salaries and wages of women are 70–75 percent of men's average income. It is true, however, that the wage gap is declining (Lobodzinska 1995; Machonin et al. 1996; Hraba, McCutcheon, and Večerník 1997; Holý 1999). Holý (1999) has revealed the factors underlying the persistent wage gap in the Czech Republic; his findings grew out of a detailed statistical analysis of income disparities between men and women based on income surveys conducted on huge samples of employees in 1996 ($N = 359,191$) and 1997 ($N = 584,510$). According to Holý, contrary to the situation in the European Union (EU) in the post-Communist countries the wage gap cannot be explained structurally, by the lower education of women, by the concentration of women in poorly paid sectors of the economy,[20] or by the high percentage of women working part time. The main reason for the lower incomes of women is their lack of leadership positions. The wage gap is also high among unskilled workers; of those with the least education, men are much better paid than women. Unlike the situation in the EU, where the wage gap increases with age, the highest wage gap in the post-Communist countries can be found among employees thirty to forty-four years old; before and after that age, incomes are more equal. It appears that the wage gap is not so much influenced by the length of working experience, but rather by the fact that women aged thirty to forty-four are the mothers of small children. Although Holý's conclusions may not necessarily be applicable to other countries in the region, they offer insight into the complexity of the problem.

Women and Politics

The post-Communist transformations also affected many aspects of the relationship between women and politics. On the subject of women and politics, it is useful to distinguish between three different topics: women's representation in politics, specific "women's issues" in politics, and the behavior of women as voters.

Much has been written about the political representation of women in the post-Communist period. One of the most remarkable consequences of the first free elections in the former Communist countries was the sharp drop in the percentage of women representatives in national parliaments. In Czechoslovakia, the percentage of women deputies fell from 30 to 6, in Hungary from 22 to 7, and in Poland from 23 to 9 (United Nations 1992). In later elections, the share of women deputies did not increase and remained substantially lower than in the decades under Communist rule. Yet the women serving in the parliaments in post-Communist East-Central Europe occupy roughly the same percentage of seats as women serving in the legislative bodies of most Western European countries (Einhorn 1993).[21]

As for women's participation in government, the breakdown of Communist rule hardly changed anything. Hanna Suchocka may have served briefly as the first woman prime minister of Poland, but generally women have rarely served in the national governments. They have tended to participate more in local politics, but even there the share of active women politicians has remained disproportionately lower than that of men (Castle-Kanerová 1992; Corrin 1992; Plakwicz 1992). Even the attempts by some women to establish political parties for women were not particularly successful. The Political Party of Women and Mothers established in 1990 at the federal level in Czechoslovakia did not gain enough support to participate in the election and was later dissolved (Heitlinger 1993). The Polish Alliance of Women Against Hardships did manage to secure 1 seat out of 460 in parliament under an extremely proportional electoral system, but it remained quite marginal politically (Jasiewicz 1992). Later, the party did not survive the introduction of the legal threshold and soon disappeared from the political scene. In Hungary, no politically active women's party came into existence.

Western political scientists have traditionally considered the low participation of women in the economy, the low educational levels of women, and the existence of legislative barriers as the main factors in the weak participation of women in politics (Havelková 1999). None of these unfavorable conditions, however, were evident in the post-Communist countries under observation in 1990s. What, then, could be the explanation? In the literature on the topic, several kinds of explanations—cultural, historical, psychological, and institutional—are offered for the underrepresentation of women in political posts. Havelková (1999) asserts that the low participation of women in Czech politics cannot be attributed to the notion that women are not socially accepted as politicians or that they are not considered well qualified for the posts. Most participants in an intellectual discourse about the topic in the Czech press were supportive of women's participation in politics and considered them as politically competent as men. The general population also saw no reason that women should not hold political office (Einhorn 1993; Havelková 1999). Goven (1993), writing about the intellectual climate in Hungary in 1980s, pointed out that some traditionalist thinkers had declared that the emancipation of women was the main reason for social problems and had promoted the idea of dividing public and private space between men and women. Yet these ideas were definitely not typical of the population of the region. On the contrary, voters appeared to be rather supportive of women's participation in politics. Moreover, women, because of their longer life expectancy than men, make up more than 50 percent of voters, so even if men were not supportive women could not be outvoted by men in the election itself.

All this being said, some cultural factors do prevent women from seeking more power within the political system. The image of politics as a dirty business requiring aggressive politicians is in sharp contrast with the traditional image of women as kind, loving persons who take care of the most important things in human lives and who are not involved in "a formal battle with man over percentages" (Havelková 1999, 148). The more the political scene is perceived as a masculine environment, the less attractive it seems as a milieu for women. And the less attractive politics becomes for women, the less often women try to enter the field, thereby placing politics in an even more masculine environment than before. Another barrier to the greater participation of women in politics is something of a counterreaction to the Communist past, which saw discredited national women's organizations operating under the direct control of the Communist Party and a quota system used in the Communist quasi-elections. Most female politicians in the post-Communist era did not want to be associated with either the leaders of the former women's unions or the women deputies assigned to their posts to manifest the regime's concern for women. The new politicians wanted to represent all their voters, not only women. As a result, the women serving in parliaments did not form any women's pressure groups or even engage in frequent discussions of gender issues. Thus the gender issues in post-Communist politics are among those considered the least important (Kitschelt et al. 1999). Women politicians and others usually explain that there are much more important problems to solve such as economic ones (Musilová 1999). The other usual explanation is presented by Čermáková (1995b) who points out that most people simply do not see men's and women's interests as different.

Although many of the factors underlying women's weak participation in politics have much to do with their attitudes toward politics, other obstacles are structural or institutional in nature and cannot be changed by any shift in attitudes. For example, Čermáková (1995b) points out that the absence of women in politics can arise from a very simple reason: lack of time. The division of labor in the household has been little changed by the introduction of democracy and market economies into the region. Women, then, continue to do most of the work in the home, which leaves them little or no time for political activities (Křížková and Tuček 1998). An institutional obstacle to the greater participation of women in politics is the political parties themselves (Einhorn 1993; *Second Periodical Report* 1999). An analysis of the success rates of women candidates in different types of elections would reveal that the majority of voters do not consider a female candidate a "lower-value" candidate than a male candidate. Yet political parties tend to consider women candidates less suitable for the highest positions on the party lists. In the system of proportional representation that is widely used in the region, the rank of a candidate on the party list[22] is the key factor determining the likely success of that candidate in winning a seat.

According to many scholars, the underrepresentation of women in top politics is the main reason the political programs of most parties do not pay much attention to specific women's issues or avoid having specific chapters devoted to gender issues. Party opinions on gender-related issues are therefore hard to pin down. Groups of parties do tend to differ, based on their general ideological orientation, on their political agenda items related to women. According to Čermáková (1995b), Christian-oriented parties lean toward advocating the traditional family structure with the woman as homemaker, stressing traditional values and morals, and generally opposing abortions. Left-wing political parties promote policies aimed at the social protection of women and children and the elimination of unemployment, and they emphasize equality and social policy. Right-wing free marketeers tend to accentuate the need for a weak state, call for lower state subsidies for families, and promote the idea of women as emancipated individuals.

Do parties have any "pro-women" programs? The definition of the term *pro-women* is very much based on the ideological position of the person trying to answer the question. But even if that person accepts the view of some ideological group—for example, the mainstream Western feminist movement—the question is still not an easy one to answer. For example, Christian democratic parties may promote the policy of protecting women against the consequences of divorces requested by husbands (a pro-women policy), while trying to outlaw abortions (an antiwomen policy). Right-wing free-marketeers may promote easy access to education and entrepreneurship for women (a pro-women policy), while also calling for drastic cuts in subsidies to publicly owned day care centers and kindergartens (an antiwomen policy). Although some analysts such as Heitlinger (1995) assert that left-oriented parties in the region tend to have generally more pro-women programs because of their emphasis on equal opportunity and the social security of families (including unmarried or divorced women with children), this type of social policy may lead to the long-term dependence of women on state welfare and discourage them from independent economic activity (an antiwomen policy).

The complicated relationship between party programs and women is also reflected in the relationship between political parties and women as voters—see Table 36, which is based on the results of surveys conducted under the International Social Science Program. The table reveals some interesting findings. The only political party in the region with support that is constantly and consistently gender-biased is the populist FKGP (Independent Smallholders Party) in Hungary. Over the survey period, the conservative and traditionalist political program of the party consistently attracted higher support from men, but was not particularly appealing to women, possibly because of its radicalism and extremism. Yet several other conservative parties—namely of Christian Democratic orientation (the KDNP in Hungary, Catholic Electoral Action in Poland, and the KDU-ČSL in the Czech Republic)—received a disproportional level of support among women in numerous surveys. Indeed, some analysts have noted that in some elections women have tended to vote more conservatively than men (Einhorn 1993). Tuček and Křížková (1998) point out that older women are one of the most conservative groups in the Czech population. The fact that all Czech women, acting on their more moderate attitudes, tend to avoid supporting

Table 36

Gender-based Differences in Voting Preferences and Voting Intentions, Post-Communist Hungary, Poland, and the Czech Republic

Country, Year	Parties Favored by Men	Parties Favored by Women
Hungary		
1990*	FKGP	FIDESZ, KDNP, SZDSZ
1991	FKGP, FIDESZ	Would not vote
1992*	FKGP, MSZP	MDF, FIDESZ, KDNP
1993	FKGP, MSZP	KDNP
1994	FKGP, SZDSZ	KDNP
1995	FKGP	FIDESZ
1996	FKGP, SZDSZ	KDNP, MSZP
1997*	FKGP	Would not vote, cannot choose
1998*	FKGP, MSZP	FIDESZ, would not vote
Poland		
1992	SLD, PSL, KPN	Center Alliance
1993	SLD. PSL, Center Alliance	Catholic Electoral Action
1994	UD, Catholic Electoral Action, Liberal Congress	SLD, Solidarity
1995	KPN, PSL	Catholic Electoral Action, SLD, UP
1996	PSL, SLD, Labor Union	Would not vote
1997*	PSL, SLD	Would not vote, cannot choose
Czech Republic		
1992	SPR-RSČ, ODA, ČSSD, LSU	KSČM, ODS
1993	—	KDU-ČSL
1994	SPR-RSČ, ODA, ČSSD	KDU-ČSL
1995	ODA, KDU-ČSL, KSČM	Would not vote
1996	SPR-RSČ, ODS	—
1997*	SPR-RSČ, KSČM	Would not vote, cannot choose
1998	SPR-RSČ, KSČM, Union of Freedom	KDU-ČSL, ODS

Source: International Social Survey Programme (ISSP), 1990–1998.
Note: Only in cases marked by an asterisk (*) were the overall gender differences in voting preferences or voting intentions statistically significant at the 95 percent level as measured by the chi-square test.

Respondents were chosen by random sampling, and the number of respondents ranged from 1,000 to 1,200 for each particular country. Hungary participated in the program beginning in 1990, Poland in 1991, and Czechoslovakia in 1992. After the split of Czechoslovakia, surveys were conducted only in the Czech Republic. Respondents were asked about past voting behavior ("What party did you vote for last election?"), and in the interelection periods they were asked about their intentions ("What party would you vote for if the election is next weekend?"). Hungary: FKGP = Independent Smallholders Party; FIDESZ = Federation of Young Democrats; MSZP = Hungarian Socialist Party; SZDSZ = Alliance of Free Democrats; KDNP = Christian Democratic People's Party; MFD = Hungarian Democratic Forum. Poland: SLD = Alliance of the Democratic Left; PSL = Polish Peasants Party; KPN = Confederation for an Independent Poland; UD = Democratic Union; UP = Union of Labor. Czech Republic: SPR-RSČ = Association for the Republic–Republican Party of Czechoslovakia; ODA= Civic Democratic Alliance; ČSSD = Czech Social Democratic Party; LSU = Liberal Social Union; KDUČSL = Christian Democratic Union; KSČM = Communist Party of Bohemia and Moravia; ODS = Civic Democratic Party.

parties considered too radical or extremist (Rendlová 1999) is probably the reason fewer women in the Czech Republic have supported the xenophobic Republicans (SPR-RSČ), the extreme-left Communists (KSČM), and the radically pro-market parties (ODA, Union of Freedom). The other side of the coin is that women's attitudes toward politics tend to be less clear than men's. In several surveys, significantly more women than men declared they would not vote or did not know what party to vote for.

In summary, gender seems to be neither an important factor explaining the voting behavior of the population nor a substantial influence on the party development of post-Communist East-Central Europe. In the 1990s, the majority of political parties did not pay much attention to women's issues in their preelection political programs. In fact, people probably did not even expect them to, because the voting intentions of most citizens are substantially influenced by ethnicity, education, class, wealth, religion, or traditions, but not too much by whether they are men or women.

Women and Abortion

The fact that gender does not constitute a cleavage in the proper sense of the word (that is, a division within society around which political conflict evolves) is best illustrated by abortion laws, an intrinsically engendered issue. A gender-based political cleavage is manifested most clearly in any political debates about potential changes in abortion regulations (Adamik 1993; Einhorn 1993). Because easy, legal access to abortion is a key element of women's reproductive rights, any attempt to restrict a woman's access to abortion (either legally, financially, or administratively) is viewed by women political activists and most of the media in Europe as an antiwoman policy. Any change in the regulations that make the access to abortion easier is considered to be a pro-women policy.

Generally, the Communist governments in East-Central Europe adopted more liberal policies toward abortion than the governments of most Western countries. By the mid-fifties, abortion was already legal—by 1956 in Hungary and Poland and by 1957 in Czechoslovakia. Abortions were permitted for those women with medical reasons and for those women who found themselves in the difficult living conditions (Fuszara 1993). Women seeking an abortion had to apply for permission to special commissions, which had the final word in every case. The overwhelming majority of applications, however, were approved. Although the governments of Czechoslovakia and Hungary, concerned about falling birthrates, made the procedure somewhat more complicated in the 1960s and 1970s, access to abortion remained relatively easy. In fact, because of the limited use of contraceptives, abortion soon became something of a contraceptive, and it gradually lost its negative social stigma. In Czechoslovakia and Hungary, the second wave of liberalization occurred in the late 1980s. New abortion laws declared that the decision to terminate a pregnancy was the exclusive right of the woman.

In Poland, by contrast, the new abortion law submitted to parliament at the very end of the Communist era, shortly before the 1989 semifree elections, was aimed at restricting access to abortions. Thus the abortion question" became part of the newborn democratic politics in Poland from the very beginning. The political battle over abortion, well documented by Fuszara (1993), was fought in the campaigns leading up to Poland's 1989 parliamentary election, 1990 presidential election, and first free parliamentary election in 1991. It was also battled out in 1992 when the new abortion law passed through the first reading in the Sejm. The proposed law declared all abortions illegal, even those sought for medical, legal, or eugenic reasons. Even many members of the ruling coalition, however, found the law too restrictive, and so after negotiations a somewhat less-restrictive version of the law was approved in 1993. It allowed abortions in cases in which the life or health of the mother was threatened, the pregnancy resulted from rape or incest, or medical tests showed that the fetus was irreparably damaged. But the general population found even this version of the law objectionable. It was widely known that restrictions on abortions were being aggressively promoted by the Catholic Church. As a result, the popularity of the church, as measured by public opinion polls, dropped substantially (Einhorn 1993). Nevertheless, the debate over abortion was not over and became an integral part of Polish politics. In the campaign leading up to the early election of 1993, abortion was a hot topic. The post-Communist Alliance of the Democratic Left, which presented itself as the main barrier to the rising power of the church in society, managed to defeat the post-Solidarity right and come to power in a coalition with the post-Communist Polish Peasants Party (PSL). A pro-abortion law was passed soon after the election in 1993. Later, in 1996, the law was further liberalized, allowing abortions for many reasons, including economic hardship. After the victory of Solidarity Electoral Action (AWS) in the 1997 election, the abortion law reverted to its more restrictive version.

The abortion debate in the other three countries studied differed from that in Poland. In Hungary, the battle over abortion lasted only about two years.

In 1990, the Christian Democratic People's Party suggested banning abortions, but the party was weak and did not obtain much support from its coalition partners. Other, more powerful attempts to restrict the right to abortion were made not by a political party but by a group of pro-life activists; they sought a ruling from the Constitutional Court on the constitutionality of liberal abortion laws. The court did not declare abortion itself unconstitutional, but ruled that the parliament must change the existing abortion law. In late 1992, by a vote of the right-wing conservative majority, the parliament passed a new abortion law that, to some extent, restricted access to abortion. It reintroduced the application procedure that included a three-day waiting period between submission of the application and the abortion itself and a compulsory pre-abortion counseling session for applicants. But it basically did not change the reasons for which an abortion could be legally realized such as health reasons, rape, or a crisis situation (Einhorn 1993). Since then, the abortion question has remained off the radar screen of Hungarian politics.

In Slovakia and especially in the Czech Republic, the abortion issue was even less prominent. The general population's dislike of any antiabortion measures prevented the relatively weak Czech and Slovak Christian Democrats from including a ban on abortion in their political agenda. Thus after the fall of communism the only change in the abortion laws—the introduction of fees to be paid by women seeking abortions in hospitals—was motivated by the efforts of the free-market parties to cut expenditures in the health insurance system rather than by concerns about any other issues. Even the activities of the newly constituted pro-life groups, which tried to restrict access to abortions by organizing antiabortion petitions and sending them to the parliaments, did not automatically gain the support of Christian Democratic deputies. Thus the abortion issue remained outside of high politics.

A common feature of the abortion debates in all four countries was the confrontation between the more antiabortion Christian Democrats and the more pro-abortion liberals. A similar ideological split, although not as sharp as the one among politicians, was observable among the voters themselves (Kitschelt et al. 1999). Indeed, attendance at religious services is a very good indicator of a person's attitude toward abortion (see Table 37). The table suggests why the political debate in Poland about abortion was so profound compared with that of other states in the region. In Poland, the general population is divided on the abortion issue into two opposing camps of approximately the same size, whereas in other countries acceptance of abortion massively prevails. Thus while in Poland it makes sense for political

Table 37

Attitudes toward Abortion and Attendance at Religious Services in Hungary, Poland, and the Czech Republic, 1994 (percent)

Country/ Attendance at Religious Services	Question: "Do you agree that pregnant woman should have the legal right to an abortion for any reason?"				
	Strongly Agree	Agree	Neither Agree nor Disagree	Disagree	Strongly Disagree
Hungary					
Regularly	39.2	17.2	17.9	8.4	17.5
Sometimes	58.3	17.6	13.1	5.1	6.0
Never	64.5	18.0	8.9	3.4	5.2
Total population	56.4	17.6	12.8	5.2	7.9
Poland					
Regularly	13.3	25.4	7.1	36.6	17.7
Sometimes	34.0	36.0	6.6	18.3	5.1
Never	44.7	36.8	2.6	11.8	3.9
Total population	20.7	29.0	6.7	30.2	13.5
Czech Republic					
Regularly	15.2	13.0	16.3	25.6	40.8
Sometimes	49.0	21.0	16.3	8.7	5.0
Never	52.9	23.4	11.3	7.3	5.2
Total population	47.8	21.6	13.5	9.4	7.8

Source: International Social Survey Programme (ISSP), 1994.
Note: Regular attendance at religious services was defined as two to three times a month or more; sometimes was defined as once a month or less. For the Polish sample N = 1,433; for the Hungarian sample N = 1,452; and for the Czech sample N = 914.

parties on the both sides of the argument to use the existing cleavage for mobilizing its potential supporters, in the other countries it could be a risky business for a party to push the antiabortion argument too far, because the antiabortion electorate is very limited. It is also clear from Table 37 that regular churchgoers tend to have much more negative attitudes toward abortion than persons who attend religious services only sometimes or never. Thus it is logical that any attempts to restrict access to abortion either came from or was at least moderately supported by parties with a Christian Democratic orientation.

Clearly, then, the political debate over abortion reflected at least to some extent a religious cleavage in these societies. But did it reflect any gender-based cleavages? Although the political battles on abortion laws are often interpreted as the clash between the interests of men and women (Adamik 1993; Einhorn 1993; Fuszara 1993), it is doubtful that this interpretation is accurate. It is true that some of the evidence seems to support the idea of a conflict between the sexes. After all, the most radical opponents of liberal abortion laws used to be the Catholic Church—that is, the clergy, who are entirely dominated by men. And the fiercest opponents of any attempt to restrict access to abortion were the activists of the organized feminist movement. Moreover, the gender cleavage is in full view when comparing the rather clearly antiabortion attitudes of the male-dominated Christian Democratic political elite with the much more moderate views of their voters who used to be a high proportion of women (Kitschelt et al. 1999).

Several other facts, however, may leave doubts about whether the abortion debate is a good example of a political issue that reflects the gender-based cleavage. First, it is not at all certain that a political elite that included more women would automatically translate into more pro-abortion attitudes among legislators. Interestingly, one of the most restrictive abortion laws in Europe was adopted in Poland under the government led by Hanna Suchocka, the first female prime minister in the post-Communist world. Second, assessing discussions between male and female politicians may not be the best way to document the conflict between men and women over abortion (note that there are a few women among the top politicians on both sides of the controversy). Politicians, both male and female, tend to be divided over many ideological issues to a greater extent than the general population. Moreover, because of their limited numbers, they may not represent the general population. For that reason, it may be better to heed the results of some surveys that shed more light on the attitudes of the general population toward abortion (Table 38).

According to the table, most Czech women tend to support the idea that women should have the right to an abortion for any reason. Czech men tend to think the same, the only difference being the intensity of their support. Even more interesting are the figures on Hungary and Poland. In both countries, slightly higher shares of women than men strongly support the right to an abortion, but women are slightly more represented in the group strongly opposed to the idea. One rather surprising outcome of the survey is the fact that in Hungary and Poland there is simply no statistically significant difference between the attitudes of men and women. Only in the Czech Republic is the difference between male and female attitudes toward abortion of any statistical significance. When compared with other factors, however, such as church-going, the gender difference remained marginal. Clearly, then, in the 1990s voters did not perceive the debates over the abortion law as a primarily gender-based issue. Therefore, women voters were

Table 38

Attitudes toward Abortion of Men and Women in Hungary, Poland, and the Czech Republic, 1994 (percent)

Country/ Sex of Respondent	Question: "Do you agree that pregnant woman should have the legal right to an abortion for any reason?"				
	Strongly Agree	Agree	Neither Agree nor Disagree	Disagree	Strongly Disagree
Hungary					
Men	54.4	18.5	14.9	4.9	7.3
Women	57.9	17.0	11.2	5.5	8.4
Poland					
Men	19.6	30.8	7.1	30.6	11.9
Women	21.6	27.4	6.4	29.9	14.8
Czech Republic					
Men	41.4	24.6	15.0	10.5	8.5
Women	54.0	18.6	12.0	8.4	7.1

Source: International Social Survey Programme (ISSP), 1994.
Note: For the Polish sample N = 1,433; for the Hungarian sample N = 1,452; and for the Czech sample N = 914.

able to support Christian Democratic parties more than male voters even though these parties tended to be more restrictive when the abortion issue came onto the political scene. This look at the abortion issue also explains perhaps why gender differences mattered so little to the newly emerging parties and did not play an important role in the post-Communist transformation process. If the abortion issue, which was the cornerstone of the gender-based political discourse in many Western countries, did not mobilize voters along the male-female division line, it is hard to believe that any other political issues would do the same. This is not to say that gender issues will not play an important role in the future, but the first decade of post-Communist politics was rather gender cleavage-free.

5

The Party System: A Product
of the Rules of the Game?

Previous chapters examined the relationship between political parties and the history, culture, and social cleavages of Hungary, the Czech Republic, Slovakia, and Poland. This chapter looks at the "juridical context"—that is, the system of laws and regulations that constitute a country's legal framework—within which the political parties are operating. Many different legal regulations influence, either directly or indirectly, the party system and its development. Political freedom itself, the first and the key condition for the existence of a democratic political system, has to be guaranteed by laws, as do freedom of speech, freedom of religion, and the other rights granted under a democracy.

Because all of the countries studied have adopted many of the same principles of democratic rule used by the Western democracies, this chapter focuses on the more specific legal norms—electoral laws—that are of special importance to the development of party structure. It is acknowledged, however, that electoral laws are not the only special laws influencing party development. Other laws regulate, among other things, the founding of new parties and the conditions under which a party can be banned or suspended.[1]

After forty years under a totalitarian system, the countries of East-Central Europe made the process of founding political parties very easy. A great many of the new parties met the requirements of the law—democratic rules for internal party organization, a written political program, and a few hundred signatures of supporters—and were officially registered. Trying to distance themselves from the practices of the Communists, the new regimes in all four of the countries studied were reluctant to use administrative measures against any political party. Even the local Communist Parties were not banned from the political life of their respective countries. Thus the legal conditions were generally favorable for the development of new parties and did not differ from country to country.

Electoral systems are intended to translate peoples' votes into seats for candidates. Of the many different electoral systems in the world, the two most basic are the majority system and the system of proportional representation. Under a majority system, a country is first divided into electoral districts. In each district, voters can choose from several candidates. The most successful candidate gains the contested seat in the elected body (such as a national parliament, regional parliament, or city council). A special type of majority electoral system in which the winning candidate is the one who receives the most votes of all the contestants (not necessarily a majority of votes) is called plurality system. Systems of proportional representation are based on idea that various ideological and social groups should be represented in parliament in proportion to their support in society. Under this system, candidates of similar ideological backgrounds form party lists, and voters vote for the different party lists rather than individual candidates. In its pure form, a system of proportional representation does not use electoral districts at all—the whole country is one electoral district. Most systems of proportional representation, however, divide the country into several electoral districts. In each district, seats are assigned to respective party lists in proportion to the votes obtained in individual districts. The national parliament is then composed of candidates who were elected in all individual electoral districts. Mixed electoral systems combine both the majority system and the system of proportional representation. Usually, some members of parliament are elected under the majority system, and the rest are elected under a system of proportional representation.

As for the electoral systems themselves, it is generally accepted that a certain relationship exists between the type of electoral system and party system development. Whether one is speaking about "sociological law," "probabilistic association," or "tendency laws," the empirically documented fact is that a two-party system is usually found in countries that use a plurality electoral system, whereas multiple parties are typical for countries with a system of proportional representation.[2] But is the kind of electoral system used dependent on a country's party structure, or is the party system a product of the rules of the game of which the electoral system is the most determining? Students of the relationship between the electoral system and party development in longtime Western democracies tend to regard the electoral system as the independent variable and the party system as the dependent variable (Grofman and Lijphart 1986). This decision is quite understandable, because, once established in a country, an electoral system (whether plurality or proportional) seems to be more stable than the party system itself. Moreover, history is littered with examples of how change in an electoral system was followed by a change in the party system. But what seems to be true for consolidated democracies may not be applicable to the situation in the post-Communist countries where electoral laws were being drafted while political parties were taking shape. The basic principles of electoral laws had to be determined by the emerging parties. Thus the parties had an extraordinary opportunity to shape the rules of the game, which in turn shaped party development.

Following this scheme, this chapter examines both the role that political parties were playing during the negotiations about the electoral laws and the effects of the adopted electoral systems on the development of the party system. As for the effects of the electoral system on party development, it is useful to distinguish between the effect of the electoral system on party behavior and its effect on voters' behavior (Sartori 1986). Also important, electoral systems generally have a reductive effect—that is, they tend to decrease the number of options available to both the parties and the voters. In this respect, the majority systems are considered more restrictive and the proportional systems less restrictive (Sartori 1986). Duverger (1964) also has pointed out that the effect of the electoral system is both mechanical and psychological. The term *mechanical* is used to describe the immediate effect of changes in the electoral law (for example, the introduction of the 5 percent threshold instantaneously prevented all parties with less than 5 percent of the vote from entering parliament). The psychological effect is more complex and slower, because many voters need time to learn, in practice, how restrictive the electoral laws are. Then, having already experienced wasted votes, they tend to turn their voting support away from the parties eliminated by the electoral law and toward parties with better chances for success.

Poland

After the famous roundtable talks in the spring of 1989, Poland became the first Communist country to break the Communist monopoly of power. The peculiarities of the electoral system, however, were not at stake. The basic question was whether the Communist Party would allow the opposition to participate politically. Facing the chaos created by the growing popular unrest, extremely high inflation, and the threat of an all-out strike, the Communist rulers were pressed to give up their privileged access to power at least partially. In a short period of time, then, negotiators for both sides reached a compromise on the nature of the electoral law. In the Sejm, 299 (65 percent) seats would be reserved for the Communist Party and their satellite parties, and the remaining 161 (35 percent) would be open to free competition. Moreover, a Senate with 100 seats was introduced to the Polish constitutional system (Perdue 1995).

The 1989 election, held under the majority system, was a landslide victory for the opposition and a catastrophe for the Communists, who did not gain a single seat in the parliament. By producing that outcome, the semi-competitive electoral system adopted in the roundtable talks fulfilled the desires of its designers: the majority of the Communists and their satellite parties remained untouched, and Solidarity was allowed to participate in power. The electoral predominance of the opposition, however, opened the floodgate to change. Because the Communists without the Peasants and Democratic Parties did not have a majority in the parliament, the creation of the first non-Communist government became possible after the former Communist allies decided to join Solidarity.

The debate that began in 1990 over the new electoral law provides solid evidence of the individual actors' profit-maximizing strategy. Taking into account the results of the last election, the Communists and their former satellites were again in agreement: they insisted on a purely proportional representation that would ensure some seats for all in future parliaments. Based on its good experience in the last election and the strength of its opponents, the Solidarity caucus suggested a mixed system (Tworzecki 1996). After his election in 1990, President Lech Wałęsa took part in the debate on the electoral law and sided with the proponents of a mixed system. The conflict, which lasted several months, included the use of presidential vetoes and parliamentary overturns; however, those who preferred the proportional representation were backed by a majority of seats in the Sejm, and therefore in the end a purely proportional system was adopted.

Once again, then, the electoral system was conformed to meet the desires of its designers. Not only did the post-Communist and former satellite parties obtain seats, but many of the small parties also gained representation. The system, because it did not offer any obstacles to any small parties wishing to enter parliament, seemed to encourage those with dissenting opinions to solve their conflict by leaving the party to which they belonged and creating their own smaller parties. Similarly, the electoral law allowed the parallel existence of parties almost identical ideologically and programmatically. Faced with this highly unrestrictive electoral formula which gave them the opportunity to choose from a whole rank of different parties, the voters did just that in the 1991 election (see Table 21). The result was an extremely fragmented political scene when no less than twenty-nine parties entered parliament. Under these circumstances, parliament found it nearly impossible to carry out its work, and in time it recognized that the electoral system was an obstacle to rational governing.

The solution seemed to be the introduction of restrictive measures. Because the use of a legal threshold provided bigger parties with an advantage, it was pushed predominantly by parties with better records in the opinion polls. Thus prior to its dissolution in 1993, parliament passed a new electoral law through the united effort of the strongest parties—the Democratic Union (UD), Alliance of the Democratic Left (SLD), Polish Peasants Party (PSL), and the Confederation for an Independent Poland (KPN)—and against the will of the weaker ones (Tworzecki 1996). The mechanical effect of the 5 percent threshold (8 percent for the coalition candidates' list) was striking in the 1993 election: the number of parties was sharply reduced to only six (see Table 22).[3] The electoral results for 1993 also documented how the psychological effect of the electoral law works slower than the mechanical effect, because a high share of voters still voted for parties that had no chance of being represented in parliament (Novák 1996).[4] The biggest losers were those parties associated with the Christian right that together received 21 percent of the vote but no seat because of their fragmentation (Sabbat-Swidlicka 1993). Learning from their experience, the unsuccessful parties began to show a greater willingness to create coalitions and to merge ideologically similar parties.[5]

Czech Republic

The juridical context also was very important in the development of party politics in Czechoslovakia. In contrast to events in Poland, the change in regime was not accompanied by major changes in the constitutional system.[6] Thus in 1989 the federal parliament inherited a very complicated structure based on the constitutional law of the Czechoslovak Federation, adopted in late 1968. The parliament consisted of two chambers: the Chamber of the People and the Chamber of Nations, which were of equal size and equal power. The 150 deputies making up the Chamber of the People were elected in both republics in proportion to the number of voters in the two republics. As a result, the chamber was composed of approximately twice as many Czech deputies as Slovak deputies. Of the 150 deputies in the Chamber of Nations, 75 were elected in the Czech Republic and 75 in Slovakia. Most bills had to be approved separately in the Chamber of the People and in each national section of the Chamber of Nations. Moreover, all constitutional changes, as well as some other bills of special importance (such as the so-called constitutional bills—for example, electoral laws and laws stating the competencies of the federation and the individual republics) had to be approved by at least a three-fifths majority of parliament. Thus only thirty-one members (10.3 percent of the total of three hundred) from either the Czech or Slovak section of the Chamber of Nations (that is, two-fifths of seventy-five plus one) could effectively block any constitutional change.

The electoral rules themselves had to be negotiated before the election of new representatives. Unlike in Poland, the negotiations over the basic principles of the new electoral system were, far from dramatic. The key factor was the decision of the Civic Forum (OF) and the Public Against Violence (VPN) to propose a system of proportional representation. Somewhat paradoxically, the leaders of these extraordinarily popular movements (as shown by the public opinion polls) did not push for a majority system, which could have resulted in a landslide victory for both parties. Rather, the system of proportional representation had been widely recognized as fairer than the majority system, because it gave different political streams a chance to emerge publicly and achieve institutionalization through parliamentary representation. Moreover, it was argued that the proportional system was used in pre-Communist Czechoslovakia. When the representatives of the Civic Forum and the Public Against Violence suggested proportional representation, all parties involved in the negotiations were satisfied. Even implementation of the 5 percent threshold, which was designed to prevent excessive fragmentation of a future parliament, was not a problem, because the participants in the roundtable talks were confident about their ability to exceed this limit.

The negotiators also decided that the laws governing election to the national councils[7] of the individual republics should be negotiated separately in the respective national political representative bodies. The Czech body adopted the federal electoral law without changes, and the Slovaks decreased the threshold from 5 percent to 3 percent but left the other provisions of the law untouched.[8] In the first free election in 1990, the restrictive effect of the 5 percent threshold was not very strong because of the plebiscitary character of the election and the extraordinarily large support for the winning movements in both the Czech Republic and Slovakia (see Tables 9 and 10). In the 1992 parliamentary election in the Czech Republic, voters' preferences were spread fairly evenly among the greater number of parties on the political scene (Table 12). The mechanical effect of the legal threshold was rather important, because several smaller parties supported by more than 3 but less than 5 percent of voters[9] were prevented from participating in parliament. In the end, the right-oriented parties (the Civic Democratic Party, Christian Democratic Union–Czechosloak People's Party, and Civic Democratic Alliance) received 42 percent of the vote, which translated into a majority of seats (53 percent) in the parliament and led to the creation of a stable government.

The split of Czechoslovakia changed the situation in the newly established Czech and Slovak republics. The federal parliament dissolved itself, and Czechoslovakia ceased to exist at the end of 1992. The constitution of the Czech Republic established a bicameral parliament. The Czech national council, formerly the Czech regional parliament within Czechoslovakia, was transformed into the lower house of parliament. The upper house of parliament, the Senate, was established by the constitution, yet senators' seats remained vacant until 1996 when the first election for the Senate was organized. The constitution of Slovakia established a unicameral parliament, which was created through the transformation of the Slovak national council.

The June 1996 election for the lower house of parliament in the Czech Republic showed that voters had learned more about the electoral law's restrictive effect (Table 16). The small parties with only a theoretical chance of gaining any seats received altogether only 11.2 percent of the vote. In fact, not even one approached the 5 percent limit. This situation explains how the coalition parties (Civic Democratic Party, Christian Democratic Union–Czechosloak People's Party, and Civic Democratic Alliance) lost their majority of seats, despite the fact that they received an even higher share of votes than four years ago (their 44 percent of the total vote translated into 49.5 percent of the seats). A sociological survey conducted twenty-four hours before the election revealed how the 5 percent limit affected the decisions of the voters. Respondents were asked not only what party they were going to vote for, but also which party they found agreeable. The fact that 35.6 percent of those whose sympathies lay with the weak

Civic Democratic Alliance (ODA) decided to vote for an ideologically similar but much stronger party—the Civic Democratic Party (ODS)—needed no commentary (Vlachová 1997).

The electoral law used for the first Senate election, scheduled for November 1996, has an interesting history in itself. The Czech constitution had already specified that the majority system was to be used in Senate elections. However, the kind of majority system to be used and even a definition of the term *majority electoral system* were the subject of constant debate on the Czech political scene from 1993 to 1995. Although various parties used different kinds of arguments to persuade both their partners and the public that their ideas best served the common good, it was obvious that the parties were working hard to set up rules favoring their own interests. The senior coalition partner, the Civic Democratic Party, aware of its position, advocated the first-past-the-post system using eighty-one single-member constituencies.[10] The junior coalition partners, afraid of ODS's strength, suggested proportional solutions that could still be considered a majority system. They insisted on the creation of twenty-seven tri-member electoral districts. Three senators would be elected for six-year terms by each district. Every two years, one of the three seats would be up for election using the two-round majority system.

The final solution was a compromise: the senators would be elected under a two-round majority system using the eighty-one single-member constituencies. If no candidate received more than 50 percent of the vote in the first round, the two candidates with the best electoral results from the first round would run on the second ballot. The winner of the second ballot would then be elected senator. This electoral law had two political consequences. First, the majority electoral system effectively eliminated the extreme parties from the Senate, because the Communists received only two seats and the Republicans none (see Table 17).[11] Second, the elections deepened the conflict between the coalition parties, especially between Václav Klaus's ODS and the Christian Democratic Union–Czechoslovak People's Party (KDU-ČSL), because after the first round, which proved to be very successful for the ODS, the leader of the KDU-ČSL refused to support ODS candidates even when they stood against the Czech Social Democratic Party (ČSSD) in the second round. The "all against ODS " strategy paid off, because a clear majority of candidates nominated by the junior coalition parties standing against ODS candidates in the second round received parliamentary seats thanks to support from the opposition voters. Thus the final result of the 1996 Senate election (although played out according to the principles of a majority system) did not have the appearance of a majority outcome (Table 17). A comparison of the percentage of votes with the percentage of gained seats offers proof that the electoral system used was not very rewarding for the winning party (ODS), but rather for the parties ranked second (ČSSD) and third (KDU-ČSL).

The debate over the nature of the electoral system was rekindled after the fall of Klaus's government, the departure of ODS internal dissenters in the spring of 1998, and the founding of a new conservative party—the Union of Freedom (US). The leaders of the Union of Freedom publicly called for the introduction of a majority electoral system, hoping it would prevent "frequent governmental changes and repeated early elections" and thereby stabilize the political system. And they raised the issue precisely when the opinion polls suggested that the Union of Freedom was the strongest party on the right side of the political spectrum.[12] The proposal put forth by the Union of Freedom was not warmly received by the other parties. Only the ODS was willing to consider it, but with reservations. No other party, including the Social Democrats, who definitely would have benefited from the change, agreed. The early parliamentary election for the lower chamber of the Czech parliament in 1998 (see Table 18) and the surprising Agreement on the Creation of a Stable Political Environment in the Czech Republic, signed by both the ČSSD and ODS, catapulted the question of the electoral system to the top of the political agenda. Aware that their three-fifths majority was needed for an eventual change in the constitution and confident about their popular support in future elections, the two most successful parties changed their attitudes radically and declared that the most efficient way to achieve "long-term political stability" (that is, the two-party system) was to change the electoral system. Although both parties had refuted the proposal made by the Union of Freedom before the election to introduce the majority system, ODS and ČSSD agreed immediately after the election that "the strengthening of the majoritarian features of the electoral system would be desirable."

The negotiations themselves were a good example of party behavior as described by Downs (1957) in his theory of party competition. The task facing the negotiators representing the two parties involved was clear: to write an electoral law that would minimize the chance of the other parties for electoral success. The negotiations between the two parties, however, were far from simple, because both parties were simultaneously trying to incorporate provisions into the bill that would increase their own electoral chances at the expense of the other negotiation partner. The situation was complicated by the fact that opinion polls documented an increase in the Communist Party's popular support at the expense of the governing Social Democrats. Moreover, the defeat of both parties in the 1998 (Table 19) and 1999 Senate by-elections by the Four-Party Coalition and an independent candidate, respectively, revealed that the majority system might not be an advantage for the ODS and ČSSD. Now wiser from these events, the ČSSD and ODS created the bi-party commission on electoral reform and adjusted their arguments appropriately.

Finally in early 2000, after a year and a half of negotiations, the two parties reached a compromise and sent the draft of the bill to the parliament. The key features of the new electoral law for the lower chamber of parliament included an increase in the number of electoral districts from eight to thirty-five and the introduction of a new system[13] for the translation of votes into seats. The system rewards big parties, particularly the winner of the election, and tends to punish smaller parties. It indirectly increases the threshold necessary for obtaining seats to 10–12 percent of the vote.

The measures taken against the smaller parties were supplemented by a reform of party finance regulations and by the introduction of new regulations on the legal threshold for coalitions. The new finance regulations limited the total amount of money that individual parties can legally obtain from supporters and donors. Simultaneously, they decreased the state subsidy per received vote and increased the state subsidy per obtained mandate. In short, the smaller parties that are already disadvantaged by the way votes are translated into seats will receive a disproportionately lower amount of money from the state while their possibility of raising money from private sources will be limited. The legal threshold for the two-party coalition was increased from 7 to 10 percent, for the three-party coalition from 9 to 15 percent, and for the four-party coalition from 11 to 20 percent. Because the legal threshold for party coalitions is now calculated as a multiple of the 5 percent legal threshold, the formation of electoral coalitions will be useless. This provision of the law was designed to harm, at least politically, the most successful critic of the opposition agreement, the Four-Party Coalition, for which the 20 percent threshold could be a threat.

Because in most of the thirty-five small electoral districts in the Czech Republic the number of seats contested is five or six, the proposed electoral system was likely to produce an unstable distribution of seats. Even a small change in a party's popular support could result in fundamental changes in the number of seats it wins. Consequently, it would be extremely difficult to estimate before an election which parties will be able to constitute a parliamentary majority, even when precise, reliable opinion poll results were available. In 2001, the Constitutional Court declared most provisions of the new electoral law unconstitutional. Parties had to restart negotiations.

Slovakia

In Slovakia, the effects of the electoral law on the formation of political parties mirrored those in the Czech Republic, and Slovak voters underwent the same learning process as their Czech counterparts. The introduction of the 5 percent threshold resulted in 23.8 percent of the vote being given to parties that were not able to exceed that limit in the 1992 election (Table 11). The 45.2 percent of the vote received jointly by Vladimír Mečiar's Movement for a Democratic Czechoslovakia (HZDS) and the Slovak National Party (SNS) provided them with a solid majority of seats in parliament. But the voters, not willing to waste their votes again, paid careful attention to the results of the preelection polls in the 1994 election. As a result, the parties with long-term popular support of around 5 percent or less failed, and the share of "wasted" votes declined to only 13 percent (Table 13). Based on these results, Mečiar's new government had to consist of three parties, which together had received 47.7 percent of the vote, in order to secure a majority of seats in parliament.

Not only voters learned how electoral laws function. Aware of its strength and tired of persistent negotiations with junior coalition partners in the government, Mečiar's HZDS came up with the idea of introducing a majority electoral system. But this proposal did not find support in the Slovak parliament and was rejected not only by the opposition but also by those who were elected on the ballots of two junior coalition partners—the Slovak National Party and the Association of Workers of Slovakia (ZRS).

In June 1998, just three months before the parliamentary election, the parliament, still dominated by Mečiar's HZDS and its allies, changed the electoral law in an attempt to aggravate the situation of their strongest opponents, the Slovak Democratic Coalition (SDK). New amendments redefined the conditions under which the electoral coalitions could gain seats in the parliament—now each party in the coalition would require more than 5 percent of the vote to win a seat in the parliament. In practice, this meant that each of the five parties that made up the HZDS's strongest rival, the SDK, would have to win more than 5 percent of the vote. Because this provision made the creation of any coalition irrational, the two strongest coalitions among the opposition—the SDK and the Hungarian Coalition—transformed themselves into political parties.

Although Mečiar's tactic seemed to fail, as evidenced by the quickly unified opposition that ultimately won the election (Table 14) and formed a new government, it did succeed in making the life of the new governing coalition very complicated in the long run. The SDK, established at breakneck speed, had no time to establish itself as a unified party; it had always worked as a rather loose coalition of ideologically and institutionally different parties. Its internal instability helped the HZDS to preserve its position on the political scene. The problems within the SDK were not immediately visible in the year after the election as the parties approached the presidential contest. Indeed, the government concentrated on unified action against the possibility of Mečiar's return to the top political position. Keeping its campaign promises, the governing coalition changed the law on presidential elections so that the new president would elected by a direct popular vote, in two rounds.

Soon after Mečiar's defeat by Rudolf Schuster in the presidential election in the summer of 1999 (Table 15), the parliament, controlled by the SDK, the SDL, the Party of Civil Understanding (SOP), and the Hungarian Coalition, passed amendments to the parliamentary election law. Basically, the newest version of the law made the creation of preelectoral coalitions meaningful again by reintroducing different thresholds for individual parties (5 percent), two- and three-party coalitions (7 percent), and four-party and bigger coalitions (10 percent). Without external pressure to keep the SDK together, its members began to act more independently, which in turn led to its gradual disintegration.

Hungary

In Hungary, the situation was somewhat similar to that in Poland. The roundtable talks between the Communist rulers and the opposition in the summer of 1989 addressed both the basic institutional arrangement and the new electoral law for the first free election. But unlike in Czechoslovakia, the negotiations were difficult. The new institutional framework rather closely followed that of the postwar Hungarian democracy (Tóka 1995a), and thus an agreement was reached rather quickly on several points such as a parliamentary type of democracy, the legal status of the president, and a unicameral parliament. A crucial point of dispute remained, however: the time and method of the presidential election. Relying on the high popularity of their reform leader, Imre Pozsgay, the Communists were in favor of direct election of the president by the people before the parliamentary election. Some opposition parties—the Alliance of Free Democrats (SZDSZ) and the Federation of Young Democrats (FIDESZ)—strongly disagreed. Using the law just passed by the (still Communist) parliament which stipulated the right of referendum, the opposition parties began to collect signatures for a referendum, including on the issue of the timing of the presidential election. The referendum decided, by a slight margin, that the president would be elected after the general election. The Communist-dominated parliament then changed the constitution before the free parliamentary elections, thereby introducing the direct election of the president. The new parliament, however, dominated by the non-Communist opposition, reversed the course once again—back to an indirect election. When another referendum (organized at the instigation of the Communists) was pronounced invalid because of low turnout, the battle over the method of electing the president was over. The Free Democrats benefited from the victory, and their candidate, Árpád Göncz, was elected president. His powers, however, remained limited.

Also difficult, but not so dramatic, was the debate over the electoral system for the parliamentary election. Because the relatively coherent political parties were aware of both the political consequences of different electoral models and their own political strength, the negotiations were very pragmatic, clearly driven by the interests of the individual parties (Ishiyama 1996). The Hungarian Democratic Forum (MDF), aware of its popularity and rather strong local organizations, preferred a system of single-member electoral districts. The urban-based Alliance of Free Democrats pushed strongly for proportional representation, which would allow it to avoid any big electoral losses in the rural single-member constituencies. The reborn historical parties, which lacked many well-known personalities, also advocated proportional representation; they were confident that they would find enough supporters nationwide to get into parliament. The compromise they finally reached called for a mixed majority/proportional system. It was backed by the Communists who were sure they could profit from a well-organized local apparatus as well as from the popularity of their well-known reform leaders (Ishiyama 1996). The parties also reached a compromise over the implementation of a legal threshold. The Communists had proposed using a 5 percent threshold; the opposition had countered with a 3 percent threshold; and both sides finally agreed on a 4 percent threshold.

Borne out of a series of compromises, the electoral law was exceedingly complicated. Of the 386 members of parliament, 176 were elected in single-member electoral districts, 152 were elected from the party lists in regional constituencies, and the last 58 were elected from the national lists of individual parties. If no candidate obtained more than 50 percent of the vote in the first round of elections in the single-member districts, a second round was organized that included all of the candidates who had received more than 15 percent in the first round (with a mandatory minimum of three candidates). This solution, designed to place at least three candidates into the second round, was incorporated under pressure from the Communists, who expected their candidate to be among the top three. They reasoned that their candidate, by facing two opposition candidates, would have a better chance of winning the runoff (Tóka 1995c). Although the mixed system that was finally adopted should have looked like a compromise between the majority and the proportional systems, in reality it strongly favored the biggest parties. Not only the single-member districts but also the way in which the votes in regional multimember districts were translated into seats obviously discriminated against the smaller parties. Another measure that worked against the smaller parties was the requirement to collect a certain number of signatures in single-member districts as a condition for nominating a candidate.

The results of the 1990 election only partially fulfilled the intentions of its designers. Although the law effectively reduced the number of parties entering parliament to only six (from the more than twenty participating in the election), the degree to which the strongest party benefited from the new legal provisions was somewhat surprising. The victorious Hungarian Democratic Forum received 24.7 percent of the vote but obtained 42.5 percent of the seats (see Table 6). The Alliance of Free Democrats, which ranked second with only 3.3 percent less than the MDF, gained about 18.3 percent less seats. All the other parliamentary parties received a lower proportion of seats than their proportion of votes, which is surprising, especially in view of the fact that almost 16 percent of the vote was lost because of the 4 percent threshold. Thus the electoral law not only prevented small parties from entering parliament, but also weakened the parliamentary opposition.[14]

Somewhat paradoxically, the Communists, highly confident about their strength at the time of the roundtable negotiations, were among those most ill-affected by the electoral law. Yet four years later, the post-Communist Hungarian Socialist Party (MSZP) had the pleasure of exploiting the electoral law when it received 54 percent of the seats with only 33 percent of the vote, whereas all the other political parties in parliament gained less seats in relation to their votes (Table 7).

The parliamentary election of 1998 was rather exceptional in the effects produced by the electoral system (Table 8). On the one hand, the system effectively kept small parties out of the parliament and diminished the parliamentary power of medium-sized parties. On the other hand, the electoral law did not reward the party with the highest share of supporters with a special premium in seats. In contrast to the previous elections, the party with the highest percentage of votes in the first round of the election—the Socialists with 32.3 percent of votes—did not obtain the highest number of seats in the parliament. This was possible only because the second most popular party, the Federation of Young Democrats–Hungarian Civic Party (FIDESZ-MPP), received almost as many votes as the Socialists in the first round (28.2 percent) and, above all, managed to win most of the second-round contests in single-member districts. If the support for both leading parties is considered together, it is clear that the electoral system continued to reward the stronger parties at the expense of the weaker ones. Together, the two strongest parties obtained 60.5 percent of the votes, but 73 percent of seats. The majoritarian effects of the Hungarian electoral law are largely moderated, however, in a situation in which the first and the second party have approximately the same strength. The reductive effect of the electoral law on the number of political parties involved in Hungarian top politics is, though, undeniable.

The electoral law also was clearly supportive of the formation of majoritarian governments backed by stable support from the majority in parliament. A byproduct of the strong majoritarian effects of the electoral law was the absence of a political war after electoral reforms were adopted, unlike in Poland, the Czech Republic, and Slovakia. The electoral law itself proved to be a very stable regulation, and the only (and relatively unimportant) change adopted later, in January 1994, was an increase in the legal threshold from 4 percent to 5 percent (Tóka 1998). Parties punished by the electoral law had no strength left to start such debates, while parties awarded by a majority of seats had no reason to contend.

6

Political Party Development
in Post-Communist East-Central Europe:
In Search of General Patterns

This concluding chapter looks at political party development in the post-Communist era a bit differently; it concentrates on trends rather than individual events, on similarities rather than differences, and describes some general patterns of development among the four countries studied. But first a caveat: the four countries, despite their differences, are historically, economically, and culturally rather close, especially when compared with some other post-Communist countries (Berglund, Hellén, and Aarebrot 1998). Therefore, any generalizations presented here may not necessarily apply to other former Communist countries.

The burning question today about post-Communist politics is: "Transition to what?" This question has neither a simple answer nor a single solution (McIntosh and Mac Iver 1993). However, a review of party development after the fall of communism in Hungary, the Czech Republic, and Poland reveals three general trends: (1) a shift from personalized and nonpolitical politics toward party politics; (2) a gradual transition from the politics of symbols, identities, and hopes toward the politics of vested interests and rational choice; and (3) the growing importance of the relationship between social structures and political parties.

Toward Party Politics

The notion that political parties are vital to the satisfactory introduction or reintroduction of democracy in post-Communist countries has been stressed by many Western politicians and political scientists (Pridham 1995), but it was not very warmly received in East-Central Europe itself after the fall of communism. In fact, almost the opposite was true. Disgust for political parties was widespread among the new political elite, as well as among the general population. The single most important reason for this disgust was quite understandable. Most people's experience with a political party had been limited to the totalitarian Communist model. Of the three most obvious roles that political parties play in a democratic society—reflecting cleavages in the social structure and therefore acting as a mechanism for translating social tensions into politics; attracting popular support through elections and thereby legitimizing the government and its actions; and recruiting and training political leaders and government decision makers—the Communist Party filled only one: recruiting and training. And even in this role, the party sometimes used methods similar to those of organized crime, including blackmail, the violent liquidation of opponents, and the persecution of excommunicated members.[1] The collapse of the Communist regime and the introduction of political freedom did not substantially improve the image of parties in the public's eye. The opinion that the primary purpose of any party was to help power seekers fulfill their desires (and thus the only difference between a one-party and a multiparty system was many party machines versus one party machine) was widespread, and the instances of politicians, even the well-known ones, switching from party to party were numerous. One should not conclude, however, that the citizens did not understand the importance of free choice and political freedom in a democracy. Although both were highly appreciated by the population, political parties were not considered an indispensable part of the new political system.

The importance of political parties was further debased by the fact that many of the new political leaders, who hailed from the dissident movements, did not believe in their usefulness and so gravitated toward nonpolitical politics as a viable alternative to classical party politics. Noting the decline in party membership, the process of party dealignment, and the rise of nonparty political movements and organizations in the West, these leaders stressed the role of citizen involvement, political movements, and nongovernmental organizations in public life. Indeed, only a few of the new actors on the political scene that mushroomed soon after the fall of the old regime even used the word *party*. Taking into account only the most influential political organizations,[2] there were three movements; two each of alliances, forums, and unions; one each of action, federation, confederation, agreement, congress, and trade union; and even one public. In accordance with their names, only the Communists and post-Communists, some former satellite parties, and the parties claiming to be successors of historical parties (the Social Democrats, Christian Democrats, Independent Smallholders, and Slovak National Party) were real "parties." Even when the broad antiregime umbrella movements were beginning to fall apart, in most cases the word *party* was carefully avoided.

But beyond names, many students of party structures and organizations point out that most political parties in the early post-Communist era really did not resemble the Western European ones. In Poland, the main political actor standing in opposition to the ruling Communists was not a party at all but a trade union. However, even after Solidarity began to split along various issues into different political groups, it did not create classical political parties. Mizgala (1994), who studied the impact of the corporatist state on the formation and development of the party system in Poland in the early post-Communist period, 1989–1993, described politics there as a system in which "political parties are seen as being incapable of preparing a policy agenda" in a situation and almost all power is concentrated in the hands of the government. Consequently, "parliamentary politics becomes, in a practical sense, a means to gain highly prized access to the executive branch in order to pursue the desired outcomes there."

Many of the various political parties were established in East-Central Europe as tools for securing individual access to power, and many existing parties split up for the same purpose. Indeed, some were called "sofa parties" because of the limited number of members. Lomax (1995), writing about obstacles to democratic politics in post-Communist Hungary, characterized many new parties as "elite parties of professional intellectuals lacking both mass membership and the social basis of traditional parties in Western democracies." Others described Hungarian parties as clubs or spiritual communities, based on sharing the same cultural identities (Markus 1994). Some political groups, such as the Federation of Young Democrats (FIDESZ), even programmatically sought *not* to be a party by avoiding the usual organizational party structures and methods of work. Similarly, the Hungarian Democratic Forum (MDF) and the Alliance of Free Democrats (SZDSZ) relied on the fame of their well-known leaders in the media rather than on the local work of their grassroots activists.

The situation in the former Czechoslovakia was no different. Although the "revolution" gave rise to many local activists from both the Civic Forum (OF) in the Czech Republic and the Public Against Violence (VPN) in Slovakia, most of them were involved primarily in local politics, their interests were divergent, and the links between them and the movement's leadership were weak. The spirit of the time is perhaps best described by the slogan popular with the Civic Forum before the 1990 parliamentary election: "Parties are for partisans, the Civic Forum is for everyone!" Soon after the election, however, it became apparent that many of the praised "advantages" of movement-type political organizations (such as greater autonomy for their individual organizations on all levels) became problems in practice. The lack of organizational ties between the center and local activists not only gave local activists freedom (which was the intention), but also allowed the center to act almost independently from its grassroots activists. Thus conflict among the various Civic Forum leaders over the possible direction of economic reforms, a crucial debate determining the future of the country, could only be observed by most of the grassroots activists. The manner in which the Civic Forum should function was another important point of political discourse. The fight between those who advocated gradual reforms and those who supported radical reforms, as well as the conflict between the movement model and the party model of organization, intensified after the election of Václav Klaus to the chairmanship of the Civic Forum. The debates culminated in the split of the Civic Forum. The founding of the Civic Democratic Party (ODS) under the leadership of Klaus, who openly pleaded for the creation of "a standard political party," seemed to be the first step toward the rehabilitation of political parties among the Czech population.

A similar process of party revival could be observed in the whole region. The main reason, however, was practical, not ideological. The more organized parties were able to more effectively mobilize their supporters and recruit volunteers during the electoral campaign, and they were less likely to shift their politics sharply after a change in leadership. Above all, organized parties were more successful in attracting popular support in the election. Thus in the 1992 parliamentary election in the Czech Republic (Table 12), five of the six most successful contestants were parties, both in name and in internal structure and organization (see Kostelecký and Kroupa 1996). The political groups in parliament not only looked like classical political parties, but also increasingly acted like them. Studies of the roles played by different actors in the Czech parliament during the period 1992–1996 revealed that the parties had become the key actors in forming parliamentary decisions (Kopecký, Hubáček, and Plecitý 1996). At the same time, the party loyalty of individual deputies was increasing.

The same was basically true in Slovakia. Although the political organization founded by Vladimír Mečiar (after his dismissal from his post as prime minister) was called the Movement for a Democratic Slovakia (HZDS), from its conception it resembled a political party in its organizational structure and in its political practices. While his opponents held government posts, Mečiar built strong local organizations and encouraged supporters to join the movement. Soon after the victorious elections in 1992 (Table 11), strong party discipline was introduced, resulting in the expulsion of several disloyal deputies from the party. After the 1994 early parliamentary elections and the repeated victory of Mečiar's HZDS and its allies (see Table 13), the dominance of political parties in Slovak politics became apparent. The most visible manifestation was the extraordinarily high level of partisan voting in the parliament, as well as the incident in which a HZDS deputy, František Gaulieder, was removed from his parliamentary seat by a vote of the coalition deputies after he left the party.[3]

The political offensive of organized parties also was evident in Poland. In his study of Poland's post-Communist party system development from 1991 to 1992, Lewis (1995) emphasized the importance of established support and strong organization in explaining the relative success of the ex-Communist Alliance of the Democratic Left (SLD) and the ex-satellite Polish Peasants Party (PSL) in the 1991 parliamentary election (Table 21). In 1991, both parties had relatively large formal memberships—60,000 and 150,000, respectively (the largest among all Polish parties). The electoral results of the early 1993 parliamentary election support his observations (Table 22). The SLD and the Polish Peasants Party substantially improved their positions to first and second, respectively. Lewis's observation that a low turnout tends to favor more organized parties seemed to apply to both elections.

When compared with the situation in the neighboring countries, the position of political parties in Hungary was stronger from the very beginning, because the anti-Communist opposition was already divided into several distinct political groups that became the core of the new parties. Szarvas (1995), who studied parties and party factions in the Hungarian parliament between 1990 and 1994, found that party factions voted together very frequently, because the individualism of the deputies was controlled by "group discipline." Indeed, the degree of unanimity in voting factions was remarkably high (between 89 and 97 percent) and resembled the situation in the Western European democracies. The total dominance of "standard parties" in the Hungarian parliament was symbolically marked by the "conversion" of the Federation of Young Democrats to a party model in 1993 and completed by the victory of the Hungarian Socialist Party (MSZP), the ex-

Communist Party that was considered to be the most professional party (of those represented in parliament) in Hungary (Lomax 1995).

The rise of political parties, however, did not stop with their victories over the poorly organized, movement-type political actors in the electoral battles. Taking advantage of the relatively weak nongovernmental organizations and the generally underdeveloped civic society in the post-Communist countries, parties proceeded to increase their influence in the narrowly defined political space. Yet they were not particularly successful in organizing themselves, and the Communists and former satellite parties continued to lose members. Although newly established parties were able to build a basic network of local organizations and to recruit some members in the early nineties (Lewis 1996), the image of politics as a dirty business quickly became a serious barrier to growth. Indeed, after several years of democratic rule most parties, including successful ones, had to struggle with a serious lack of party activists and apathy among the rank-and-file party members. Yet despite parties' inability to better penetrate society organizationally, they successfully increased their influence into most spheres of public life. Meanwhile, they remained rather elite, internally dominated by the core group at headquarters and increasingly powerful (Ágh 1998). The ongoing economic transformation created an extraordinarily supportive environment for this development.

All the parties that succeeded in the first free elections naturally sought reelection. For successful parties, the first step toward achievement of their strategic goals was to monopolize power on the electoral scene in order to reduce their chances of being replaced by the other political actors. This tactic, which was used by bigger parties against smaller parties, was described in Chapter 5 in its discussion of the influence of electoral laws on party development. The electoral legislation adopted by parliaments and dominated by political parties generally "favored parties over meso-political organizations, for example, over organized interests and civil society associations" (Ágh 1998). Having dominated national parliaments, parties had the strength to set the rules of the electoral game. Their subsequent success in elections was used to legitimize their right to interfere in any aspect of public life, including those aspects quite unrelated to the political sphere. In all conflicts between parties and any nongovernmental organization or professional association, parties did not miss the chance to claim that they, unlike their opponents, were elected by voters, which gave only them the mandate to decide about anything.

Parties also sought to reduce the opportunity for independent candidates and ad hoc political associations to participate in local elections. In the

Czech Republic, for example, when the parties dominating parliament realized from the local election results that they could easily be defeated by independent candidates in most municipalities, they changed the electoral law. The new provision required independent candidates or an association of independent candidates to collect supportive signatures from a certain percentage of voters in the municipality before the election in order to participate in the contest at all. As the number of signatures increased in tandem with the growing size of the municipalities, it became much easier to establish new nationwide political parties that ran as independents in the mid-sized and bigger cities (Kostelecký 1996). Similarly, the law adopted in early 2000 governing election to the Czech Republic's regional parliaments allows, quite illogically, only nationwide political parties to participate in the regional electoral races.

In addition to their struggle against potential competitors on the political scene, parties had to gain access to the media and to financial resources. All four countries studied experienced a battle over the media, although they differed in its intensity and timing. Poland had less difficulty in this area because of its tradition of decentralization and power sharing that made any attempt by parties to monopolize control over the media less probable. By contrast, in Hungary, the Czech Republic and Slovakia, the battle over the media was always a big part of party politics. In Hungary, the conflict over control of the media was especially heated in 1991 and 1992 when the conservative government attempted to gain direct control of the electronic media. In Slovakia, the struggle over the media was particularly important after the HZDS's electoral victory in 1994. Mečiar's government proceeded to transform public television into a conduit for pro-government propaganda. On the other hand, Mečiar's opposition was backed by the private station TV Markíza and most of the daily newspapers.[4] In the Czech Republic, political parties influenced the media in a more sophisticated way than direct control. They sought to influence public TV by interfering in its broadcast (including the list of participants) of the popular and influential political debates. This interference became publicly known after the resignation of the director of public TV in early 2000. The private electronic media were influenced through broadcasting boards, members of which were nominated by the parliament—that is, by the parties.

The most obvious sign of the growing power of political parties was their deep penetration into the economy. The ongoing process of economic transformation gave the parties an extraordinary opportunity to take advantage of their position as decision makers at both the national and the local levels of government. The governing parties not only made numerous decisions to privatize state-owned industries, but also exercised influence over not-yet-privatized companies and those semi-owned by the state. Thus political parties, on the lookout for funds for their campaign coffers, became an easy target for bribery by potentially big investors and semi-state-owned companies. Moreover, parties served as a kind of patron organization for members looking for business opportunities in the privatization of enterprises.

The increasingly shady relations among political parties, privatization, and business had at least two political consequences. The ways in which parties dealt with their financial matters increasingly transformed them into what Ágh (1998) aptly calls "cartel parties"—that is, mostly top-down institutions held together by the mutual economic and power interests of their memberships and rather hostile to newcomers. The second consequence was that many of the political issues raised by competing parties only pretended to be an expression of some societal conflict; in reality, they were simply fights over financial resources and business influences among competing business-political groups. Because the process of privatization took longer than expected and because, in the meantime, the first generation of reformers was replaced by the opposition, almost no relevant parties were able to avoid the pattern just described.

Despite the frequency with which the parties in power in the countries studied underwent financial scandals of various types, the parties involved usually were not punished too much (if at all) by the voters in the next elections. Ágh (1998, 209) even argued that, after privatization, the separation of political and economic interests would be impossible. He foresaw only two options for countries in East-Central Europe: either the "Italian road" as a partist democracy with a clientele system and structural connections between politics and business, or the "Austrian model" as some kind of neo-corporatist democracy[5] with regulated relationships and without an articulated separation of these two worlds.

As this section has looked back at the decade of post-Communist political development, it has become more than clear that political parties as institutions emerged from the process as the single most successful political institution.

Toward Rational Choice Based on Interests

Shortly before the results of the parliamentary election in 1992 were officially proclaimed, pensioners sitting on a bench in one of Prague's parks were asked by a journalist whom they voted for and why. One of the old ladies replied, "I voted for Klaus because he has good posture. I was always told I should have good posture when I was a child and I do really appreciate somebody who walks with good posture."

Her answer demonstrates the value of considering voters' rationality or irrationality. Theoretically, two extremes are possible. Voters can be perceived as completely irrational, driven by momentary feelings, sympathies, and hopes in their electoral decisions, or they can be considered entirely rational, able to evaluate their social position, define their personal and group interests, analyze the political programs and the credibility of individual parties, and finally vote for the party that will maximize their personal benefits. For a study of party development in the post-Communist era, the rational choice approach seems far more promising than any other, because it allows the formulation of a logical framework within which, among other things, the relationships among different economic, social, and political phenomena can be evaluated and the causes and the consequences identified (Przeworski 1991; Kitschelt 1992; Pacek 1994). The use of the rational choice approach may not be legitimate, however, because its application requires the presence of several conditions. This discussion will leave aside the main condition—the assumption that people are profit-seeking individuals,[6] which seems confirmed by the numerous empirical economic studies as well as by people's own daily experience—and will concentrate on the other prerequisites.

It is commonly assumed that people's voting preferences are based on their rational reflections of the relationship between themselves and the world that surrounds them. After all, if their electoral decisions were absolutely independent of what was going on outside of their own minds, there would hardly be much to study. In reality, though, the origins of many political attitudes are endogenous, with only a few or even no identifiable links to the social structures and ongoing processes in society. Thus Przeworski (1991), studying the interconnections between different strategies of economic reform and the popular reaction to them, notes that popular confidence plays a crucial role in economic reform and stresses that "this confidence is to a large extent endogenous. The reason is that people do not know in fact how costly and how long the transition will be." This finding is empirically well documented by the results of opinion polls conducted in March 1990 in both the Czech Republic and Slovakia that is, before (!) any economic reforms began and any consequences could be perceived. Even though unemployment was virtually absent in either republic, 34 percent of the Slovak respondents agreed that "unemployment should be avoided even at the cost of significantly restraining or even suspending economic reform," and 47 percent of them agreed that "the state should bear complete responsibility for finding employment for every citizen." The respective percentages for Czech respondents were 19 percent and 32 percent (Skalnik Leff 1997). Similarly, Bútorová, Gyarfásová, and Kúska (1996) note that a sociological survey conducted before large-scale privatization began in Czechoslovakia revealed that the attitudes of the Slovak population toward this process were rather mistrustful and disapproving.

Another condition that must be met to use the rational choice approach in politics is that people, once they are able to evaluate their position in society and their real interests, must be able to understand the basic principles of democracy, recognize the differences among parties and, finally, cast their votes in their interests. In the period shortly after the fall of communism, this condition probably was not met. It is not surprising that people facing the reality of huge political, economic, and social changes and having no or only limited experience with a democracy and a market economy were rather disoriented. Many people had a naive belief that the shift to a market economy would quickly bring about a much-improved material base. Former Polish prime minister Jan Krzysztof Bielecki was quoted as saying, "We obtained the agreement for the building of a market economy from a people not completely aware of what a market system stands for" (Donnorummo 1994). The lack of understanding of the basic rules of the new system was also well documented by the results of various sociological surveys. When asked in an international comparative research survey conducted in 1991 about their opinions on what is most important in a democracy, the respondents from post-Communist countries differed sharply from their Western European counterparts. Their responses suggested that they equated democracy more with economic prosperity and security than with liberal democratic values. More specifically, 42 percent of Poles and 35 percent of Hungarians surveyed thought the most important feature of a democracy was economic prosperity, and only 13 percent and 21 percent considered the most important feature to be a system of justice that treats everyone equally—the most frequent answer in the Western countries surveyed (McIntosh and Mac Iver 1993).

The examples of voters' confusion over political issues are numerous. For example, many people in the Czech Republic prefer housing to be "all private" and yet strongly approve of state rent subsidies no matter the cost. Similarly, larger-than-marginal groups of respondents have declared that the economy in general should be "all state-owned" and that small businesses should be "all private" (Kostelecký 1995c). In another example, a large share of Slovak voters "supported the existence of an independent Slovakia within a federal Czechoslovakia" and opted for Slovakia to become a member of the North Atlantic Treaty Organization (NATO) while maintaining neutrality (Bútorová, Gyarfásová, and Kúska 1996).

Given the economic situation just before the economic reforms and the one in the first months or even years after the reforms were implemented, such voter confusion is not surprising. In Poland, where the situation was the most drastic, the annualized consumer price index during the last five months of 1989—that is, before the onset of economic reforms—stood at about 3,000 percent and inflation for the year at 640 percent (Balcerowicz 1994). What kind of rational economic decisions could one make under such conditions? Although the macroeconomic conditions in Hungary and Czechoslovakia were not as bad as in Poland, how could the voters rationally decide whether to support the political party devoted to shock therapy or the party advertising a more gradual approach toward economic reforms? Or whether the best privatization method was the direct sale of state enterprises to managers, employees, and foreign firms, or the voucher method of privatization?[7]

An additional complication is the fact that interests, however they are defined, can be both short term and long term. For example, a cut in subsidies or the lifting of price controls on food may immediately result in a price increase that nobody deserves, but it also can lead to an end to food shortages and to better-quality products, because new producers and importers will emerge with the possibility of making a profit. Even the price of food can fall in the long run if the competition increases. In another example, one party may promise state employees a substantial increase in wages, but what if such a pay hike also increases inflation and devalues higher salaries? And yet another example: How can voters rationally assess the credibility and competence of political parties that came into existence only several months earlier? In fact, the situation in the early post-Communist societies shows that it is exceptionally challenging to determine which decision is a rational one. Moreover, the absorption of the civic society by the state made it very difficult for individuals to define their particular interests because of the missing connections between individual and group interests.

The situation just described has had several consequences. The great importance of the subjective factors that influence the voting decision, a fact stressed by many students of early post-Communist politics, is one of the most visible. While describing the situation in Hungary, Glatz (1995) points out that subjective factors influence political thinking to a greater degree in Hungary than in Western Europe and that habitual attitudes are much more significant for the politically active generations than in the West. Similarly, Körösényi (1991) describes early post-Communist Hungary as a segmented society with various cleavages "which are not institutionalized, but live in the inherited attitudes, instincts and memories of the people." Marody (1995), characterizing the different stages of the emergence of a party system in Poland, reminds his readers that the first Polish political parties elected in 1989 arose from either ideological or personal divisions in the parliament. In his empirical study of the process of the development of political preferences, Raciborski (1993) identifies four basic ideological orientations of voters: social democratic, nationally Catholic, liberal, and populist. The choice of party is close to a voter's ideological orientation, but the ideological orientation itself is not a product of the voter's position within the social structure. Similarly, investigators have pointed out the importance of ideological rather than social or economic cleavages in explaining the voting behavior of both Czech (Kostelecký 1993a) and Slovak voters (Szomolányi and Mesežnikov 1995). Finally, Musil (1995), in trying to summarize the reason for the political split between the Czech Republic and Slovakia, stresses the importance of the long-term ideological differences between these two nations and their political relevance in the post-Communist period.

Because voters in East-Central Europe encountered difficulty in rationally defining individual or group material interests, they searched for other frames of reference that could make the voting decision easier. As a result, a large group of voters derived their political attitudes from their national, regional, or religious identity or from their attitudes toward history. The electoral results reflected this situation. Several nationalist parties emerged in the region and gained seats in the respective parliaments, and some historical parties were reestablished. Religious affiliation became one of the strongest underlying factors influencing voters' decisions (Körösényi 1991; Kostelecký 1994). The political issues connected with these sorts of collective identities were among the most controversial, even overshadowing conflicts over the economic reform strategy. Many scholars point out that in Poland, Slovakia, and Hungary the main political division in the first period after the fall of communism was not based on the polarity between supporters and opponents of the free market (Körösényi 1991; Kitschelt 1992; Gortat and Marciniak 1995; Szomolányi 1995; Tóka 1995a). The Czech Republic is sometimes noted as the exception to this general observation, because its main political cleavages were based primarily on economic issues from the very beginning (Brokl 1996; Krause 1996). Meanwhile, Czechs were dealing with another phenomenon: identity politics, stemming from the existence of a common state with Slovakia.

Another frame of reference used by voters was the so-called valence issues—that is, the issues that revolve more around the question of "Who can do this job better?" than around differences in actual policies (Evans and Whitefield 1993). Simply put, unable to distinguish which political program is better, voters try to distinguish who is more competent to serve as leader. The empirical research suggests that in most of the post-Communist countries studied the voters' evaluation of a politician's competence influenced voting decisions more than the voters' evaluation of their own personal situation. This was true both in the Czech Republic and in Slovakia for the 1990 and 1992 elections (Yancis 1994) and for Hungary in the 1990 election (Tóka 1995a).

As the transformation proceeded, however, the situation began to change. From the political point of view, the most visible outcome of the economic reforms in all of the post-Communist countries was the rise of social and economic inequalities (Večerník 1996). But because all the societies studied were rather egalitarian under communism, even the relatively quick rise in inequalities in the region did not lead to extreme differences between the poor and the rich such as those found in the developing world. In fact, quite the opposite was true; comparative sociological surveys conducted in 1992 revealed that inequalities in Czechoslovakia, Poland, and Hungary were less significant than those in Western Europe. Nevertheless, the people perceived a rise in inequalities, and perceptions are what really matters in politics (Brokl 1996). The real increase in inequalities was further strengthened by the feeling of relative deprivation. The economy may have been recovering and the gross domestic product and household real incomes may have been rising, but people felt poorer when comparing their incomes with the more quickly rising ones of their more educated, harder working, or simply more fortunate neighbors. According to empirical analyses of sociological surveys, people indeed tended to perceive the inequalities as bigger than they were in reality (Körösényi 1995; Machonin et al. 1996). The changes generated by the economic reforms included the creation of a group of private owners and the growth of unemployment. The changes also led to increasing differences between those working in the private sector, where salaries were more or less based on market evaluation, and those working for the state, where salaries were more dependent on state redistribution.

The political consequences of the changes became more visible as the social differences became more obvious. While studying the development of the relationships between political attitudes and social stratification in the Czech Republic between 1991 and 1993, Machonin et al. (1996) concluded that attitudes are increasingly determined by the position of the respondent in the social structure. Similarly, Kéri and Levendel (1995), writing about the development of the Hungarian political spectrum after the 1990 parliamentary election, note that "the monthly opinion polls indicated that the social backgrounds of the individual parties were slowly being clarified." Večerník (1996), referring to the results of sociological surveys, points out that the link between people's economic situation and their self-placement on the political spectrum has been growing stronger for several years in all four of the countries studied. Also, the importance of the classical class cleavage increased as the workers tended to vote more frequently for the left-oriented parties (Matějů and Řeháková 1997). Finally, it is reported that survey respondents' political self-identification as a liberal or conservative also has become more closely connected with party choice (Šimoník 1996). Although politics is not one-dimensional and several different factors shape voting decisions, the increasing importance of purely economic factors is a reality on both the individual and the aggregate levels. Voters of lower social status—that is, those who consider themselves to be losers in the reform process—have increasingly tended to vote for left-oriented parties. Similarly, the popularity of left-wing parties is rising among the people living in regions with higher unemployment ("Bulletin of Electoral Statistics" 1994; Kostelecký 1994; Pacek 1994).

The other consequence of the sometimes painful process of learning how a democracy and market economy work was the growing pragmatism behind and rationality of voting decisions. The daily problems of life seemed to take precedence over questions of morality, the Communists' guilt for the totalitarian regime, or even nationalism. Körösényi (1995), in explaining the victory of the Hungarian Socialists, points out that "the electorate—at least the part of it that decided the election—is, by and large, pragmatic: ideological slogans, questions of historical justice, and a moral approach to the past leave it cold." For Hungarian Socialists, the image of good administrators proved to be more important than their "politically incorrect" history.

Indeed, as early as 1992, opinion polls suggested that Hungarian voters did not hold prior Communist membership against those who were believed to have done a good job while in office. Thus former Communists Miklós Németh and Gyula Horn were judged to be the best and the second-best candidates, respectively, for the position of prime minister (Pataki 1992). And apparently this was a trend in the region. In the 1995 presidential election, traditionally strong anti-Communist Poles favored longtime Communist apparatchik Aleksander Kwaśniweski over the former leader of the anti-Communist opposition Lech Wałęsa and were indifferent to arguments from Walesa who warned the nation about the danger of a return to communism. Similarly, the strong decommunization campaign of some Hungarian parties before the 1993 parliamentary election did not pay off among the voters (Wiatr 1993). Quite the contrary, the post-Communists, perceived as a party that cares "about the interests of the ordinary man and not of an abstract society" (Marody 1995), somewhat surprisingly won the contest.

In the Czech Republic, the former Czech minister of economy and trade, Vladimír Dlouhý, a member of every post-Communist government until 1997 and the most popular politician in the country for several years, was praised for his professional qualities and his work. Apparently, though, about 70 percent of the respondents who appreciated his work did not care that he became minister of the first postrevolutionary Government of National Understanding as a nominee of the Communist Party, which he left only after several months in office to join, somewhat paradoxically, the right wing of the Civic Forum. Dlouhý's fortune began to decline in 1996, when the economy felt the first tremors of the foreign trade deficit for which he was held responsible.

Finally, a more pragmatic and rational choice-oriented approach by the voters was demonstrated by the sinking fortunes of highly ideological nationalist parties such as the Slovak National Party and the Confederation for Independent Poland. Moreover, the Society for Moravia and Silesia in the Czech Republic practically disappeared, and Istvan Csurka's Hungarian Justice and Life Party produced a poor record.

Party development in Slovakia only partially fits the scheme just described. During the period 1989–1992, the crucial question in Slovak politics was national sovereignty, and the majority of Slovak politicians dealt with all political issues, including the biggest post-Communist ones such as the establishment of a democratic system, economic reform, and the future orientation of foreign policy, in relation to the fundamental "national question." Every proposal by the Czechoslovak federal government and every bill discussed in the federal parliament of Czechoslovakia were evaluated from the point of view of Czech-Slovak relations. In this political environment it became quickly obvious that the main divisive issue within Slovak politics was that of the level of Slovak national sovereignty within (or out of) a common state with Czechs.

It is very hard to judge the interests aimed at strengthening the sovereignty of the nation in terms of rationality. Some people calling for Slovak independence were perfectly rational, such as those members of the political elite hoping to obtain lucrative diplomatic or administration posts. Other supporters of Slovak independence were completely irrational, such as those who believed in the immediate economic recovery of the Slovak economy after the split of Czechoslovakia. They believed that the split would put an end to the subsidies from Slovakia to the Czech Republic. They failed to consider, however, the considerable money transfers from the Czech Republic to Slovakia. Similarly, the arguments of the opponents of Slovak independence were both irrational (an independent Slovakia would fall into total chaos and would be immediately attacked by Hungarian and Russian troops) and rational (the Slovak economy would weaken and Slovak companies would lose many of their Czech customers).

Although one would expect the political behavior based on the conflicts surrounding sovereignty and statehood to change after the creation of an independent Slovakia, quite the opposite was true. Perhaps because of the process of nation building and the problems associated with the split of Czechoslovakia and the constitution of the independent state, "politics based on the search for identity rather than on the recognition of interest" was still observed in 1994 by Slovak political scientists (Malová 1995). According to the Slovak sociologist Soňa Szomolányi (1995), in this respect Slovakia was somewhere between the Central European and southeastern European models[8]—a position caused mainly by the political split between the "standard" and "nonstandard" parties. The opposition, made up of the "standard" parties, represented the whole spectrum of parties from conservative through Christian Democratic and liberal to social democratic and socialist based on the classical political cleavages in society. The governing coalition of "nonstandard parties" was very unclear in its program[9] and hardly capable of being defined politically.

Although those who voted for the ruling coalition had a generally lower level of education than those who voted for the opposition, the split in Slovak politics was not based primarily on social cleavages but rather on different attitudes and values. For example, it has been reported that voters for the government coalition tended to lean toward authoritarianism—their most important feature (Mesežnikov 1995). As conflicts between Mečiar's

government and the opposition deepened, the links between social structures and party structures became even vaguer. A rather heterogeneous and
ideologically fuzzy bloc of governing parties led by Mečiar stood against a
bloc of opposition parties similarly heterogeneous and ideologically un-
specified. They were connected by not too much more than the common desire to remove Mečiar from office.

The founding of the Party of Civil Understanding (SOP) only six months
before the parliamentary election scheduled in September 1998 did not help
to clarify the Slovak political scene, because the SOP remained as vague in
its political orientation as the two largest political parties. The astonishing
rise in the opinion polls in early 2000 of Smer, a party founded by popular
former SDL deputy Robert Fico, is exactly the same story; the one-man
party with almost no political program became the second most popular
party in the country soon after its founding. It seems that Slovak politics is
still quite far from politics based on rational choice and on the interests of
different social groups—that is, if one does not consider the interests and
rational choices of most of the political elite seeking either to maintain or
to obtain cozy political posts.

Toward a More Clearly Structured Politics? A "Limited Convergence" Hypothesis

Although no party system anywhere is literally frozen in place (despite the
accurate and popular thesis proposed in 1967 by Lipset and Rokkan on
frozen party systems in Western Europe), the speed and the depth of party
system changes in post-Communist East-Central Europe clearly cannot be
compared with the situation in any consolidated Western democracy. The
observed highs and lows of individual parties, the party splits and merges,
the high volatility of voter behavior, and the inconsistent party policies and
frequent changes in ideological positions may well lead students of these
processes to doubt the quality of the democratic system or even the future
of democracy itself in the post-Communist world. This section will argue,
however, that the four countries studied have manifested an observable pattern of developing more structured and stable politics. This argument may
serve as a source of limited optimism about the stabilization of the new
democracies. In any case, it is necessary to keep in mind the dynamic character of the party systems that moved through several distinct stages during
the 1990s. Given the variations in individual countries, it is hardly possible

to speak about any general "rule" shaping the political development of the region, but some trends are definitely common to all the countries observed.

Soon after the fall of communism, the political spectrums of the observed countries were highly polarized. The main political and ideological split was represented by the cleavage between the Communists and the opposition, sometimes described as the difference between us and them. Following this basic scheme, the first elections had a rather plebiscitary character in which voters had to decide between the Communist past and the non-Communist future. The fact that many possible and rather different non-Communist futures existed, was not the key issue in the election. The situation in Hungary was somewhat different probably because of the more liberal character of the Communist regime in the 1980s. Although opinion polls in mid-1989 showed that a reformed Communist might win the free election, such a win was not perceived as a fatal threat for the future of the country and did not lead an ideologically and organizationally divided opposition to join into a kind of grand anti-Communist coalition as in the neighboring countries. After communism was generally rejected by the voters in the first free elections, the question about how the society should look in the future became more prominent.

The emerging party systems, however, were not very easy to survey. The main problem was that the link between social structures and political parties was not well established during the first post-Communist years. In fact, Wessels and Klingemann (1994) use the term *flattened societies* to describe the early post-Communist situation in which unclear and quickly changing social structures prevented citizens from defining their political interests. The cleavage theory assumes that some divisions within society are reflected by political parties. But for this to happen, such divisions have to be recognized by the voters. Thus relevant here are three different structures that may or may not correspond. These structures are: the structural (objective) divisions among various groups of voters, the ideological (subjective) divisions in the voters' minds, and the institutional, ideological, and policy divisions among political parties. In a typical Western European frozen party system, some of the social divisions were perceived as politically relevant by the voters and were simultaneously reflected by the political parties. The result was a functional and relatively stable political system, because the social divisions, which gave ground to both the subjective perceptions of voters and the party system, did not change quickly in a normal situation. The post-Communist transformations, however, were anything but a normal situation. Just after the fall of communism in the region, not only was the link "'social divisions–voters' perceptions–party system'" not established, but also all segments of the scheme were undergoing simultaneous change. Yet what sometimes looked like almost total chaos to the distant observer proved over the long run to have some logic. Some of the social divisions, such as ethnic or religious differences, were perceived by the majority of voters as politically relevant from the very beginning, and thus they constituted cleavages in the proper sense of the word. As the economic transformations proceeded, the rise of inequalities, the differing perspectives of various social groups of the labor market, and the gradual creation of a class of employers also were increasingly perceived as politically relevant. Thus many existing noneconomic cleavages persisted while economic cleavages gradually developed, and the once almost uniform anti-Communist ideological space became richer and more clearly structured.

Although other approaches to structuring ideological space in post-Communist East-Central Europe in the 1990s have been used, two features are common to practically all attempts to find some analytical framework to describe the post-Communist ideologies and politics. The first common feature is the inappropriate use of the traditional one-dimensional left–right continuum in which the right is associated with conservatism, traditions, and a free-market economy, and the left is connected with modernity and a higher regulatory role for the state in the economy (Kitschelt 1992). Although the traditional one-dimensional, left–right scheme was used successfully for many decades in describing the main political division within the majority of Western societies, it has not been without its critics. Gellner (1991, 497), for example, noticed that the use of this scheme tends to hide the fact that there are in fact two quite different right-wing ideologies. One is represented by a "commitment to an unframed free market," and the other is represented by a "commitment to hierarchy, authority and tradition." The mix of both types of right-wing ideologies constituted the "traditional Right" in the nineteenth and twentieth centuries, although this connection seems to be illogical, and it is likely that both right-wing ideologies were in strong opposition to each other. Similarly illogical, however, seems to be the ideology of the "traditional Left," because it combines an emphasis on individual freedom with an emphasis on the regulatory role of the state in the economy. The conceptual disconnection of economic and noneconomic aspects of the traditional one-dimensional left–right scheme appears to be useful anywhere, but particularly so when studying the ideological space in an early post-Communist society. Most students of the post-Communist political space, regardless of whether they started from some theoretical considerations or were just performing empirical analyses of political attitudes, came to the same conclusion. Generally, the proposed analytical frameworks are two-, three-, or even four-dimensional, and political parties and their voters can be placed somewhere on the ideological space according to their position vis-á-vis the main ideological cleavages represented by the individual axes of the scheme.

The second feature common to all attempts to generalize the post-Communist ideological space is the presence of the economic dimension in any explanatory scheme. It is used to describe the different attitudes of both politicians and voters toward the role of the state in the economy. Although many scholars and others agree that the economic dimension or cleavage is important, opinions vary greatly about the other possible dimensions. In discussions of Poland, the church–state cleavage (also called religiosity versus secularism or particularism versus universalism) is most often mentioned as a second axis in any explanatory scheme, independent on the economic dimension (Wiatr 1992; Jasiewicz 1993; Raciborski 1993; Zukowski 1993). However, other dimensions of Polish political ideologies also have been identified such as the split between nationalism and a pro-Western option (Gebethner 1993; Jasiewicz 1993), the split between authoritarianism and parliamentary democracy (Jasiewicz 1993), and the cleavage based on different attitudes toward decommunization (Jasiewicz 1993). The search for other noneconomic dimensions of political ideologies is not so complicated in the other three countries studied. In Hungary, the main noneconomic cleavage is represented by the division between the traditional "Christian-national" and "liberal-cosmopolitan" streams in Hungarian politics (Lomax 1995; Bigler 1996), sometimes referred to as the traditionalist/collectivist versus the modernist/individualist cleavage (Tóka 1995a). In Slovakia, the second dimension of political space is described as the division between those supporting and those opposing authoritarianism and nationalism. And finally, in Czech politics the main noneconomic political cleavage is that found between traditionalism and libertarianism (Brokl 1994) or, in other words, between those who incline toward tradition and order and those who prefer modernity and cultural individualism (Kostelecký 1995b).

Is there anything common to all these noneconomic dimensions of the political space? All of the dimensions mentioned appear to be various expressions of the basic difference between those who believe that individuals should have the right to determine their own values and to follow their own norms and those who oppose this right, believing that the values to be shared and norms to be followed should be collective. Because many collective identities, values, and norms exist, the noneconomic dimensions along which political space is structured also can be numerous. For example, nationalists believe that whatever is good for the nation is good for each citizen of the state. Traditionalists believe that whatever is traditional is good for everybody. Supporters of a big role for the church in society believe that such a role will also be a blessing for nonbelievers. And authoritarian leaders and their voters believe that their solutions are best for everyone. In fact, the classical economic cleavage is also about freedom in the economic choices of both individuals and corporations, because support for the free market means nothing other than support for more freedom for economic actors based on their own profit-maximizing decisions. State paternalism, by contrast, is a sort of implementation of collective decisions intended to serve the collective well-being.

The four major political orientations identified by Jasiewicz (1997) in Poland (which are also present in the Czech Republic and Hungary and partially in Slovakia) fit well into the basic framework of existing ideological space presented here. The liberal democratic sector is defined by support for a free market combined with an emphasis on individual freedom and a secular and nontraditionalist state. Conservatism and a Christian Democratic orientation are defined by pro-free-market attitudes together with support for traditions and respect for Christian norms and values in the state. The basic characteristic of social democratic ideas is a greater state role in the economy, together with an emphasis on individual freedom and secularism. Finally, the authoritarian (populist) ideology is defined by a combination of authoritarian and nationalist attitudes with support for state intervention in the economy.

When the explanatory scheme described here is generalized to the maximum degree possible, the ideological space within which both voters and political parties can be placed looks like the diagram in Figure 1. The basic political orientations displayed in Figure 1 are very similar to those in Western European politics. In this respect, the post-Communist countries studied are clearly close to the classical Western European model of politics. The problem, however, is that the ideological divisions in the Western European model (what people think about politics, what values they share, what they believe in) may not have the same meaning in East-Central Europe. In classical Western European form, ideological divisions reflected the interests of socially defined groups in politics. In other words, political ideologies mirrored social structures. On the other hand, political parties were established to represent the political ideologies found in the realm of

Figure 1

Major Ideological Dimensions of Politics in Post-Communist East-Central Europe.

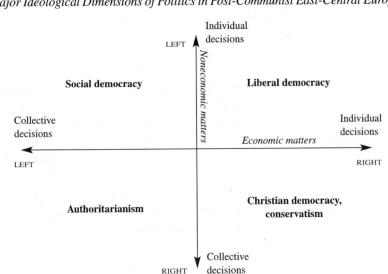

practical politics. Thus in an ideal case, real politics mirrored the theoretical causal chain social structure–ideological space–political parties in a way that was both internally consistent and functional: different interest groups within the society created their own different political ideologies and own parties. But is such an ideal situation found in the post-Communist countries? Here a look at the relations among social structures, ideologies, and political parties may be helpful.

Describing the relationship between the development of social structures and the political attitudes and beliefs of voters seems to be the easier part of the problem. It has been documented that over the 1990s the political attitudes and beliefs of voters in the post-Communist countries increasingly were in accord with the personal characteristics of their social groups. However, the relationship between the social position of individual voters and their ideological preferences was relatively weak in comparison to that found in the classical cleavage model in the era of mass parties. For example, it is still true that a surprisingly large share of homeowners believe that tenants' rent should be regulated by the state, and a high percentage of poor pensioners support the privatization of the health care system, but the general trend is toward fewer such views. A tenant may believe that the rental sector works best when free-market rents are in effect, but, if ever unemployed while living in a flat with state-regulated rent, the tenant may look much more favorably on more state involvement in the housing sector. Another person could generally support the idea of individual freedom to use drugs, but turn toward a more restrictive and authoritative approach if faced with drug-related crime in the neighborhood.

Although people's political beliefs are far from a simple reflection of their position in the social structure, the latter has a growing influence on their position in ideological space. People may attain their ideological beliefs from almost anywhere, but life experience is always important. And the previous life path, the contemporary situation, and the possibility of opportunities in the future are increasingly based on a person's position in the social structure. As for voters' attitudes toward the scope of the state's involvement in the economy, the most important structural factors are education, income, age, status, class, and the center–periphery cleavage. In all the countries studied, higher education predicts a higher adherence to free-market principles and less state involvement in the economy. People who are better off financially also tend to support the free market to a greater extent than others. Similarly, younger generations, voters with higher social status, white-collar workers, entrepreneurs, and people living in more prosperous centers lean toward the free-market end of an economic axis in the scheme. The noneconomic cleavages seem to be even more connected to the ascriptive characteristics of individuals and structurally defined social groups. The most important indicators of the position of voters on the noneconomic axis of the ideological scheme are education, religiosity, age, ethnicity, and urban–rural cleavage. Less-educated, older, and more religious people tended to support more traditional and authoritative ideologies. Similarly, the rural population leans toward the more traditionalist and collectivist ideologies. Ethnic structure becomes a prominent factor underlying the ideological divisions in ethnically heterogeneous countries.

The relations between social structures and the ideological positions of voters may be relatively easy to describe, but the chaotic political party scene of the early 1990s is not. Because the big umbrella type of opposition movements was not able to maintain either political or organizational unity, many new parties were established, various factions within the existing parties emerged, parties split and merged, and many deputies in parliament moved from one party to another. Although some splits were based on bad personal relations rather than different attitudes to political issues, and many parties were established following the logic that it is better to be the chairman of a small party than the deputy chairman of a larger one, the ideological differences among various political parties or groups of parties gradually became more visible. In fact, the existing ideological space framed the political activity of existing parties and defined, to a great extent, their main allies and opponents. Although several of the new ad hoc alliances and coalitions were unrelated to the ideological positions of the involved parties, they did not represent mainstream party behavior and, moreover, usually did not last for long. When several small parties sought to appeal to a constituency in competition with other small parties ideologically similar, the typical party strategy was either to present itself as the best representative of its own political ideology or present itself as the strongest opponent of the most antagonistic political ideology.

Some parties proved more viable and gained popular support in elections; others failed to exceed thresholds and, without parliamentary representation, soon became politically marginal. The more successful parties tended to dominate their own ideological space, the less successful ones tended to disappear or merge with the more successful ones. Sometimes only the most publicly known representatives of unsuccessful parties joined the bigger parties. Could a process resembling natural selection lead in theory to the establishment of a relatively transparent but limited system of big parties, each representing one of the main political ideologies? Natural selection, however, was only part of the story on the party scene. Two other complications in effect made the whole process of party system formation more complex and less predictable.

The first complication was the fact that parties not only merged but also split. Moreover, after the initial splits of the umbrella-type anti-Communist movements, most of the party divisions were not based on profound ideological differences between splitting parties but rather were the consequence of fierce battles over party leadership, personal aversions among party leaders, and an intolerance of minority opinions within the party. Because practically all early post-Communist parties were rather weak organizationally, dependent more on the fame of their most popular leaders than on strong local and regional party organizations, popular party figures not satisfied with their position within the party hierarchy found it relatively easy to build a new party. Many of the new splinter parties did not differ much from their mother party. Trying to disassociate themselves from their ideological counterparts, new parties tended to emphasize minor or even alleged differences, which made it even more difficult for voters to understand the party system.

The second complication in party development was the fact that many parties were not affiliated with any particular ideology. Indeed, many of them had no history, no political traditions, and only a limited membership, and were under the strong influence of party leaders. Taking advantage of these factors, those leaders were able to change even substantial aspects of their party's program in order to achieve a temporary political advantage without much opposition from within the party or the party constituency. Some leaders were even fonder of formally proclaiming the basic tenets of a party ideology in order to maintain support from ideologically oriented core voters, but acting freely with few ideological constraints in practical party policies. Some parties even changed their basic ideological positions in an attempt to fill the empty ideological space left by some declining party.

Now let us return to the theoretical causal chain of classical cleavage theory, which begins with the structural (objective) divisions among various groups of voters, proceeds to the ideological (subjective) divisions in the voters' minds, and ends with the institutional, ideological, and policy divisions among political parties. The discussion in this chapter leads to the conclusion that this model only partially works in post-Communist East-Central Europe. Although ideological divisions are increasingly anchored in social structures, party systems reflect both objective and subjective divisions only to a limited extent. Because of the institutional instability of parties, the "early freezing hypothesis" formulated by Olson (1993), may be partially applicable.[10] In other words, even though the social structures and ideological divisions among voters are "freezing," as well as the mutual relationship between those two, the party systems are not yet firmly connected to the rest of the society. Thus party systems could even be "early frozen"—that is, relatively stable but not really properly serving as translators of social tensions and cleavages into politics.

All this leads back to the question: To what extent is it realistic to expect party systems in East-Central Europe to resemble the classical Western European cleavage model? The problem is that the Western European party systems themselves have undergone profound changes over the last few decades. Such changes have usually taken the form of a decline in party memberships, an erosion of links between social groups and parties, an increase in the volatility of voters' electoral decisions, and an expansion of the corporatist pattern of policy making (Lane and Ersson 1991). Moreover, party systems tend to be more unstable than they used to be. New political parties such as the Greens entered the political arena for the first time in the seventies (Richardson and Rootes 1995), and the traditional parties in Western Europe have been losing their ideological and organizational stability.

A comparison of the situations in Western Europe and East-Central

Europe reveals, then, that party development in Western Europe (labeled the "new politics" by Müller-Rommel 1989; Müller-Rommel and Poguntke 1995) has taken almost the opposite path from that taken by party development in post-Communist Hungary, the Czech Republic, Slovakia, and Poland. While links between social groups and political parties have been eroding in Western Europe, they have been gaining strength in East-Central Europe. While West European parties have been gradually losing the loyalty of their voters, the links between East-Central European parties and the voters have begun to assume some solidity. While West European parties have been losing their long-term dominance in the public sphere to nongovernmental organizations, citizens associations, and nonpartisan trade unions, East-Central European parties have been increasingly dominating all other types of organizations.

It even seems that the famous convergence theory was reborn and partially fulfilled in the political sphere in Europe after the breakdown of communism.[11] In the first half of the 1990s, obvious convergence tendencies were observable when one compared the development of Western European and Eastern European party systems. Up to the mid-1990s, the "limited convergence" scheme seemed to fit the reality well. In the second half of the 1990s, however, party system development in both parts of Europe was more parallel than converging.

In any case, it is clear that the party systems of East-Central Europe resemble those of Western Europe much more now, in the beginning of the new millennium, than they did in the early 1990s. It is almost certain that the East-Central European party systems will never become the classical cleavage-based party systems from the era of mass parties. It is probably safe to count, however, on the centrifugal and unifying forces of the process of European integration and predict that party systems in the region will tend to become more similar to what will come to be considered the "European standard." The problem is that no one can say authoritatively now which way the process of European integration will go and what all that can mean for the future of European party systems.

Toward Political Stability?

Up to now, this chapter has focused on how political parties and electorates are structured. Now let us turn to the problem of political stability in East-Central Europe. In the broadest sense, political stability refers to the stability of a democratic regime. From that point of view, all four of the countries studied (with some reservations about Slovakia under Mečiar's government) are rather stable democracies: their parliaments are adopting legislation; their courts are independent; they are holding free and fair elections; their electoral results are respected; and within them, power is transferred peacefully. If political stability is viewed in a narrower sense—that is, as the stability of governments, political parties, electoral preferences, and the political attitudes of the population—the answer is obviously more complex. The political attitudes and the values shared by the population since the fall of communism are usually reported to be rather stable (Zukowski 1993; Bútorová, Gyarfásová, and Kúska 1996; Šimoník 1996; Matějů and Řeháková 1997). So if the political attitudes are rather stable, what factors explain the relatively big changes in the electoral results from one election to the next? For example, how can one explain the quite different results produced by the 1991 and 1993 elections in Poland, the 1990 and 1994 elections in Hungary (the elections in both Poland and Hungary were sometimes described as prime examples of a left turn in post-Communist politics), the 1990 and 1992 electoral results in Slovakia (which resulted in the displacement of the reformers by the nationalists), and the 1992 and 1996 parliamentary elections in the Czech Republic (the former establishing a stable, pro-reform government based on a coalition of right-oriented parties, the latter becoming the starting point of the government's weakness and instability).

Part of the explanation lies in the growing rationality of the electorate. Various sociological surveys and opinion polls conducted in the first years after the fall of communism documented that of the different values propagated by the Communist ideologists, social equality was one of the few that was accepted by the majority of the population (Machonin et al. 1996). In the first elections, however, the electorate voted overwhelmingly for parties advocating a departure from the Communist economic model through radical reforms, the logical consequence of which had to be a rise in inequalities. In fact, the winning parties were not very transparent about their economic policy, because they did not stress the possible negative consequences of reforms. Moreover, the elections themselves were, to a great extent, about noneconomic issues, and thus many voters voted against communism, unaware that they were simultaneously voting for shock therapy. After the voters learned more about how the economic reforms worked, what the consequences of implementing the different political programs would be, and who would probably be winners and losers in the process, their attitudes and party choices tended to be more consistent and, as a result, a turn toward more left-oriented parties stressing values such as social security and social equality should not be surprising.

Based on the number of seats gained in the parliament, the extent of the left turn seems impressive, but the effect of the electoral laws should not be forgotten. In Hungary, because the electoral law gave a disproportionately high number of seats to the winning party, the left turn was far more dramatic in terms of seats than in terms of votes. The increase in voting support for the Hungarian Socialist Party from 10.9 percent in the 1990 election (Table 6) to 33.0 percent in the 1994 election (Table 7) resulted in an increase in the MSZP's proportion of seats from 8.6 percent to 54.1 percent. Likewise in Poland, the left turn was not nearly so dramatic as it looked from the change in the proportion of seats in parliament, especially when taking into account the fact that the almost 21 percent of the vote given to the various small parties with a Christian right orientation were not translated into seats because none of them exceeded the legal threshold. Consequently, the impressive results achieved by Solidarity Electoral Action (unifying various Christian Democratic parties) in the 1997 parliamentary election (Table 24), much like the 1998 results achieved by the Federation of Young Democrats–Hungarian Civic Party (FIDESZ-MPP) in Hungary (Table 8), did not necessarily mean a shift in political preferences toward the religious right. In the Czech Republic, no left turn has occurred at all, despite the fact that the Social Democrats (ČSSD) received four times more votes in the 1996 election (Table 16) than in the 1992 election (Table 12). (Most of those votes came from former supporters of several smaller left-wing parties thought to be unable to exceed the 5 percent threshold in the 1996 election.) Similarly, the electoral victory of the ČSSD in the 1998 election (Table 18) was not backed by anything that could be seriously called a left turn in the preferences of voters, because the ratio of votes for the right and for the left remained similar to that in the 1996 election.

The main argument here, then, is that, after the first few messy years of the transition from communism to a democratic society with a market economy, the divisions of the electorate in accordance with its basic political orientations have stabilized considerably in all four of the countries studied. Moreover, the observed growing correspondence between the positions of the voters in the social structure and their political attitudes could further increase the stability of the political party systems in these countries. As for the parties themselves, the stability of individual parties within the political spectrum based on both the party's internal institutional stability and the stability of its electoral support has grown considerably. Political analysts in the region, however, report that although party loyalty is generally increasing, the index of volatility measuring the scope of change in voters' party preference is still higher than in Western Europe (Körösényi 1995; Tóka 1995a).

That said, the index of volatility may not be a good indicator, because it is partially dependent on the number of parties. The more parties, the higher is the probability of shifting party loyalty. If only two parties exist, a change of party loyalty means no less than a switch to supporting a former opponent. If twenty-nine parties are represented in the parliament, including four agrarian ones (like in Poland between 1991 and 1993), the switch from one agrarian party to another constitutes a smaller change than a switch from, say, Eurooptimist to Eurosceptic within the British Conservative Party. The empirical data support the fact that a change of party loyalty is more likely between ideologically close parties than between ideological antipodes (Kéri and Levendel 1995; Šimoník 1996; Vlachová 1997). Facing a relatively stable electorate divided into four main ideological groups, parties would be more likely to seek more votes from the parties that are ideologically similar. Voters for the smaller parties threatened by the legal thresholds in the electoral rules would probably gradually switch their support to larger parties. Thus a relatively stable spectrum of a limited number of political parties, each representing one major ideological stream, is likely to be the outcome of the post-Communist social, economic, and political developments in the Czech Republic, Poland, and Hungary.

But for both political analysts and practitioners, the jury is still out on Slovakia. In view of the various political scandals and the astonishing changes in the policies of individual political parties, political attitudes and party choices have been surprisingly stable in Slovakia. If the loyalty of Slovak voters to political parties has been based on a search for identity and an attraction to charismatic party leadership, then the stability of the country's political attitudes and party choices has a very limited number of roots in the social structure and in collective interests—a fact that enables parties to espouse fuzzy ideological positions and political programs. In short, the future development of the party system in Slovakia remains open to question. And the example of Slovakia may serve as a warning signal to those studying the political systems of Hungary, the Czech Republic, and Poland to guard against the temptation to be excessively optimistic. It is obvious that the transition from Communist totalitarian regimes to stable democracies is a more complicated process than was expected at the beginning of nineties and is far from the only possible outcome.

Notes

Introduction

1. The term *East-Central Europe* used here and later in the text refers to the Central European countries that found themselves on the eastern side of the iron curtain during the cold war. Because the debate about the definition of the term *Central Europe* best remain outside this book, readers are encouraged to choose from any of the existing definitions or to create their own, but it is hoped that the definition chosen will include all four countries studied here: Hungary, the Czech Republic, Slovakia, and Poland. Readers seriously interested in "the problem of Central Europe" will find more in Schöpflin and Wood (1989) and Todorova (1996).

2. A negative side effect of that concentration is the existence of the implicit but widespread notion of "exceptionalism," which is usually manifested by an exaggerated emphasis on the "uniqueness" of the development of individual countries.

1. An Overview of Party Development (1850–1989)

1. For more information about the history of the region, see, for example, Kann and David (1984) or Johnson (1996).

2. Under the curie system, parliament was divided into several sections (curies), each section of which represented some social group such as the nobility, entrepreneurs, and big farmers.

3. In the Czech Lands, the number of people working in industry and services outnumbered those working in agriculture, fisheries, and forestry in 1900, and the same became true for Slovakia in 1950, Hungary in 1951, and Poland in 1957 (see Musil 1995).

4. The party adopted "Realists" as part of its name in trying to persuade voters that the party would be more "realistic" than ideological.

5. An all-national party is one that declares itself to be the only party representing a large group within a nation. For example, the all-national Slovak People's Party declared itself to be the only political representative of the Slovak nation within multiethnic Czechoslovakia.

181

6. The Slavic nations include Belorussia, Bulgaria, the Czech Republic, Slovenia, Slovakia, Poland, Russia, Ukraine, Serbia, and Croatia.

7. The Treaty of Trianon is the short name used for the Treaty of Peace between the Allied and Associated Powers and Hungary signed in 1920. This international treaty officially terminated the state of war between Hungary and its former war enemies and fixed new frontiers of Hungary. As a consequence, Hungary lost two-thirds of its former territory and about one-third of its Hungarian-speaking population.

8. The Soviet-inspired Independent Popular Front officially intended to "unify progressive forces" to rebuild Hungary after the war. The front included political parties (the Communist Party, Social Democratic Party, Independent Smallholders Party, and National Peasant Party), trade unions, and other mass organizations. But, in fact, the Independent Popular Front was created to limit free political competition and to help the Soviets and local Communists control the political situation. The same strategy was used in both Poland and Czechoslovakia.

9. Czechoslovakia also gained Subcarpathian Ruthenia from Hungary in 1919.

10. According to the 1921 population census, out of the total population of 13,613,172, "Czechoslovaks" numbered 8,760,937 (about 6,750,000 Czechs and 2,011,000 Slovaks), Germans 3,123,568, Hungarians 745,431, Ruthenians and Ukrainians 461,849, Jews 354,342 and Poles about 75,000.

11. The Communist Party of Czechoslovakia was the only big party that did not fit the otherwise obvious scheme of an ethnically divided party system. The party was the only party in Czechoslovakia that unified all ethnic groups within one organization.

12. The National Fascist Community polled 2 percent of the votes in the 1935 parliamentary election.

13. The Munich Agreement, signed by Germany, Italy, Great Britain, and France in 1938, forced prewar Czechoslovakia to "give" its borderland to Germany. The agreement of both Great Britain and France with the plan proposed by Adolf Hitler was perceived as betrayal of Czechoslovakia's Western allies.

14. They were the Communist, National Socialist, People's, and Social Democratic Parties.

15. Poland had fourteen different prime ministers between 1918 and 1926 (Donnorummo 1994).

16. Encouraged by the fact that the Red Army was approaching Warsaw, Poles in the city stood up against the Germans, who still ruled the city. The Soviets, however, failed to help the insurgents, leaving the Germans to defeat the insurgents and almost completely demolish the city of Warsaw.

17. In Hungary, the unified candidate list was approved by 95.6 percent of voters in 1949 and 98.2 percent in 1953 (Grzybowski 1991a). In the Czech Lands, it was approved by 87 percent in 1948 and 98 percent in 1954, and in Slovakia by 85 percent in 1948 and 98 percent in 1954 (*Československé děejiny v datech* [Czechoslovak history in dates], 1986).

18. Dessewffy and Hammer (1995) point out that the first postwar hospital in Hungary was built in 1963. And according to Musil (1995), because of massive industrialization in the fifties, the share of the tertiary sector even decreased in the Czech Lands, not reaching the standard of 1930 even by 1980.

19. Charta 77, an organization of dissidents founded in early January 1997, began its activities by publishing a manifesto that blamed the Communist regime for breaking international treaties on human rights signed by Czechoslovakia. From 1977 to 1989,

Charta 77 published many documents on human rights and became the cornerstone of practically all antiregime opposition groups.

20. In 1973, member states of the Organization of Petroleum Exporting Countries (OPEC) agreed to drastically decrease the production of oil in order to substantially increase the price of oil on the world market. As a result, most oil-importing countries in Western Europe and America experienced serious economic troubles in the early seventies.

21. Mikhail Gorbachev was elected the secretary general of the Communist Party of the Soviet Union in 1985. He committed himself to a substantial change in the Communist Party policy, later known as *perestroika* (reconstruction). The new policy of *perestroika* included limited democratization of the public sphere, more freedom for the media, economic reforms, and change in Soviet foreign policy.

22. They were the anniversary of the Soviet invasion on August 21, 1968, the anniversary of the founding of Czechoslovakia on October 28, 1918, and the anniversary of the self-burial of student Jan Palach on January 15, 1969.

23. The astonishing fact that Communist leaders ordered the police to cruelly beat the students collected to remember a student who was killed by the Nazis at the antiregime student demonstration fifty years ago suggests that they were either entirely out of touch with reality or (more probable) all the events were orchestrated by the leaders of the secret police in order to discredit the orthodox leadership of the party and force it to leave. Indeed, the parliamentary commission created after the regime change to investigate the role of different actors in the event proved that the secret police had prepared their response in advance. Yet the purpose of their plan remains unclear.

2. A New Day: Parties in the Post-Communist Period (1990 to the present)

1. FIDESZ became world famous for establishing an age limit for potential party members: only people thirty-five years old or younger were allowed to be members. This limit was later abandoned.

2. In the first round a majority of votes was needed to gain a seat; in the second round a simple plurality of votes was sufficient.

3. The Agrarian Alliance obtained a seat owing to a victory in an individual contest in a single member constituency. Four candidates were endorsed by other parties to the candidate lists of six major parties. Moreover, six independent candidates entered the parliament.

4. The government had the hidden support of the SZDSZ. In return, SZDSZ candidate Arpad Gönz was elected president with the support of the MDF.

5. Jószef Antall's remark that he considered himself to be the prime minister of "fourteen million Hungarians" (ten million live in Hungary and the rest in neighboring countries) was noted with the highest suspicion by Hungary's neighbors.

6. The federal parliament inherited a very complicated structure based on the Constitutional Law of the Czechoslovak Federation adopted in late 1968. The parliament consisted of two chambers: the Chamber of the People and the Chamber of Nations, which were of equal size and of equal power. The 150 deputies making up the Chamber of the People were elected in both republics in proportion to the number of voters in the

respective republics (Czech deputies outnumbered Slovak deputies by about two to one). Of the 150 deputies in the Chamber of Nations, 75 were elected in the Czech Republic and 75 in Slovakia. Most bills had to be approved separately by the Chamber of the People and by each "national section" of the Chamber of Nations. Moreover, all constitutional changes as well as some other bills of special importance (so-called constitutional bills—for example, electoral laws and laws stating the responsibilities of the federation and individual republics) had to be approved at least by a three-fifths majority. Thus only thirty-one MPs from either the Czech or the Slovak section of the Chamber of Nations (that is, two-fifths of seventy-five plus one) could effectively block any constitutional change.

7. In the first year of reform the rate of inflation was 58 percent in Czechoslovakia compared with 586 percent in Poland (Jeffries 1993, 386 and 440).

8. In the period between the parliamentary election (June 1990) and December 1991, the rate of unemployment increased from 0.2 percent to 4.1 percent in the Czech Republic, but from 0.2 percent to 11.8 percent in Slovakia (*Statistical Yearbook of the Czech and Slovak Federative Republic* 1992).

9. Both the Green Party and the Democratic Party were represented in the Slovak national council but not in the federal parliament, because only a 3 percent legal threshold was applied for the national council and a 5 percent threshold was applied for the parliament.

10. The parliaments of the individual republics—the Slovak and Czech national councils—became increasingly important during the Czecho-Slovak constitutional negotiations and outlived the federal parliament after the election. Symptomatically, all leading political figures in Slovakia ran for the seats on the Slovak national council. For that reason, figures for national councils are presented. In any event, the electoral results for the federal parliament were much the same.

11. The president is elected by the parliament, and a three-fifths majority is required.

12. In the political struggle between the government and the president, the democratic rules were not respected, and the government unabashedly used state-controlled television for its propaganda. Moreover, it is suspected of misusing the intelligence service as a tool against its opponents. A prime example of such political behavior was the kidnapping on August 31, 1995, of President Michal Kováč's son, a crime that police investigators were unable to pursue because the intelligence service refused to cooperate.

13. At this point, the Civic Democratic Party was a senior coalition party, and the Civic Democratic Alliance and the Christian Democratic Union–Czechoslovak People's Party were junior coalition parties.

14. The term *less orthodox* is used here instead of reformers in order to stress the very real difference between reformers within the Czech Communist Party and reformers in the other countries studied.

15. Although the Senate as an upper chamber of Parliament was introduced by the new Czech constitution in January 1993, it did not come into being until November 1996, because no agreement had been reached on the details of its electoral system.

16. Inflation grew from 17.7 percent in 1986 to 244.0 percent in 1989, and the net hard currency debt was as high as $37.5 billion in 1989 (Jeffries 1993).

17. Under Bielecki, the economic policy of the government did not change.

18. In each province, the voter had two votes. The exceptions were Warsaw and Katovice, where voters had three votes and where three senators were elected.

19. Inflation decreased from 43 percent in 1992 to 35 percent in 1993; GDP growth for 1993 was estimated at 3.8 percent.

20. This general rule does not apply to political parties and movements representing ethnic minorities.

3. The Party System: A Product of a Country's History and Culture?

1. This list of continuities ends with clearly cultural categories. Because of mutual overlaps and the difficulty of distinguishing whether certain factors influencing party development are historical or cultural, these two categories are discussed together.

2. Although "decommunization" proved to be a rather important political issue, at least in Poland and the Czech Republic in early 1990s, the opinion that the new regimes should turn their attention to the future rather than engage in a battle with the past prevailed. Therefore, no trials of former Communist Party leaders were organized, in contrast to the active persecution of such leaders in the Balkans.

As for ordinary members, even the Czechoslovak Screening Law (*Lustrační zákon*), which some Western scholars and journalists often erroneously refer to as a prime example of the collective punishment of ordinary Communist Party members, does not fit into the category of extensive persecution. The main purpose of the law was to prevent high Communist Party officials and anyone who cooperated with the Communist secret service from reaching the highest posts in the new state administration. Several former rank-and-file Communist Party members, later members of various parties, were members of many governments, including the most right-oriented.

3. Hungary was the exception in this respect because no non-Communist political parties were in the front organization.

4. In spite of maintaining of the word *Czechoslovak,* the party has worked and is working exclusively in the Czech Lands and not in Slovakia.

5. This suspicion itself is a clear example of the popular reaction to certain historical events: the left wing dominated Social Democrats helped the Communists to take power in 1948. Later, however, the Social Democrats were forced to merge with the Communist Party, and many of its leading members were persecuted.

6. A partial exception to this rule was Solidarity. Although it was not a party, it was nevertheless well organized on both the local and regional levels.

7. This research was carried out by means of a set of independent variables describing the level of urbanization, regional GDP, unemployment, scope of foreign investment, level of illiteracy in 1930s, strength of Andrej Hlinka's prewar Slovak People's Party, religious composition, abortion rate, and education of the population.

8. The term *pro-market parties* refers to political parties that favor market-based solutions to economic problems as opposed to parties that prefer more state involvement in the economy.

9. Some or perhaps most of traditional political orientations of the regions could have some structural reasons behind them—for example, the various paths and periods of the Protestant Reformation, urbanization, industrialization, and secularization. Nevertheless, this does not change the basic idea that political traditions are rather autonomous regardless of the ways in which they have evolved and thus cannot be regarded as simple reflections of the present social and economic situation in the regions.

10. Indeed, the Czechs went down the same path during the nineteenth and early twentieth centuries vis-à-vis the Viennese government.

11. In both the early 1920s and the early 1990s, one of the most popular definitions of "sovereign" was a situation in which Slovaks would be drinking Slovak milk that came from Slovak cows.

12. Similarly, the traditional Czech text on the Czechoslovak presidential flag— *Pravda vítězí* (the truth wins)—had to be supplemented with the Slovak version— *Pravda víťazí*—after the protests of Slovak deputies. Later, both were replaced with neutral Latin, *Vincit veritas,* after Czech deputies protested the bilingual version.

13. Moravians in the parliament argued that the restoration of land that was historically Moravian was a neccessary "remedy of historical injustice."

14. Polish society's traditions of independence and autonomy represesent a fundamental difference between the Polish and Czech outlooks. Whereas in Poland any substantial change in the country's situation is met with strong social resistance, Czech society has repeatedly proved to be much more flexible in dealing with change. For that reason, the German Nazis, Soviets, Communists, and post-Communist reformers have always had to work much harder in Poland than in the Czech Lands to impose their regimes.

15. Although the general trend in the developed world in the second half of the twentieth century was a declining role for industry and a larger one for services in the economy (that is, the developed world was moving into the postindustrial phase of economic development), the economic development of the Communist countries followed a different path. The "second" wave of industrialization imposed by the Communists in the 1950s adversely affected the size of the "postindustrial" tertiary sector, which was larger in the 1930s than during the entire Communist period.

4. The Party System: A Reflection of Social Cleavages?

1. The figures about ethnic composition here and later in the text are cited from Bugajski (1994).

2. One type of center–periphery conflict may evolve between Budapest and the other cities (the population of Budapest equals that of twenty other big Hungarian cities). Similarly, there is predisposition to the center–periphery conflict between the more-developed west and the less-developed east.

3. In the most economically devastated regions of the (industrial) northeast the party received less-than-average support (Körösényi 1991).

4. Even after the introduction of the 5 percent legal threshold aimed at limiting the number of political parties in parliament, minorities have held some seats in parliament, because they are exempt from the need to fulfill this demand.

5. People declaring Moravian or Silesian ethnicity are considered Czech here.

6. The 1991 census declared a specific Romany ethnicity for the first time. Because many of the Roma declared themselves to be either Czech, Slovak, or Hungarian, the number of Roma as defined by the census is probably underrepresented; it could in fact be as much as five times greater.

7. A party had to exceed the 5 percent legal threshold in at least one of the republics in order to be eligible for any seats in the federal parliament. No pro-minority exceptions to this rule were applied in either the Czech Republic or Slovakia.

8. Brno, the second largest city in the Czech Republic, had served as the capital of Moravia.

9. The Protestant Reformation evolved from various reform movements within the Catholic Church that criticized, among other things, the corrupt practices of the church (such as selling indulgences) and demanded worship in native languages instead of Latin and a return to biblical principles in church practice. In Central Europe, the most influential Reformation movements were those inspired by John Hus (1372–1415), Martin Luther (1483–1546), and John Calvin (1509–1564). Eventually, the upheaval fomented by the Protestant Reformation led to the split of the Catholic Church into Catholic and Protestant parts and to a series of religious wars in Europe. The reaction of the Catholic Church to the Protestant Reformation, known as the Counter-Reformation, included the strengthening of Catholic doctrines with the help of a new religious order—the Jesuits.

10. The National Revival movement aimed to revive the Czech nation, its language, and national culture after two centuries of the Germanization pressure of Habsburg rule. The National Revival movement reached its peak in the nineteenth century.

11. Both Slovak Lutherans and Calvinists adopted Czech as their liturgical language and used the Czech translation of the Bible (Kann and David 1984). The use of the Czech language, which is generally similar to Slovak language, helped the Slovak Protestant elite to avoid assimilation into their Hungarian-dominated environment.

12. It is true, however, that similar trends were observable in Western Europe, where churches enjoyed more or less complete freedom. It is difficult to distinguish the influence of persecution from the general trend of secularization.

13. The term *liberal* is used here in the European sense of the word—that is, in Europe liberalism typically stresses individual freedom such as the freedom to carry out business unrestricted by government regulations. In this sense, liberalism is considered a right-wing political ideology as opposed to the socialist and social democratic ideologies that tend to emphasize the regulatory role of the state in the economy.

14. Note that "traditionalist" was not construed to be opposition to the free market. The classification presented here is based on a two-dimensional division of political space in the Czech Republic along the axes of traditionalist/modernist and state redistribution/free-market. Four possible combinations exist.

15. The Communists did, however, succeed in defining classes in the classical Marxist sense—labor versus capital, employees versus owners.

16. Tables 29–31 rely on data derived from Machonin et al. (1996), who kindly granted permission to reproduce the numbers shown here. The data came from an international comparative survey, "Social Stratification and Elite Circulation in Eastern Europe after 1989," conducted by national teams led by Donald J. Treiman and Ivan Szelenyi from the University of California at Los Angeles.

17. In Western Europe, class typically does not influence voting participation but has a great deal of influence on which party voters choose. In the United States, the inverse is true: class typically influences voter participation, but once voters appear at their polling station their voting decisions are not influenced by class to the extent found in Western Europe. A similar situation was found in Hungary.

18. The financial status of pensioners, which have always belonged to the poor, is not taken into account here.

19. Unemployment figures should be read carefully, however, because bias may be present in the statistics, caused by the hidden or unregistered unemployment of women (Koncz 1993). However, Fodor (1997), using data from the comparative research project "Social Stratification in Eastern Europe after 1989," shows that the proportion of

"early retired" women in 1993 did not exceed that of men, nor was staying home as housekeepers a source of hidden unemployment of women.

20. One well-documented fact is that some of the lower-paying sectors of the economy (primary education, health care, social services) are dominated by women. They are counterbalanced, however, by the high proportion of women working in some booming, high-paying sectors such as banking and insurance.

21. The exception is the Scandinavian countries where women occupy 30–40 percent of the seats in parliaments.

22. Generally, in the systems of proportional represented used in the majority of European countries, voters do not vote for individual candidates in single-member electoral districts but vote for a whole list of party candidates in a multimember electoral district. The higher a candidate is on the party list, the more chance he or she has to obtain a seat.

5. The Party System: A Product of the Rules of the Game?

1. Party financing in the post-Communist countries, another topic worthy of analysis, is in a state of disarray (Lewis 1996). One cannot understand the mechanisms of financing by simply comparing existing legal regulations. In fact, because the art of party financing is usually kept out of the sphere of public accessibility, its legality cannot be either ascertained or disputed. As a result, party financing is omitted here despite its potential importance.

2. For more information about electoral laws and their political consequences, see Grofman and Lijphardt (1986). For a detailed discussion of the relationship between electoral laws and party systems, see Giovanni Sartori's article (1986) in Grofman and Lijphardt's volume.

3. The legal thresholds do not apply to ethnic minorities, so the German minority received a few seats in addition to the six parties mentioned.

4. Altogether 34.5 percent of the total number of votes was given to parties that did not gain any seats in parliament.

5. The liberal democratic Union of Freedom (UW) and the Christian Democratic Solidarity Electoral Action were examples of this phenomenon.

6. The only exception was abolishing the article that declared the Communist Party's leading role in society. This constitutional change was passed almost unanimously by the (still) Communist parliament.

7. The national councils served as the parliaments of the individual republics of the federation.

8. Before the 1992 election, the Slovak National Council adopted an amendment to electoral law that increased the threshold from 3 to 5 percent.

9. The small parties collectively received 19.1 percent of the vote.

10. First-past-the-post, also known as the Westminster system, is a plurality system that uses single-member electoral districts and one-round elections. The seat is won by the candidate with the highest number of votes.

11. Facing likely defeat, the Republicans decided not to participate and appealed to their voters to boycott the elections.

12. The preelection opinion poll conducted by STEM in March 1998 suggested that

29.5 percent of the public favored the Social Democrats and 18.3 percent preferred the Union of Freedom, while only 11.4 percent supported Klaus's ODS (STEM 1998).

13. The new system represents a compromise between the d'Hondt system pushed by ČSSD and the Imperiali system favored by the ODS. Under the classical d'Hondt system, the votes for individual parties in each multimember electoral district are consecutively divided by 1, 2, 3, 4, 5 (in the Imperiali system the dividing numbers are 2, 3, 4, 5). The individual mandates are then assigned consecutively to the parties with the highest numbers from the division. The compromise proposed by the ODS and the ČSSD consisted of replacing the divisor 1 by the number 1.42. Although the ČSSD and ODS labeled the new system as "compensatory d'Hondt" (and sometimes even erroneously refer to it simply as d'Hondt), a more precise and less confusing label would be the Koudelka system, named after the system's inventor, Zdeněk Koudelka.

14. The MDF, for example, obtained slightly less than three times as many votes as the FIDESZ but almost eight times as many seats.

6. Political Party Development in Post-Communist East-Central Europe: In Search of General Patterns

1. It is true, however, that the practices of the Communist Party differed from country to country and were changing from time to time.

2. These are limited to those that entered the parliament in the first post-Communist elections in Czechoslovakia and Hungary and, in Poland, those with more than 5 percent of the vote.

3. Because there was serious doubt about the legality of this act, the Constitutional Court was asked to decide. The court ruled that the dismissal of Gaulieder from the parliament by a vote of deputies was unconstitutional. That decision, however, was not respected by the parliament.

4. See Krivý (1999) for a description of how the support of different media influenced the results of the 1998 election in Slovakia.

5. Corporatism is a system in which business and producer interest organizations are official participants in the policy-making process. It is usually connected with the pre–World War II systems in Italy and Spain. Neocorporatism is modern-day corporatism in which the participants in the policy-making process are not only producer interest organizations but also other interest groups such as trade unions and consumer associations. The term *neocorporatism* is used these days to describe the political systems of Austria, Sweden, Belgium, the Netherlands, Switzerland, and Norway.

6. Profit in this sense may not necessarily mean money. It also may be described as the desire to live better, however "better" is defined.

7. Voucher privatization was one of the methods used to effect the mass privatization of state-owned assets. Vouchers, which were distributed to the population at almost no cost, could be used to purchase shares in privatized companies. Voucher privatization allows the government to transfer former state-owned companies into the hands of local citizens who usually did not have enough funds to buy shares in competition with foreign investors.

8. These two models of political development were observable in the post-Communist states. Political conflicts in southeastern Europe (the Balkan countries) typically re-

volved around ethnic cleavages and were based mostly on identity issues. In Central Europe, political conflicts around material interests were more typical.

9. The attitudes of HZDS's junior coalition partners—the Slovak National Party and the Association of Workers of Slovakia—toward Slovakia's potential membership in NATO are a prime example of this political ambiguity. Even though the junior coalition partners were part of a government whose prime foreign policy goal was (officially) to join NATO, they urged their supporters to vote against the move in the NATO referendum.

10. Olson's early freezing hypothesis is derived from the freezing hypothesis developed earlier by Lipset and Rokkan (1967). While studying the development of the party system in Western Europe, Lipset and Rokkan noticed that after a turbulent period of social and political change social structures and the party structure were stabilized enough to be labeled *frozen*. A "frozen party system" therefore tends to be very stable. Within that system, parties reproduce themselves, and they are able to absorb effectively new issues and political conflicts. The "early freezing hypothesis" refers to the fact that party systems themselves can "freeze" even before any relationships between social structures and party structures can be established.

11. Convergence theory states that the social, political, and economic systems of all industrial societies, whether capitalist or communist, will converge because of the dominant effects of technological development.

Works Cited

Adamik, Maria. 1993. "Feminism and Hungary." In *Gender Politics and Post-Communism,* ed. N. Funk and M. Mueller. London: Routledge.

Ágh, Attila. 1995. "The Emergence of Democratic Parliamentarism in Hungary." In *Lawful Revolution in Hungary,* ed. Béla Király and András Bozók. New York: Columbia University Press.

———. 1998. "The End of the Beginning: The Partial Consolidation of East Central European Parties and Party Systems." In *Comparing Party System Change,* ed. Paul Pennings and Jan-Erik Lane. London: Routledge.

Almond, Gabriel A., and Sidney Verba, eds. 1989. *The Civic Culture Revisited.* Newbury Park, Calif.: Sage Publications.

Angresano, James. 1992. "Political and Economic Obstacles Inhibiting Comprehensive Reform in Hungary." *East European Quarterly* 26 (March): 55–76.

Balcerowicz, Leszek. 1994. "Poland: The Economic Outcomes." *Economic Policy* (December): 72–97.

Berglund, Stan, Tomas Hellén, and Frank H. Aarebrot, eds. 1998. *The Handbook of Political Change in Eastern Europe.* Cheltenham, Northampton, England: Edward Elgar.

Bigler, Robert M. 1996. "Back in Europe and Adjusting to the New Realities of the 1990s in Hungary."*East European Quarterly* 30 (June): 205–234.

Blackwood, Lee. 1990. "Czech and Polish National Democracy at the Dawn of Independent Statehood, 1918–1919." *European Politics and Societies* 4 (fall).

Brokl, Lubomír. 1994. "Politická kultura a politický prostor České republiky" (Political culture and the political space of the Czech Republic). *Lidové noviny,* November 11.

———. 1996. "Parlamentní volby 1996" (Parliamentary elections 1996). *Sociologický časopis* 32 (4): 389–406.

Bugajski, Janusz. 1994. *Ethnic Politics in Eastern Europe.* New York: M. E. Sharpe.

"Bulletin of Electoral Statistics and Public Opinion Research Data." 1994. *East European Politics and Societies* 8 (spring): 369–378.

Bútorová, Zora, Olga Gyarfásová, and Miroslav Kúska. 1996. *Current Problems of Slovakia on the Verge of 1995–1996* (Report of the Sociological Survey). Bratislava: FOCUS.

Castle-Kanerová, Mita. 1992. "Czech and Slovak Federative Republic. The Culture of

Strong Women in the Making?" In *Superwomen and the Double Burden,* ed. C. Corrin. London: Scarlet Press, 1992.

Čermáková, Marie. 1995a. "Gender, společnost a pracovní trh" (Gender, society, and the labor market). *Sociologický časopis* 31 (1): 7–24.

———. 1995b. "Women and Family—The Czech Version of Development and Chances for Improvement." In *Family, Women, and Employment in Central-Eastern Europe,* ed. B. Lobodzinska. Westport, Conn.: Greenwood Press.

———. 1997. "Postavení žen na trhu práce" (Women in the labor market). *Sociologický časopis* 33 (3): 389–404.

Československé dějiny v datech (Czechoslovak history in dates). 1986. Prague: Nakladatelství Svoboda.

Cipkowski, Peter. 1991. *Revolution in Eastern Europe: Understanding the Collapse of Communism in Poland, Hungary, East Germany, Czechoslovakia, Romania, and the Soviet Union.* New York: Wiley.

Clarc, G. L. 1981. "Law, the State, and the Spatial Integration of the United States." *Environment and Planning A* (13): 197–232.

Corrin, Cris, ed. 1992. *Superwomen and the Double Burden.* London: Scarlet Press.

Cox, Kevin R. 1979. *Location and Public Problems.* Chicago: Maaroufa Press, 1979.

Davies, Norman. 1981. *God's Playground.* Oxford: Clarendon Press, 1981.

Dessewffy, Tibor, and Ferenc Hammer. 1995. "The Transition in Hungary." In *1990 Election to the Hungarian National Assembly,* ed. Gábor Tóka. Berlin: Ed. Sigma.

Donnorummo, Robert. 1994. "Poland's Political and Economic Transition." *East European Quarterly* 28 (June): 259–279.

Downs, Anthony. 1957. *An Economic Theory of Democracy.* New York: Harper.

Duverger, Maurice. 1964. *Political Parties.* London: Methuen.

Dziewanowski, Marian K. 1976. *The Communist Party of Poland: An Outline of History.* Cambridge: Harvard University Press.

Ehrlich, Eva, and Gábor Revesz. 1995. *Hungary and Its Prospects, 1985–2005.* Budapest: Akademiai Kiado.

Einhorn, Barbara. 1993. *Cinderella Goes to Market. Citizenship, Gender, and the Women's Movement in East Central Europe.* London: Verso.

European Bank for Reconstruction and Development. 1994. *Transition Report on Economic Transition in Eastern Europe and the Soviet Union.* October.

Evans, Geoffrey, and Stephen Whitefield. 1993. "Identifying the Bases of Party Competition in Eastern Europe." *British Journal of Political Science* 23 (4).

Felak, James R. 1994. *At the Price of the Republic: Hlinka's Slovak People's Party, 1929–38.* Pittsburgh: University of Pittsburgh Press.

Fodor, Eva. 1997. "Gender in Transition: Unemployment in Hungary, Poland and Slovakia." *East European Politics and Societies* 11 (fall 1997): 470–500.

Funk, Nanette, and Magda Mueller. 1993. *Gender Politics and Post-Communism.* London: Routledge.

Fuszara, Malgorzata. 1993. "Abortion and the Formation of the Public Sphere in Poland." In *Gender Politics and Post-Communism,* ed. N. Funk and M. Mueller. London: Routledge.

Garver, Bruce M. 1978. *The Young Czech Party.* New Haven: Yale University Press.

Gebethner, Stanislaw. 1993. "Osemnascie miesiecy rozczlonkowanego parlamentu" (Eighteen months of fragmented parliament). In *Polska scena polityczna a wybory,* ed. Stanislaw Gebethner. Warsaw: INP UW and ISP PAN.

Gellner, Ernest. 1991. "Civil Society in Historical Context." *International Social Science Journal* 43(3): 495–510.

Glatz, Ferenc. 1995. "Multiparty System in Hungary, 1989–94." In *Lawful Revolution in Hungary,* ed. Béla Király and András Bozóki. New York: Columbia University Press.

Gortat, Radzislawa, and Piotr Marciniak. 1995. "On the Road to Democracy: The Emergence of Political Parties in Poland." In *Party Formation in East Central Europe: Post-Communist Politics in Czechoslovakia, Hungary, Poland, and Bulgaria,* ed. G. Wightman. Aldershot, Hants, England: Edward Elgar.

Goven, Joanna. 1993. "Gender Politics in Hungary: Autonomy and Antifeminism." In *Gender Politics and Post-Communism,* ed. N. Funk and M. Mueller. London: Routledge.

Grofman, Bernard, and Arend Lijphart, eds. 1986. *Electoral Laws and Their Political Consequences.* New York: Agathon Press.

Grzybowski, Marian. 1991a. "The Transition from One-Party Hegemony to Competitive Pluralism: The Case of Hungary." In *The New Democracies in Eastern Europe,* ed. S. Berglund and Dellenbrant. Aldershot, Hants, England: Edward Elgar.

———. 1991b. "The Transition of the Polish Party System." In *The New Democracies in Eastern Europe,* ed. S. Berglund and Dellenbrant. Aldershot, Hants, England: Edward Elgar.

Havelková, Hana. 1999. "The Political Representation of Women in Mass Media Discourse in the Czech Republic, 1990–1998." *Czech Sociological Review* 7 (2): 145–166.

Heitlinger, Alena. 1993. "The Impact of the Transition from Communism on the Status of Women in the Czech and Slovak Republic." In *Gender Politics and Post-Communism,* ed. N. Funk and M. Mueller. London: Routledge.

———. 1995. "Women's Equality, Work, and Family in the Czech Republic." In *Family, Women, and Employment in Central-Eastern Europe,* ed. B. Lobodzinska. Westport, Conn.: Greenwood Press.

Holý, Dalibor. 1999. "Analýza mzdové disparity mužů a žen na podkladě výběrového šetření mezd zaměstnanců" (Analysis of wage disparity between men and women based on sample surveys of employees' wages). *Statistika* (2): 53–68.

Hraba, Joseph, Allan L. McCutcheon, and Jiří Večerník. 1997. "Životní šance mužů a žen v období transformace. Srovnání České a Slovenské republiky" (Gender differences in life chances during the post-Communist transformation. Comparison of the Czech and Slovak Republics). *Sociologický časopis* (4): 405–421.

Inglehardt, Ronald. 1988. "The Renaissance of Political Culture." *American Political Science Review* 82 (December): 1203–1230.

Ishiyama, John T. 1996. "Electoral Systems Experimentation in the New Eastern Europe: The Single Transferable Vote and the Additional Member System in Estonia and Hungary." *East European Quarterly* 29 (January): 487–507.

Jasiewicz, Krzystof. 1992. "Poland." *European Journal of Political Research* 22 (December): 489–504.

———. 1993. "Polish Politics on the Eve of the 1993 Elections." *Communist and Postcommunist Studies* 26 (December): 387–411.

———. 1997. "Polish Politics in the First Year of Aleksander Kwasniewski's Presidency." *East European Studies.* Woodrow Wilson Center, Washington, D.C., March–April.

Jeffries, Ian. 1993. *Socialist Economies and the Transition to the Market.* London: Routledge.

Jehlička, Peter, and Luděk Sýkora. 1991. "Stabilita regionální podpory tradičních politických stran v Českých zemích (1920–1990)" (Stability of voting patterns of the main political parties in the Czech Lands). *Sborník ČGS* 96 (2): 81–95.

Johnson, Lonnie R. 1996. *Central Europe; Enemies, Neighbors and Friends.* New York: Oxford University Press.

Kann, Robert A., and Zdeněk V. David. 1984. *The Peoples of the Eastern Habsburg Lands, 1526–1918.* Seattle: University of Washington Press.

Katz, Richard, and Peter Mair. 1992. *Party Organizations.* London: Sage Publications.

Kéri, Lazslo, and Adam Levendel. 1995. "The First Three Years of a Multi-Party System in Hungary." In *Party Formation in East Central Europe: Post-Communist Politics in Czechoslovakia, Hungary, Poland, and Bulgaria,* ed. Gordon Wightman. Aldershot, Hants, England: Edward Elgar, 1995.

Kirchheimer, Otto. 1966. "The Transformation of the Western European Party System." In: *Political Parties and Political Development,* ed. J. LaPalombara and M. Weiner. Princeton: Princeton University Press.

Kitschelt, Herbert. 1992. "The Formation of Party Systems in East Central Europe." *Politics and Society* 20 (March): 7–50.

Kitschelt, Herbert, Zdena Mansfeldová, R. Markowski, and G. Tóka. 1999. *Postcommunist Party Systems. Competition, Representation and Inter-Party Cooperation.* Cambridge: Cambridge University Press.

Kolosi, Tamás. 1984. "Status and Stratification." In *Stratification and Inequalities,* ed. R. Andorka and T. Kolosi. Budapest: Institute for Social Sciences.

Kolosi, Tamás, Ivan Szelényi, Szonja Szelényi, and Bruce Western. 1992. "The Making of Political Fields in Postcommunist Transition" (Dynamics of Class and Party in Hungarian Politics, 1989–1990). In *Postcommunist Transition,* ed. András Bozóki, András Körösényi, and George Schöpflin. New York: St. Martin's Press.

Koncz, Katalin. 1993. "Hungary: Growing Unemployment of Women." *Women's International Network News* 19 (autumn): 1–2.

———. 1995. "The Position of Hungarian Women in the Process of Regime Change." In *Family, Women, and Employment in Central-Eastern Europe,* ed. B. Lobodzinska. Westport, Conn.: Greenwood Press.

Kopecký, Petr, Pavel Hubáček, and Petr Plecitý. 1996. "Politické strany v českem Parlamentu (1992–1996): Organizace, chování, vliv" (Political parties in the Czech Parliament (1992–1996): Organization, behavior, influence). *Sociologický časopis* 32 (4): 439–456.

Körösenyi, András. 1991. "Revival of the Past or New Beginning? The Nature of Postcommunist Politics." In *Democracy and Political Transformation,* ed. Gyorgy Szobszlai. Budapest: Hungarian Political Science Association.

———. 1995. "The Reasons for the Defeat of the Right in Hungary." *East European Politics and Societies* 9 (winter).

Kostelecký, Tomáš. 1993a. "Analysis of the Election Results as a Part of the Political Geography" (in Czech). Ph.D. dissertation, Faculty of Science, Charles University, Prague.

———. 1993b. "Parliamentary Elections 1992 in the Czech Republic in the Eyes of a Geographer: No Great Surprises." *Geografické rozhledy* 2 (1): 4–6.

———. 1994. "Economic, Social and Historical Determinants of Voting Patterns in the

1990 and 1992 Parliamentary Elections in the Czech Republic." *Czech Sociological Review* 2 (2): 209–228.

———. 1995a. "Changing Party Allegiances in a Changing Party System: The 1990 and 1992 Parliamentary Elections in the Czech Republic." In *Party Formation in East-Central Europe: Postcommunist Politics in Czechoslovakia, Hungary, Poland, and Bulgaria,* ed. G. Wightman. Aldershot, Hants, England: Edward Elgar.

———. 1995b. "Political, Economic, and Social Behaviour during the Postcommunist Transformation in the Czech Republic—The Regional Perspective" (in Czech). Working paper no. 5, Institute of Sociology, Prague.

———. 1995c. *Social and Economic Consequences of Privatisation Survey 1995. Codebook.* Prague: ICCR Prague Foundation.

———. 1996. "Komunální volby jako mechanismus výběru místních politických elit" (Municipal election as a mechanism of the local elite recruitment). In *Geografická organizace společnosti a transformační procesy v České republice* (Geographical organization of the society and the transformation processes in the Czech Republic), ed. M. Hampl. Prague: Přírodovědecká fakulta, University Karlovy.

Kostelecký, Tomáš, and Petr Jehlička. 1991. "The Development of Czechoslovak Green Party since the Elections 1990." *Environmental Politics* 1 (1): 72–94.

Kostelecký, Tomáš, and Aleš Kroupa. 1996. "Party Organization and Structure at National Level and Local Level in the Czech Republic since 1989." In *Party Structure and Organization in East-Central Europe,* ed. P. Lewis. Aldershot, Hants, England: Edward Elgar.

Kostelecký, Tomáš, Petr Jehlička, and Luděk Sýkora. 1993. "Czechoslovak Parliamentary Elections 1990: Old Patterns, New Trends and a Lot of Surprises." In *The New Political Geography of Eastern Europe,* ed. John O'Loughlin and Herman van der Wusten. London: Belhaven Press.

Kovács, Mária. 1992. "Jews and Hungarians: A View after the Transition." East European Studies Occasional Paper No. 35, Woodrow Wilson International Center for Scholars, Washington, D.C.

———. 1994. *Liberal Professions and Illiberal Politics.* Washington, D.C.: Woodrow Wilson Center Press; and New York: Oxford University Press.

Kovács, Zoltan. 1993. "The Geography of Hungarian Parliamentary Election 1990." In *The New Political Geography of Eastern Europe,* ed. John O'Loughlin and Herman van der Wusten. London: Belhaven Press.

Kozera, Nicole. 1997. "Czech Women in the Labor Market: Work and Family in a Transition Economy." Working Paper No. 6, Institute of Sociology, Prague.

Krause, Kevin. 1996. "Systém politických stran v České republice, demokracie a volby roku 1996" (System of political parties in the Czech Republic, democracy and elections in 1996) *Sociologický časopis* 32 (4): 423–438.

Krivý, Vladimír. 1995. "The Parliamentary Elections 1994: The Profile of Supporters of the Political Parties, the Profile of Regions. In *Slovakia Parliamentary Elections 1994,* ed. Sona Szomolányi and Grigorij Mesežnikov. Slovak Political Science Association.

———. 1999. *Čo prezrádzajú volebné výsledky? Parlamentné volby 1992–1998* (What electoral results reveal? Parliamentary elections 1992–1998). Bratislava: Institute for Public Issues.

Krivý, Vladimír, Viera Feglová, and Daniel Balko. 1996. *Slovensko a jeho regiony. Sociolokultúrne súvislosti volebného správania* (Slovakia and its regions. Social and cultural context of electoral behavior). Bratislava: Nadácia Media.

Krivý, Vladimír, et al. 1994. *Slovensko a jeho regiony: vzorce volebného správania a ich sociokultúrne pozadie* (Slovakia and its regions: Patterns of electoral behavior and their social and cultural background). Bratislava: SÚ SAV.

Křížková, Alena, and Milan Tuček. 1998. "Zaměstnání versus rodina—dělba rolí v rodině" (Employment versus family—the division of labor in family). In "Česká rodina v transformaci. Stratifikace, dělba rolí a hodnotové orientace" (Czech family in transformation: Stratification, the division of roles, and value orientation), ed. Milan Tuček et al. Working Paper No. 3, Institute of Sociology, Prague.

Kuchařová, Věra. 1999. "Women and Employment." *Czech Sociological Review* 7 (2): 179–194.

Lane, Jan-Erik, and Svante O. Ersson. 1991. *Politics and Society in Western Europe.* 2d ed. London: Sage Publications.

Lenski, Gerhard. 1954. "Status Crystallization: A Non-Vertical Dimension of Social Status." *American Sociological Review* (19): 405–414.

Lewis, Paul G. 1995. "Poland's New Parties in the Postcommunist Political System." In *Party Formation in East Central Europe: Postcommunist Politics in Czechoslovakia, Hungary, Poland and Bulgaria,* ed. G. Wightman. Aldershot, Hants, England: Edward Elgar, 1995.

———. 1996. "Models of Party Development and Prospects for Political Change in Contemporary Poland." In *Party Structure and Organization in East-Central Europe,* ed. P. Lewis. Aldershot, Hants, England: Edward Elgar, 1996.

Linz, Juan. 1978. "Il sistema patritico spagnolo." In *Rivista Italiana di Scienza Politica* (The Spanish political system). Bologna: Societe editrice il Mulino.

Lipset, Seymour Martin, and Sten Rokkan, eds. 1967. *Cleavage Structures, Party Systems, and Voter Alignments: Cross-National Perspectives.* New York: Free Press.

Lobodzinska, Barbara, ed. 1995. *Family, Women, and Employment in Central-Eastern Europe.* Westport, Conn.: Greenwood Press.

Lomax, Bill. 1995. "Obstacles to the Development of Democratic Politics." In *Hungary: The Politics of Transition,* ed. Terry Cox and Andy Furlong. London: Frank Cass.

Machonin, Pavel, et al. 1996. *Česká společnost v transformaci* (Czech society in transformation). Prague: Sociologické nakladatelství.

Malová, Darina. 1995. "The Relationship between the State, Political Parties and Civil Society in Postcommunist Czecho-Slovakia." In *Slovakia Parliamentary Elections 1994,* ed. Sona Szomolányi and Grigorij Mesežnikov. Bratislava: Slovak Political Science Association.

Markus, G. G. 1994. "Parties, Camps and Cleavages in Postcommunist Hungary." In *Social Democracy in Postcommunist Europe,* ed. Bruno Coppiers, Kris Deschouwer, and Michael Waller. London: Frank Cass.

Marody, Mira. 1995. "Three Stages of Party System Emergence in Poland." *Communist and Postcommunist Studies* 28 (2): 263–270.

Matějů, Petr, and Blanka Řeháková. 1997. "Obrat doleva nebo proměna vzorců volebního chování sociálních tříd?" (Left turn or changing patterns of class voting patterns). *Social Trends, Working Papers.* No. 2.

Matykowski, Roman, and Anna Tobolska. 1994. "The 1991–1993 Parliamentary Elections in Poland: From the Birth of Democracy to the Success of the Palaeosystem." Institute of Socio-Geography and Spatial Planning, Adam Mickiewicz University, Poland.

McIntosh, Mary E., and Martha A. Mac Iver. 1993. "Transition to What? Publics Confront Change in Central and Eastern Europe." East European Studies Occasional Paper No. 38, Woodrow Wilson International Center for Scholars, Washington, D.C.

Mesežnikov, Grigorij. 1995. "The Programs of Political Parties in Slovakia: Practice and Declarations." In *Slovakia Parliamentary Elections 1994*, ed. S. Szomolányi and G. Mesežnikov. Bratislava: Slovak Political Science Association.

Millard, Frances. 1994a. *The Anatomy of the New Poland: Post-Communist Politics in Its First Phase.* Aldershot, Hants, England: Edward Elgar.

———. 1994b. "The Polish Parliamentary Election of September 1993." *Communist and Postcommunist Studies* 27 (September): 295–313.

Mitchell, Brian R., ed. 1975. *European Historical Statistics, 1750–1970.* New York: Columbia University Press.

———. 1992. *International Historical Statistics: Europe 1750–1988.* Basingstoke, Hants, England: Macmillan.

Mizgala, Joanna J. 1994. "The Ecology of Transformation: The Impact of the Corporatist State on the Formation and Development of the Party System in Poland, 1989–93." *East European Politics and Societies* 8 (spring): 358–368.

Možný, Ivo. 1991. *Proč tak snadno. Některé rodinné důvody sametové revoluce* (Why so easy. Some family roots of the Velvet Revolution). Prague: Sociologické nakladatelství.

Müller-Rommel, Ferdinand, ed. 1989. *New Politics in Western Europe: The Rise and Success of Green Parties and Alternative Lists.* Boulder: Westview Press.

Müller-Rommel, Ferdinand, and Thomas Poguntke, eds. 1995. *New Politics.* Brookfield, Vt.: Dartmouth.

Musil, Jiří, ed. 1995. *The End of Czechoslovakia.* Budapest: Central European University Press.

Musilová, Martina. 1999. "Equal Opportunity as a Matter of Public Interest." *Czech Sociological Review* 7 (2): 195–204.

Novák, Miroslav. 1996. "Volby do Poslanecké sněmovny, vládní nestabilita a perspektivy demokracie v ČR" (Election to lower house of the Parliament, government instability, and perspectives of democracy in the Czech Republic). *Sociologický časopis* 32 (4): 407–422.

Olson, David. 1993. "Political Parties and Party Systems in Regime Transformation: Inner Transition in the New Democracies of Central Europe." *American Review of Politics* 14 (winter).

Pacek, Alexander. 1994. "Macroeconomic Conditions and Electoral Politics in East Central Europe." *American Journal of Political Science* 38 (August): 723–744.

Parysek, J. J., Z. Adamczyk, and R. Grobelny. 1991. "Regional Differences in the Results of the 1990 Presidential Election in Poland as the First Approximation to a Political Map of the Country." *Environment and Planning A* 23: 1315–1329.

Pataki, Judith. 1992. "Hungarians Dissatisfied with Political Changes." *RFE/RL Research Report* 1 (November): 66–70.

Perdue, William. 1995. *Paradox of Change.* Westport, Conn.: Praeger.

Plakwicz, Jolanta. 1992. "Poland. Between Church and State: Polish Women's Experience." In *Superwomen and the Double Burden*, ed. C. Corrin. London: Scarlet Press.

Pridham, Geoffrey. 1995. "Political Parties and Their Strategies in the Transition from Authoritarian Rule: The Comparative Perspective." In *Party Formation in East-*

Central Europe: Postcommunist Politics in Czechoslovakia, Hungary, Poland and Bulgaria, ed. G. Wightman. Aldershot, Hants, England: Edward Elgar.

Průcha, Václav. 1995. "Economic Development and Relations, 1918–89." In *The End of Czechoslovakia,* ed. J. Musil. Budapest: Central European University Press.

Przeworski, Adam. 1991. "Political Dynamics of Economic Reforms: East and South." In *Democracy and Political Transformation,* ed. Gyorgy Szobszlai. Budapest: Hungarian Political Science Association.

Pungur, Joseph. 1992. "Protestantism in Hungary: The Communist Era." In *Protestantism and Politics in Eastern Europe and Russia,* ed. Sabrina Ramet. Durham: Duke University Press.

Raciborski, Jacek. 1993. "Determinanty Procesu Krystalizacji Preferencji Wyborczych" (Determinants of the process of the crystallization of electoral preferences). In *Polska scena polityczna a wybory* (The Polish political scene and elections). Warsaw: INP UW and ISP PAN.

Rendlová, Eliška. 1999. "The Gender Paradox in Public Opinion Survey." *Czech Sociological Review* 7 (2): 167–178.

Richardson, Dick, and Chris Rootes, eds. 1995. *The Green Challenge.* London: Routledge.

Sabbat-Swidlicka, Anna. 1993. "The Polish Elections: The Church, the Right, and the Left." *RFE/RL Research Report* 2 (October): 24–30.

Sartori, Giovanni. 1986. "The Influence of Electoral Systems: Faulty Laws or Faulty Method?" In *Electoral Laws and Their Political Consequences,* ed. Bernard Grofman and Arend Lijphart. New York: Agathon Press.

———. 1990. "A Typology of Party Systems." In *The West European Party System,* ed. Peter Mair. Oxford: Oxford University Press.

Schöpflin, George. 1993. "The Road from Post-Communism." In *The New Institutional Architecture of Eastern Europe.* London: Macmillan.

Schöpflin, George, and Nancy Wood. 1989. *In Search of Central Europe.* Totowa, N.J.: Barnes and Noble Books.

Second Periodical Report of the Czech Republic on the Fulfillment of the Convention on the Elimination of All Forms of Discrimination against Women (ed. Alena Nedomova). 1999. Prague: Czech Government.

Selle, P., and L. Svasand. 1991. "Membership in Party Organizations and the Problem of Decline of Parties." *Comparative Political Studies.* Vol. 23.

Šiklová, Jiřina. 1993. "Are Women in Central and Eastern Europe Conservative?" In *Gender Politics and Post-Communism,* ed. N. Funk and M. Mueller. London: Routledge.

Šimoník, Pavel. 1996. "Politické spektrum v České republice." *Sociologický časopis* 32 (4): 457–469.

Skalnik Leff, Carol. 1997. *The Czech and Slovak Republics. Nation versus State.* Boulder: Westview Press.

Statistical Yearbook of the Czech and Slovak Federative Republic. 1992. Prague: Czech Statistical Office.

STEM. 1998. *Trendy 3/98.* Prague.

Surazska, Wisla. 1993. "Local Government in Poland; Political Failure and Economic Success." In *The New Localism,* ed. Edward Goetz and Susan Clarke. London: Sage Publications.

Szarvas, László. 1995. "Parties and Party Factions in the Hungarian Parliament." In *Hun-*

gary: The Politics of Transition, ed. Terry Cox and Andy Furlong. London: Frank Cass.

Szomolányi, Soňa. 1995. "Does Slovakia Deviate from the Central European Variant of Transition?" In *Slovakia Parliamentary Elections 1994,* ed. Sona Szomolányi and Grigorij Mesežnikov. Bratislava: Slovak Political Science Association.

Szomolányi, Soňa, and Grigorij Mesežnikov, eds. 1995. *Slovakia Parliamentary Elections 1994.* Bratislava: Slovak Political Science Association.

Titkow, Anna. 1993. "Political Change in Poland: Cause, Modifier, or Barrier to Gender Equality." In *Gender Politics and Post-Communism,* ed. N. Funk and M. Mueller. London: Routledge.

Todorova, Maria. 1996. "Hierarchies of Eastern Europe: East-Central Europe versus the Balkans." Occasional Papers, East European Studies No. 46, Woodrow Wilson International Center for Scholars, Washington D.C., May.

Tóka, Gábor, 1995a. "Parties and Their Voters in 1990 and 1994." In *Lawful Revolution in Hungary,* ed. Béla Király and András Bozóki. New York: Columbia University Press.

———. 1995b. "Seats and Votes: Consequences of the Hungarian Election Law." In *1990 Election to the Hungarian National Assembly,* ed. Gábor Tóka. Berlin: Ed. Sigma.

———. 1995c. "The Impact of the Religion Issue on the Electoral Preferences in Hungary, 1990–1991." In *Wahlen in Zeiten des Monbruchs,* ed. O. W. Gabriel and K. G. Troitzch. Berlin: Peter Lang.

———. 1998. "Hungary." In *Handbook of Political Change in Eastern Europe,* ed. Sten Berglund, Tomas Hellén, and Frank Aarebrot. Aldeshot, Hants, England: Edward Elgar.

Toth, Olga. 1993. "No Envy, No Pity." In *Gender Politics and Post-Communism,* ed. N. Funk and M. Mueller. London: Routledge.

Tuček, Milan, and Alena Křížková. 1998. "Rodina: postoje a hodnoty" (Family: attitudes and values). In *Česká rodina v transformaci. Stratifikace, dělba rolí a hodnotové orientace* (Czech family in the transformation. Stratification, role division, and value orientations), ed. Milan Tuček et al. Working Paper No. 3. Prague: Institute of Sociology.

Tuček, Milan, et al. 1998. *Česká rodina v transformaci. Stratifikace, dělba rolí a hodnotové orientace* (Czech family in the transformation. Stratification, role division, and value orientations). Working Paper No. 3. Prague: Institute of Sociology.

Tworzecki, Hubert. 1996. *Parties and Politics in Post-1989 Poland.* Boulder: Westview Press.

United Nations. 1992. *The Impact of Economic and Political Reform on the Status of Women in Eastern Europe.* New York: United Nations.

Vajdová, Zdenka. 1996. "Functions of the Executive: Power, Leadership, and Management." In *Local Democracy and the Processes of Transformation in East-Central Europe,* ed. H. Baldersheim et al. Boulder: Westview Press.

Vajdová, Zdenka, and Tomáš Kostelecký. 1997. "Politická kultura lokálních společenství: případ tří měst" (Political culture of local communities: The case of three Czech cities). *Sociologický časopis* 33: 457–469.

Večerník, Jiří. 1996. *Markets and People. The Czech Reform Experience in a Comparative Perspective.* Aldershot, Hants, England: Avebury.

Vinton, Louisa. 1993. "Correcting Pilsudski: Walesa's Nonparty Bloc to Support Reform." *RFE/RL Research Report* 2 (September): 1–9.

Works Cited

Vlachová, Klára. 1997. "Co říkají volby do Sněmovny o české politické scéně." *Social Trends* 1 (3).

Wade, Larry L., Alexander J. Groth, and Peter Lavelle. 1994. "Estimating Participation and Party Voting in Poland: The 1991 Parliamentary Elections." *East European Politics and Societies* 8 (winter): 94–121.

Wandycz, Piotr S. 1990. "Poland's Place in Europe in the Concepts of Pilsudski and Dmowski." *East European Politics and Societies* 4 (fall): 451–468.

Watson, Peggy. 1993. "Eastern Europe's Silent Revolution: Gender." *Sociology* 27(3): 471–487.

Weiner, Elaine. 1997. "Assessing the Implications of Political and Economic Reform in the Post-Socialist Era: The Case of Czech and Slovak Women." *East European Quarterly* 31 (3): 473–502.

Wessels, Bernhard, and Hans-Dieter Klingemann. 1994. "Democratic Transformation and the Prerequisites of Democratic Opposition in East and Central Europe." Wissenschaftszentrum Berlin für Sozialforschung. FS III: 94–201.

Wiatr, Jerzy J. 1993. *Wybory Parlamentarne 19 Wrzesnia 1993: Przyczyny I Nastepstwa* (Parliamentary Elections 19 September 1993: Causes and Consequences). Warsaw: Agencja Scholar.

Yancis, Lisbeth. 1994. "Economic Discontent and Political Behavior." In *Current Economics and Politics of (ex) Czechoslovakia,* ed. J. Křovák. New York: Nova Science Publishers.

Zajicek, Anna M., and Toni M. Calasanti. 1995. "The Impact of Socioeconomic Restructuring on Polish Women." In *Family, Women, and Employment in Central-Eastern Europe,* ed. B. Lobodzinska. Westport, Conn.: Greenwood Press.

Zarnowski, Janusz. 1990. "The Evolution of Polish Society since 1918." *East European Quarterly* 24 (June): 227–235.

Zukowski, Tomasz. 1993. *Polska scena polityczna a wybory* (Polish political scene and elections). Warsaw: INP UW and ISP PAN.

Zuzowski, Robert. 1991. "The Origins of Open Organized Dissent in Today's Poland: KOR and Other Dissident Groups." *East European Quarterly* 25 (March): 59–90.

———. 1993. "Political Culture and Dissent: Why Were There Organizations like KOR in Poland?" *East European Quarterly* 27 (winter): 503–522.

INDEX

abortion issue, 100, 101, 118, 131–36;
  Czechoslovakia, 131–32; Czech Republic,
  133, 134*t*, 135, 136*t*; Hungary, 131,
  132–33, 134*t*, 135, 136*t*; Poland, 131, 132,
  133–34, 134*t*, 135, 136*t*; Slovakia, 133
ad hoc political associations, 157–58, 175
age, generational cleavages, 114–17; voters,
  111–12
Agrarian Alliance, 42*t*, 105, 183*n*
agrarian parties, common features, 103;
  Czechoslovakia, 21, 22, 24; Czech
  Republic, 105–6; education, 112; Hungary,
  9; Slovakia, 105–6; suffrage, 103. *See also*
  Catholic parties
Agrarian Party, 53; changes name, 67; Czech
  Republic, 105–6
agrarian populism, 93
Agreement on the Creation of a Stable
  Political Environment in the Czech
  Republic, 145
agriculture, collectivization, 30;
  Czechoslovakia, 103–4; economic
  reforms, 71; employment, 104, 104*t*;
  Hungary, 40, 41–42, 46, 103–4; Poland,
  103–4; Polish parties, 67, 69, 69*t*; Polish
  voting patterns, 81; reprivatization, 40,
  41–42; Slovakia, 103–4
agriculture-industry cleavages, 91, 95, 103–6
Alliance of the Democratic Left (SLD),
  abortion issue, 132; education, 112;
  elections of 1991, 69*t*; elections of 1993,
  70, 71*t*; elections of 1995, 72, 73, 73*t*;

elections of 1997, 74*t*; membership, 156;
  religious indicators, 101
Alliance of Free Democrats (SZDSZ),
  avoiding party label, 154; characterized,
  41; elections of 1990, 150; elections of
  1994, 44*t*; elections of 1998, 45, 45*t*;
  generational voting, 115; image, 84;
  presidential elections, 149; proportional
  representation, 149; social status, 111
Allies, Poland, 27
all-national movements, 86, 181*n*
Antall, Jószef, 41, 43, 84, 183*n*
anti-Semitism, Hungary, 17. *See also* Jews
appliances, household, 120–21, 121*t*
Arrow Cross Party, 17
Association for the Republic—Republican
  Party of Czechoslovakia (SPR-RSČ),
  education, 113; elections of 1992, 52–53,
  52*t*; elections of 1996, 60*t*; elections of
  1998, 63, 63*t*; gender bias, 130*t*, 131;
  generational voting, 116; majority system,
  144–45, 188*n*
Association of Workers of Slovakia (ZRS),
  disappearance, 55; educational levels, 114;
  elections of 1994, 54, 54*t*; electoral laws,
  147; generational voting, 116; social
  cleavage, 113
atheism, 97, 98, 99; voting patterns, 103
Austria-Hungary, Galicia, 15; population, 12*t*
Austrian model, 159
Austrian Monarchy, Hungary, 8, 9; Polish
  territories, 14, 15

201